Domestic Violence and Child Protection

also edited by Nicky Stanley

Students' Mental Health Needs
Problems and Responses
Edited by Nicky Stanley and Jill Manthorpe
Foreword by Barbara Waters
ISBN 978 1 85302 983 7

of related interest

Childhood Experiences of Domestic Violence
Caroline McGee
Foreword by Hilary Saunders
ISBN 978 1 85302 827 4

Domestic Violence
Guidelines for Research-Informed Practice
Edited by John P. Vincent and Ernest N. Jouriles
ISBN 978 1 85302 854 0

Making an Impact – Children and Domestic Violence
A Reader
Marianne Hester, Chris Pearson and Nicola Harwin
ISBN 978 1 85302 844 1

Preventing Violence in Relationships
A Programme for Men Who Feel They Have a Problem
with their Use of Controlling and Violent Behaviour
Gerry Heery
ISBN 978 1 85302 816 8

Good Practice in Working with Victims of Violence
Edited by Hazel Kemshall and Jacki Pritchard
Good Practice Series 8
ISBN 978 1 85302 768 0

Developing Good Practice in Children's Services
Edited by Vicky White and John Harris
ISBN 978 1 84310 150 5

Social Work with Children and Families
Getting into Practice, Second Edition
Ian Butler and Gwenda Roberts
ISBN 978 1 84310 108 6

Domestic Violence and Child Protection

Directions for Good Practice

Edited by Cathy Humphreys
and Nicky Stanley

Jessica Kingsley Publishers
London and Philadelphia

First published in 2006
by Jessica Kingsley Publishers
116 Pentonville Road
London N1 9JB, UK
and
400 Market Street, Suite 400
Philadelphia, PA 19106, USA

www.jkp.com

Library of Congress Cataloging in Publication Data
Domestic violence and child protection : directions for good practice / edited by Cathy Humphreys and
Nicky Stanley.
    p. cm.
    Includes bibliographical references and index.
    ISBN-13: 978-1-84310-276-2 (pbk. : alk. paper)
    ISBN-10: 1-84310-276-5 (pbk. : alk. paper) 1. Child welfare—Great Britain. 2. Family violence—Great
Britain. 3. Child abuse—Great Britain. 4. Children of abused wives—Great Britain. 5. Social work with
children—Great Britain. 6. Family social work—Great Britain. I. Humphreys, Catherine. II. Stanley, Nicky,
1955-
    HV751.A6D66 2006
    362.760941—dc22

                                                    2005037573

British Library Cataloguing in Publication Data
A CIP catalogue record for this book is available from the British Library

ISBN 978 1 84310 276 2

This book is dedicated to Ray
for his continuing support and encouragement
and to Rachel for her tolerance and many hours of child care.

Contents

List of Figures

Introduction

Cathy Humphreys and Nicky Stanley

Promising developments are now beginning to emerge in the professional response to the needs of children living with domestic violence. These interventions are in contrast to the previous history of child welfare services which have been castigated for their generally poor record in responding to domestic violence. Archival research on child-care agency files since the early 1900s points to decades of attention to children's needs which has excluded recognition and consideration of violence towards mothers (Gordon 1988). Further research on statutory case files in both the US (Stark and Flitcraft 1988) and the UK (Humphreys 2000; Maynard 1985) demonstrates that the trend continued. Women have been either urged to stay with their abusive partners for the sake of the children (Maynard 1985) or more recently blamed for their 'failure to protect' through not separating from violent men (Humphreys 1999). The link to direct child abuse was slow to emerge (Farmer and Owen 1998; Stanley 1997) and the destructive effects of children witnessing domestic violence underestimated (Brandon and Lewis 1996). The problems for black and minority ethnic women accessing services were minimised (Imam 1994), the issues for disabled women relocating ignored (Pryke and Thomas 1998), and there was a consistent slippage away from the man's violence to focus on the mother's problems (Mullender 1996). In some states in the US, this position has been taken to the extreme with women facing legal charges when they do not separate from violent men (Magen 1999).

The consistency of this pattern points to a profound separation in the discourses of child abuse and woman abuse which underpins structural and organisational barriers to an integrated response to the issue. An integrated response is one which centralises the following principles: first, the development of policy and practice which directs responsibility to perpetrators and their abuse; second, a commitment to work with domestic violence survivors – (usually) women and children – from diverse backgrounds to ensure their safety and well-being. This will require attention to their separate needs as well as recognition that the child's safety will usually (though not always) be linked to that of the mother. This book aims to offer positive models of policy and practice which can bridge the gaps between the two discourses while acknowledging the difficulties in achieving this.

Service and legislative developments

The women's movement, and specifically the 30-year campaign by Women's Aid in the UK, has played a pivotal role in highlighting the issue of domestic violence. The network of more than 250 refuges in England providing safe housing for women and children has been expanding over the past ten years to provide outreach services and a 24-hour helpline run in conjunction with Refuge, England. More recently, a children's website has been launched (www.thehide out.org.uk) and Scotland has led the way with a £6 million grant for children's services following an active campaign (Listen Louder) in which children were active participants (see Chapter 5). The estimate of at least 750,000 children in England and Wales living with domestic violence indicates that this is not an issue which should be on the margins of practice (Department of Health 2002).

However, the level of multi-agency development which we are now witnessing in the UK, combined with the rise in the attention to children's needs, has been assisted by the active efforts of health workers, police, housing departments, social services and children's charities. The growth of awareness of domestic violence among those working for statutory agencies heralds the first stage in 'mainstreaming' the issue, a development to which it is hoped that this book will contribute. No longer is concern about this issue confined to the women's voluntary sector. In fact, at the time of writing, the women's voluntary sector and survivors are finding it increasingly difficult to have their voices heard in many multi-agency forums in the UK.

Further legislative developments occurred while this book was being written. Of particular importance was the Children Act 2004. While it will not override the legislation for the protection of children under the Children Act 1989, it changes the delivery of services to children and their families at the local level. Multi-agency working through children's trusts, the development of local plans for services for children and young people and mechanisms for sharing the data between professions and agencies working with children will be established. At the time of writing it is unclear what impact this will have for the response to children living with domestic violence.

A further development in the UK has been the amendment to the definition of harm introduced by the Children and Adoption Act 2002. This provided the new category of 'impairment suffered from seeing or hearing the ill treatment of another' and therefore makes more explicit in cases of domestic violence the local authority's duty to either investigate whether there has been significant harm or risk of significant harm to a child under part IV section 47 of the Children Act 1989, and/or whether to provide services under section 17 to children and their families in need of support. Chapter 9 in this book provides further discussion of the developments in child contact legislation which also impinge upon protecting children from domestic violence.

The Domestic Violence, Crime and Victims Act 2004 was implemented in the UK in July 2005. The Act represents a strengthening of legislation in the area of non-molestation, occupation and restraining orders and is therefore progressive. However, it also represents a missed opportunity to make a significant difference to domestic violence intervention by providing the proactive legislation now seen in some countries in Europe where there are measures to exclude the perpetrator of domestic violence from the home for periods of time following an incident. An amendment (s. 38A [2]) to the Children Act 1989 does allow the local authority to seek an exclusion order but only under the very limited circumstances where there is an interim care order or emergency protection order in place and, even then, only when the informed consent of the mother or child's carer has been gained.

At a strategic level, the Crime and Disorder Act 1998 is also worth noting as it imposes a duty on responsible authorities – namely the police, local authorities and more recently primary care trusts – to audit crime in their areas, including domestic violence. These authorities have been responsible for a considerable increase in activity and resources channelled into work on domestic violence at a local level across England and Wales and, in future, they will need to work closely with local children's safeguarding boards and children and young people's strategic partnerships for planning children's services.

To date, there have been questions raised about whether all progress, both legislative and in relation to children and domestic violence, has been positive. In particular, concerns have been raised that the only message which has been communicated relates to children's roles as victims of domestic violence. This book aims to extend the debate beyond that message by emphasising the value and the means of achieving approaches which are preventive, which support victims to find safety and which address the consequences and future risks of domestic violence for children. It includes a number of international examples of positive practice and policy which broaden the perspective and offer alternatives to seemingly entrenched models for responding to this complex issue.

Gender and domestic violence

Issues of gender and diversity need to be addressed in any discussion of domestic violence. There is a danger of producing simplistic, unnuanced accounts in which women are treated as a homogenous category of victims of violence and abuse, men are always perpetrators, and children's needs are consistently aligned with their mothers. Such accounts have been the brunt of heavy criticism particularly by those (Featherstone and Trinder 1997) who argue that these constructions represent an essentialist form of feminism which underplays the complexity of gendered relations and denies female violence. While counter-arguments can be proffered that texts have been misread and the attention to diversity laundered out, such criticisms raise the question of how complexity can be understood without falling into the trap of a gender-neutral analysis.

Several issues need to be disentangled. At the point where domestic violence, and particularly violence against women, is moving onto the child welfare agenda as a significant concern, it is possible to discern a push for a gender-neutral analysis, which suggests that men are equally the victims of violence and that the level of violence perpetrated by women is being underplayed. The evidence needs to be examined carefully.

When victim reports from the British Crime Survey confidential self-completion questionnaires are examined under expanded definitions of domestic violence, which include emotional and financial abuse as well as physical force and threats but not sexual violence, its prevalence becomes more evenly distributed between men and women (Walby and Allen 2004). Thirteen per cent of women and 9 per cent of men report being subjected to domestic violence in the past year. However, when the most heavily abused are considered, based on the frequency of attacks, the range of forms of violence and the severity of injury, women are overwhelmingly the most victimised. Among people subjected to four or more incidents of domestic violence from the perpetrator, 89 per cent were women. There were an estimated 635,000 incidents in 2001/2002 in England and Wales, of which 81 per cent were attacks on women (Walby and Allen 2004). Moreover, women are twice as likely to be injured, and three times as likely to report living in fear than men (Mirrlees-Black 1999). When homicide is considered, 37 per cent of women homicides were committed by a partner or former partner, as against 8 per cent of male homicides (Mirrlees-Black 1999). At least 54 per cent of rape and serious sexual assault is perpetrated by a male partner or former partner (Walby and Allen 2004). Domestic violence incidents and recorded crime again show overwhelmingly gendered patterns, with 90 per cent of incidents involving a female victim and a male perpetrator (Scottish Executive 2003). Issues of diversity may also be important. A Home Office survey (1996) analysed by Mirrlees-Black (1999) showed 12 per cent of disabled women aged

16–29 had experienced domestic violence in 1995 compared with 8.2 per cent of non-disabled women of the same age.

The data suggest that language and an analysis which underplays this dominant pattern of violence towards women minimises the seriousness of the problem. The forms of 'intimate terrorism' which represent the most concerning and dangerous patterns of violence are also the ones which should be coming to the attention of child protection authorities.

However, acknowledging this dominant, gendered pattern of violence can give rise to problems in identifying minority patterns of abuse, many of which may be very dangerous to children and the adults involved. Women's violence towards their male partners, women's abuse of children, the abuse of women by other female relatives or the man's new partner, women's violence in lesbian relationships, male violence in gay relationships, relationships in which both the woman and man are violent and abusive towards each other, abuse by carers of disabled women, and non-domestic violence by unrelated people (usually, though not always, men) all impact on children living in neighbourhoods where violence and abuse are common. Failing to acknowledge the diverse forms of violence in families may limit professionals' capacity to safeguard children.

Language which reflects both the dominant pattern and this diversity is difficult to find. 'Domestic violence' as a term does not designate a particular gender, though it has come to be understood as reflecting the dominant pattern of violence towards women. It nevertheless is an inclusive term which highlights the criminal nature of much abuse and will be used throughout this book to refer to both the gendered pattern of violence against women, as well as to other diverse ways in which adult violence impacts upon children. Within the principles outlined here, the qualifying term 'usually' is therefore important in acknowledging the dominant pattern while recognising that this is not the only form of abuse within families. At times, gender-neutral language will be used in relation to perpetrators and survivors; at other times female terminology will be used to refer to women survivors and male terminology for perpetrators. 'Domestic abuse' is also used in some chapters where authors consider it represents more accurately the wider pattern of practices used to enforce power and control by one person over another (see the power and control wheel, Figure 3.1, p.57).

About this book

The book is divided into four parts which cover the different areas of knowledge and practice required for an integrated approach to domestic violence and child protection. Following an initial exploration of the evidence base in this field, the book addresses children's needs and initiatives aimed at meeting those needs; the protection of women and children through both service responses and legal systems; and, finally, work with perpetrators. Part One introduces the reader to the current state of the relationship between domestic violence and child protection, focusing primarily on the UK. Chapter 1 by Cathy Humphreys provides an overview of the evidence base in this field which has developed rapidly in the last ten years. This chapter draws attention to issues of post-separation violence and the ways in which domestic violence and its effects on children are associated with mothers' mental health needs and substance misuse. The chapter also considers what is known about the longer-term impact of domestic violence on mother–child relationships and highlights the role of resilience. In Chapter 2, Nicky Stanley and Cathy Humphreys focus on the service response to the linked issues of domestic violence and child protection and considers the factors which inform and shape multi-agency work.

Part Two addresses children's needs and large-scale initiatives which are responding to those needs. Chapter 3 by Audrey Mullender uses children's own accounts to forefront their views and experiences. The material presented here reinforces the relevance of child protection, the diverse range of children's needs, the demand for prevention programmes and the importance of recognising children's strengths and resilience. In Chapter 4, Jane Ellis, Nicky Stanley and Jo Bell map the delivery of prevention programmes in schools and youth centres and explore the thinking which underpins this development. Chapter 5 by Claire Houghton describes a Scottish campaign run by the voluntary sector which harnessed children's voices and experiences to the processes of policy and service development in the field of domestic violence.

Part Three focuses on the protection of women and children, exploring a range of service responses including some Australian examples of positive practice in this field. In Chapter 6, Marianne Hester considers how practitioners can incorporate routine questions into their practice to open up the issue of domestic violence for women and children. Similarly, Jan Breckenridge and Claire Ralfs' chapter draws on work undertaken in Australia to offer guidance for practitioners in a range of front-line settings providing an initial response to domestic violence. Chapter 8 by Elaine Farmer discusses research undertaken in the statutory sector which highlights the ways in which the effects of domestic violence can be marginalised in this context. The final two chapters in this part of the book focus on legal systems. In Chapter 9, Christine Harrison outlines the relevance of child protection to child contact arrangements and explores whether and how contact centres function as a means of protecting children. Private law is also considered in the Australian context by Thea Brown who in Chapter 10 considers the management of the legal process when allegations of abuse arise in the context of divorce. This chapter introduces the reader to new models of intervention which are being trialled and evaluated in Australia and Canada and provides evidence for their effectiveness.

Part Four addresses work with perpetrators. In Chapter 11, Lorraine Radford, Neil Blacklock and Kate Iwi from the West London Domestic Violence Intervention Project (DVIP) describe an approach to assessing the risks posed to women and children by violent men which has been developed by a voluntary agency in West London working in partnership with local authority social services departments. The following chapter by Marius Råkil discusses the work of Alternative to Violence (ATV), a project based in Oslo, which provides services for men, women and children and adolescents who have developed problems with violence. ATV has set up a specific service for men who are fathers which aims to enable them to address the effects of living with violence and abuse on their children. This section on perpetrators concludes with a chapter by Brian Littlechild and Caroline Bourke, which considers how the strategies of power and control which perpetrators use with their victims can also shape their relationships with child protection workers, limiting professionals' capacity to protect women and children.

This book is aimed at a range of readers including practitioners, policy makers, students and academics. While there is still much to criticise in the service response to the intertwined issues of children's welfare and domestic violence, the contributors have used the evidence base in their respective areas to provide positive examples of practice and guidance. They point to the dynamic nature of the work and the fact that the structures, legislation and guidance are changing as we write. We need to ensure that in this shifting arena of work that we not only 'do no further harm', but also that our interventions provide a route to safety and recovery for children and survivors and engage effectively with perpetrators of abuse.

References

Brandon, M. and Lewis, A. (1996) 'Significant harm and children's experiences of domestic violence.' *Child and Family Social Work 1*, 33–42.

Department of Health (2002) Women's Mental Health: Into the Mainstream. London: The Stationery Office.

Farmer, E. and Owen, M. (1998) *Child Protection Practice: Private Risks and Public Remedies*. London: HMSO.

Featherstone, B. and Trinder, L. (1997) 'Familiar subjects? Domestic violence and child welfare.' *Child and Family Social Work 2*, 3, 147–60.

Gordon, L. (1988) *Heroes of Their Own Lives*. New York: Viking.

Humphreys, C. (1999) 'Avoidance and confrontation: The practice of social workers in relation to domestic violence and child abuse.' *Journal of Child and Family Social Work 4*, 1, 77–87.

Humphreys, C. (2000) *Social Work, Domestic Violence and Child Protection*. Bristol: The Policy Press.

Imam, U. (1994) 'Asian children and domestic violence.' In A. Mullender and R. Morley (eds) *Children Living with Domestic Violence*. London: Whiting and Birch.

Magen, R. (1999) 'In the best interests of battered women: Reconceptualising allegations of failure to protect.' *Child Maltreatment 4*, 2, 127–35.

Maynard, M. (1985) 'The response of social workers to domestic violence.' In J. Pahl (ed) *Private Violence and Public Policy*. London: Routledge, pp.125–40.

Mirrlees-Black, C. (1999) *Domestic Violence: Findings from a New British Crime Survey Self-Completion Questionnaire*. London: HMSO.

Mullender, A. (1996) *Rethinking Domestic Violence: The Social Work and Probation Response*. London: Routledge.

Pryke, J. and Thomas, M. (1998) *Domestic Violence and Social Work*. Aldershot: Ashgate Publishing.

Scottish Executive (2003) *Recorded Crime in Scotland, 2002*. Edinburgh: Scottish Executive.

Stanley, N. (1997) 'Domestic violence and child abuse: Developing social work practice.' *Child and Family Social Work 2*, 3, 135–45.

Stark, E. and Flitcraft, A. (1988) 'Women and children at risk: A feminist perspective on child abuse.' *International Journal of Health Services 18*, 97–118.

Walby, S. and Allen, J. (2004) *Domestic Violence, Sexual Assault and Stalking: Findings from the British Crime Survey*. Home Office Research Study 276. London: Home Office Research, Development and Statistics Directorate.

Part One

Defining the Issue and Setting the Scene

Chapter 1

Relevant Evidence for Practice

Cathy Humphreys

Introduction

The complexity of the evidence base is a striking feature of work in this area. While the impact of domestic violence on children is the most obvious body of knowledge for practitioners to access, assessing the child's vulnerabilities as well as their ability to survive adversity requires a broader lens which explores a range of other issues. These include: the compounding effects of direct physical and sexual abuse; the heightened vulnerability of women during pregnancy; the particular problems of child abduction and forced marriage; risks associated with post-separation violence; the complexities which occur when domestic violence impacts on women's mental health; the links with substance use; and the ways in which these problems together undermine the mother child relationship and the father–child relationship. A range of other issues are also relevant, particularly the assessment of perpetrators of domestic violence. However, this area will be explored in depth in later chapters, while other issues such as child contact and the effects on children living with domestic violence will be touched on here but developed in more detail by other authors in this volume (see Chapter 9, for example). Separate bodies of knowledge and practice have developed around different issues. This chapter aims to bring that evidence together to inform the development of a more holistic approach to practice.

The effects on children living with domestic violence

Children have their own perspectives on what living with domestic violence is like for them and Chapter 3 explores their views in depth. However, some information is needed here to provide the backdrop against which work with children living with domestic violence occurs.

First, children and young people can rarely be protected from the knowledge that domestic violence is occurring. Up to 86 per cent of children are either in the same or adjoining rooms during an incident of domestic violence (Abrahams 1994). The first national prevalence study of 2869 young adults indicated that 26 per cent had witnessed violence between their parents at least once and for 5 per cent the violence was frequent and ongoing (Cawson 2002). Of these children, 23,500 each year will live in a refuge with their mothers escaping from the violence (www.womensaid.org.uk). This suggests very high numbers of children living with violence and abuse, pointing to a chronic social problem.

Second, children witnessing incidents of domestic violence may be at risk of significant harm – an issue now recognised in the UK by an amendment to the definition of harm in the Children Act 1989 which now includes 'impairment suffered from seeing or hearing the ill treatment of another' (Adoption and Children Act 2002). Throughout the 1990s, these risks to the well-being of children living with domestic violence began to be documented and a comprehensive body of knowledge started to develop (Hester, Pearson and Harwin 2000; Laing 2001; Mullender and Morley 1994). While there remain gaps in the evidence, the research consistently shows that children living with domestic violence have much higher rates of depression and anxiety (McClosky, Figueredo and Koss 1995), trauma symptoms (Graham-Bermann and Levendosky 1998), and behavioural and cognitive problems (O'Keefe 1995) than children and young people not living with these issues. The impact on children at different developmental stages shows the broad range of ways in which children react to their environments. While children of pre-school age tend to be the group who show the most behavioural disturbance (Hughes 1988) and are particularly vulnerable to blaming themselves for adult anger (Jaffe, Wolfe and Wilson 1990), babies living with domestic violence are subject to high levels of ill health, poor sleeping habits and excessive screaming (Jaffe *et al.* 1990). Problems for children can compound over time as they live with the multiple problems associated with the destructive effects of domestic violence. A summary is provided by Rossman who states: 'Exposure at any age can create disruptions that can interfere with the accomplishment of developmental tasks, and early exposure may create more severe disruptions by affecting the subsequent chain of developmental tasks' (Rossman 2001, p.58). At worst, children may be traumatised by hearing or seeing their mothers being sexually assaulted (McGee 2000) or murdered (Hendricks, Kaplan and Black 1993; Richards and Baker 2003).

These disturbing patterns have a number of implications for professionals working in the field of child protection. They suggest that potentially many children may be at serious risk of harm when they are living with domestic violence. However, given that this is a chronic social problem affecting a very large number of children, it is also impossible for all these children and their families to be routed through intensive assessments and child protection investigations. The response to domestic violence therefore needs to be located both in child protection services and in the context of family support delivered through community-based services; such a model avoids the conflicts which can develop between approaches offering advocacy and support and investigations of significant harm. Jan Breckenridge and Claire Ralfs' chapter in this volume (Chapter 7) also emphasises the role of front-line workers in responding to the needs of women and children.

The evidence base provides some important guidance for deciding when the seriousness of the domestic violence requires a statutory investigation. This is extremely difficult territory to negotiate when too often severity is restricted to severe physical violence, 'the atrocity story' (Humphreys 2000). Survivors constantly remind us that the long-term effects often lie in the emotional abuse and psychological violence – physical violence does not need to occur often for its intimidating presence to be experienced on a daily basis (Bagshaw and Chung 2000). Similar warnings have arisen in relation to children's needs, emphasising that living in environments of low warmth and high criticism may be as damaging, or even more damaging, than individual incidents of violence and abuse (Department of Health 1995). In exploring the evidence base further, this issue needs to be kept at the forefront.

The patterns of direct abuse

The relationship between the direct abuse of children and domestic violence needs to be highlighted, particularly as the research would suggest that children who are both living with domestic violence and also being physically or sexually abused show higher rates of distress (Hughes 1988; O'Keefe 1995; Sternberg et al. 1993). The UK prevalence study of children and young people showed that eight out of ten young people who suffered serious physical abuse had also experienced domestic violence, and for nearly half (43%) the domestic violence was constant or frequent (Cawson 2002). The same study also showed that, of the 27 young people who reported being sexually abused, 21 said they lived with domestic violence. Other studies show the same patterns emerging (Farmer and Pollock 1998; also see Chapter 8). The severity of violence is also relevant. Ross (1996) for example found that in a US study of 3363 parents there was an almost 100 per cent correlation between the most severe abuse of women and the men's physical abuse of children.

When studies show that between 30 and 66 per cent of children who suffer physical abuse are living with domestic violence (Edleson 1999), the association is such that where there is domestic violence, questions need to be raised about child abuse, and where there is child abuse, questions need to be raised about domestic violence. Hester and Pearson (1998) show that systematically asking questions dramatically changes the amount of violence disclosed. This issue is explored in greater depth in Chapter 6. While the association with direct forms of child abuse needs to be recognised, simplistic assessments which assume that only children who are being directly abused are at serious risk of harm need to be avoided (see Brandon and Lewis 1996).

Pregnancy as a time of risk

The risks of attack during pregnancy are of particular concern (Mezey and Bewley 1997) and are indicative of highly dangerous perpetrators. These attacks represent a form of 'double intentioned violence' (Kelly 1994) as they incorporate both acts of woman abuse and child abuse. One study showed that women subjected to domestic violence in pregnancy were four times more likely to miscarry than women who were not abused (Schornstein 1997). Women reporting attacks in pregnancy are more at risk of moderate to severe violence and homicide (Campbell *et al.* 1998) with the Canadian national survey showing women abused in pregnancy four times more likely to report severe violence which included beatings, choking, attacks with weapons and sexual assault (Jameison and Hart 1999). The risk does not cease with the pregnancy with some studies suggesting that the postpartum period is the time of greatest risk for moderate to severe violence (Gielen *et al.* 1994). The number of women with very young children living in refuges – half the children in refuges are under five (Saunders and Humphreys 2002) – suggests both the extent of the problem and the vulnerability of these women and their children.

Such findings highlight the significance of developing a more proactive public health response which places greater emphasis on the role of health professionals such as GPs, obstetricians, gynaecologists, health visitors and midwives in exploring domestic violence with women during pregnancy and recognising that such violence is also a form of child abuse.

The problem of abduction and forced marriage

A range of issues arise for children and young people from black and minority ethnic backgrounds to which they are more (though not exclusively) vulnerable than children living in white British families. These issues, which have tended to be neglected in the context of children living with domestic violence, are those of child abduction and forced marriage, and a growing body of evidence is starting to illuminate these questions.

Forced marriages occur where duress is experienced in the forms of emotional pressure, threats, abduction, imprisonment, physical violence and sometimes murder (Samas and Eade 2003). They need to be distinguished from arranged marriages where there is consent from both parties. Forced marriage is an act of violence in itself, and is frequently the precursor for further acts of domestic violence since, when the person's will or consent is overridden in the first instance, it provides the basis for this to occur again in the future. It has been reported in minority communities within the UK including South Asian communities, a variety of West African communities, traveller communities and communities from European countries such as Greece and Turkey (Sen, Humphreys and Kelly 2003). In 2003–2004, there were 250 reported forced marriage cases, of which 50 per cent were children under 16. These reported figures are clearly the tip of the iceberg, with Southall Black Sisters in London alone reporting 200 enquiries per year (Southall Black Sisters 2001). When the number of under-16-year-olds in the reported figures are considered, the intersection of this issue as one of both child abuse and domestic violence becomes clear.

The seriousness of the issue is highlighted by the number of runaways among young Asian women: these tend to cluster around the age of 16 when many may feel compelled to marry (Bhugra, Desai and Baldwin 1999). The number of attempted suicides by teenage Asian girls is also associated with forced marriages, and Yazdani (1998) found that this issue was raised by a number of the young women in her study. To date, the response of child protection workers to these issues has often been seen to be inadequate, overplaying the role of mediation and underplaying the level of risk and violation of the young women's rights to protection (Southall Black Sisters 2001). Mediation is particularly inappropriate when the vast majority of families deny that the marriage is forced, directly contradicting the victim's report and the fears which led them to seek help in the first instance (Khatkar 2002).

While child abduction may be an element in forced marriages, a history of domestic violence is also the most cited feature in child abduction cases (Plass, Finkelhor and Hotaling 1997). There has been a 78 per cent increase in international child abduction since 1995, with Reunite (the primary voluntary sector agency in this area) reporting a 93 per cent increase in abduction cases between 1995 and 2003. Some of this is attributable to an actual increase in child abduction, some of it due to a change in language whereby the resident parent (in the majority of cases, the mother) escaping domestic violence and the attendant problems for children are now often referred to as 'child abductors' and are coming under the auspices of the Hague Convention (McLean 1997). In 1997, approximately two-thirds of Hague Convention applications in the UK involved the primary carer (mostly mothers) removing or retaining their children without the permission of the other parent (McLean 1997). For the most part, these were women returning to the UK as their country of origin following incidents of domestic violence and/or child abuse.

On the other hand, a substantial proportion of cases where fathers abduct children occur against a background of continuing power and control in an ongoing pattern of domestic violence (Grief and Hegar 1991). A study set in child contact centres showed that in 65 per cent of cases the resident parent's fear of child abduction was one of the reasons for contact occurring in a child contact centre (Aris, Harrison and Humphreys 2002). The backdrop to these women's fears included: previous threats that her ex-partner would take the children; the father having extended family living in other countries with whom he was in close contact; and legal and cultural injunctions from these countries which gave the father and his family rights in respect of the children's residence in cases of divorce. Women's fears in these cases need to be taken extremely seriously. The impact on children of child abduction may be severe and long lasting (Grief and Hegar 1991; Plass *et al.* 1997).

Post-separation violence

A significant group of women and children will be no safer when they leave violent homes. While the data from the British Crime Survey (BCS) self-report study (Walby and Allen 2004) showed that separation was the best avenue of escape from domestic violence, for 37 per cent of women the violence either increased, took a different form (e.g. stalking), remained the same, or commenced following separation. A study of 180 women using outreach and refuge services found that 76 per cent of the separated women suffered further abuse and harassment when they first left. Police had to be called to incidents of violence and stalking in 36 per cent of cases and, for 36 per cent of the women, violence and abuse continued (Humphreys and Thiara 2002). The Canadian Violence Against Women Survey found that 19 per cent of women were physically assaulted following separation, and for 35 per cent the violence escalated upon separation (Johnson 1998). In Humphreys and Thiara's study, post-separation violence and abuse appeared to be less of a problem proportionally for black and minority ethnic women in the first six months. However, more white women found that it was a problem which reduced over time, or which they could escape from, while black and minority women who experienced it in the short term continued to experience it in the long term as well.

Men who are most violent when living with women continue to be the most violent following separation. This includes both physical violence (Burgess *et al.* 1997; Morrison 2001) and serious psychological abuse (Davis and Andra 2000; Mechanic, Weaver and Resick 2000). The child protection concern here is that, in situations of more extreme violence where women report that they are often pressured by statutory workers to separate (Humphreys 1999), this may be a particularly ineffective and dangerous strategy unless there is a highly integrated strategy of multi-agency support organised. Murder and rape are threats and real possibilities in the post-separation period for a small but important group of women. The multi-agency domestic violence murder reviews showed that 76 per cent involved separation (Richards and Baker 2003), and at least 29 children have been killed in the last decade by their fathers post-separation (Saunders 2004). In most cases there had been a prior history of domestic violence.

Child contact arrangements provide the greatest opportunity for the continuation of post-separation violence. The BCS self-report study showed that in 19 per cent of cases where there was child contact it had been court ordered and that, similar to the findings of Humphreys and Thiara (2002), one-third of women with child contact arrangements reported experiences of abuse and threats to either themselves or their children. This is an issue explored further in Chapter 9, but is highlighted here to draw attention to the evidence which indicates that separation carries its own risk and provides no simplistic solutions. This is a key message for practitioners who, in their anxiety to protect children, may insist on separation as a means of avoiding care proceedings.

Domestic violence and mothers' mental health

Children come to the notice of statutory services when further complex problems associated with their adult carers come to light. This section focuses on the problems which arise when, alongside or as a consequence of domestic violence, women develop mental health problems, specifically those of depression, symptoms of trauma and self-harm and suicide attempts (Humphreys and Thiara 2003). These 'symptoms of abuse' increasingly emerge as the violence and abuse becomes chronic and entrenched (see Golding 1999). While some men may be affected, the dominant pattern remains that of women developing mental health problems, because they are the ones generally subjected to the more severe forms of abuse (Walby and Allen 2004). A consistent pattern is discernible with the identified rates of depression among women who are subjected to domestic violence varying between 38 per cent and 83 per cent, depending from where the sample was drawn (Cascardi, O'Leary and Schlee 1999). A similar picture emerges in relation to symptoms of trauma where an overview by Jones, Hughes and Unterstaller (2001) of 42 studies found worryingly high rates of post-traumatic stress disorder (PTSD) associated with domestic violence. These include three symptom clusters of: flashbacks (reliving the experiences); numbness and denial (emotionally shutting down); and hypervigilance, inability to sleep (anxiety states). Taken together, these symptoms which represent a normal response to fear can become entrenched and deeply debilitating (Herman 1992).

The evidence of suicide attempts and self-harm is equally concerning. Again, rates vary considerably between research settings. A US study by Stark and

Flitcraft (1995) found that, of 176 women identified through medical records at an accident and emergency department, 52 (30%) had been subject to domestic violence during the sample year. For black women in the US study, the rate was considerably higher than for white women, featuring in 48.8 per cent of the suicide attempts as against a rate of 22.2 per cent for white women. This is an issue which is now consistently noted in the UK and there are now a number of studies showing elevated rates of self-harm and suicide attempts among Asian women under 30 (Bhugra *et al.* 1999; Soni-Raleigh 1996).

Case file research often exposes the poor quality of assessment in many of these cases (Humphreys 2000). As the mother's mental health problems emerge, domestic violence – which may be an extremely significant if not causal factor (see Golding 1999) – drifts into the background. For instance, Stanley and Penhale (1999) found that all 13 women in their study of children identified at risk of significant harm due to their mother's mental health problems had also been the subject of domestic violence. The children's problems however were identified in relation to the mother's mental health, not in relation to the domestic violence they had experienced.

Worryingly, in a small number of cases, the perpetrator of violence has been treated by professionals as 'the cornerstone of the family' with the woman increasingly placed in a marginal position in relation to her children and others around her, as the perpetrator's power in the domestic domain became entrenched (Humphreys 2000). Women with mental health needs are often reluctant to seek help because of fears that they will be judged as inadequate mothers and their children will be 'taken away' (Stanley *et al.* 2003). Such fears feed and intensify the pressures and isolation experienced by women who are threatened with care proceedings if they remain in violent relationships.

However, there is also evidence surrounding the potential of many women to recover their mental health when they are no longer living with violence (Campbell, Sullivan and Davidson 1995; Surtees 1995), and the extent to which they are given access to services which help them recover their mental health is an important issue for child protection professionals to explore. Many women also make particularly valiant efforts to continue 'good enough parenting' under adverse conditions and their strengths in this process need to be recognised and built upon (Radford and Hester 2001). That said, this is a particularly complex area of child protection intervention where the potential for change and harnessing multi-agency support to intervene with the perpetrator, while simultaneously accessing extensive support for both women and children, requires high level case management and assessment skills.

Domestic violence and substance use

A further complexity in relation to the quality of mothering or fathering which children experience lies in the recognition that children are often living with the dual adult problems of domestic violence and problematic substance use.

A particularly good example of this link is provided in the UK by the Cheshire Social Services database of 3321 case files open to statutory children and families' workers during a one-week period. It showed that in 41 per cent of cases where domestic violence was reported, substance abuse was a factor in over half of the families. In only 10 per cent of the substance use cases was domestic violence not considered a factor. A further case-study analysis in four long-term teams in London found that problematic substance use featured in 34 per cent of these cases. These families were four times as likely to have reported domestic violence as those cases where there was no substance use identified (Harwin and Forrester 2002).

However, the way in which these connections are made is a crucial aspect of the assessment which should affect the mode and focus of intervention. There have been particular problems in linking these dual problems. First, among the researchers on children and domestic violence in the UK, there has not been significant attention given to the issues of substance use either for survivors or for perpetrators of domestic violence. This is partly due to concerns that any suggestion which points to heightened rates of drug and alcohol problems among perpetrators of abuse can lead to a misunderstanding that alcohol or drug abuse must therefore *cause* domestic violence. The vast majority of research evidence in this area is clear in finding that this is *not* the case (see Humphreys *et al.* 2005). A further problem is that the literature on children who live with substance abuse rarely explores the gendered patterns of substance use and the ways these interact with domestic violence and other forms of violence. Separate discourses have often resulted in the overlap between these areas being overlooked (see, for example, Home Office 2003). It is rarely specified in the research literature whether it is the mother or father (or father figure) who has the substance problem, and which of the parents is involved in the abuse, either of their partner or of the children (Leonard 2002).

Children living with either one or both parents with problematic substance use show heightened rates of distress (Cleaver, Unell and Aldgate 1999; Gorin 2004; Kroll 2004) and the descriptions of emotional and behavioural problems are very similar to the patterns identified for children living with domestic violence (Hester *et al.* 2000; Laing 2001). This is unsurprising given the level of overlap between substance use and domestic violence. It also suggests that children living in stressful family environments react in similar ways showing high rates of depression, cognitive and behavioural problems (Gorin 2004).

The assessment of significant harm in families with substance use problems also overlaps with the complexities of domestic violence intervention. Substance use by mothers or fathers may not be particularly problematic if it is circumscribed, not chaotic and not necessarily impairing the functioning of the mother or father as a parent. Substance use exists on a continuum (Guy and Harrison 2003) and child-care practitioners need to acknowledge the extent to which the behaviour is widespread and common while remaining alert to its potential impact on patterns of violence and children's welfare.

Kroll's meta-review (2004) of seven studies of children and young people's experiences of living with mothers and fathers with substance use problems highlighted the problems of violence and abuse and suggested that the primary problem for many of these children was the violence and abuse they were experiencing in their families. The presence of substance use should therefore not shift the focus from the violence children are living with, even though it is often when their mother (or primary carer) becomes disabled through substance use problems that serious child protection concerns are raised (Harwin and Forrester 2002; Humphreys 2000). Commenting on the children's perspectives across the seven studies of parental substance use, Kroll comments:

> Practical help and physical protection featured more in some studies than others. Witnessing and managing violence, however, were persistent worries, and the impact of family disharmony was often seen as more of a problem than the substance use. (2004, p.137)

Substantial evidence exists across a range of settings of the higher risks of alcohol and drug problems for domestic violence survivors (Gleason 1993; Hutchinson 2003). There are many explanations for the association between women's experiences of domestic violence and their patterns of substance use. A commonly cited one, supported by the evidence base (Zubretsky 2002), is that many women use alcohol and drugs to cope with the attacks to which they are subjected as a form of self-medication. A study by Barnett and Fagan (1993) showed different patterns of drinking between men and women. Men drank twice as much as women during an incident (30% versus 17.8%), but women's drinking was twice as common following the abusive attack (48% versus 24%).

The significant overlap between the problematic use of alcohol and drugs by a substantial number of perpetrators of domestic violence is also now uncontested (Hutchinson 2003; Mirrlees-Black 1999). The British Crime Survey 2000 indicated that 44 per cent of domestic violence offenders were under the influence of alcohol and 12 per cent were affected by drugs during the domestic violence incident (Kewshaw et al. 2000). However, it is also important to note that less than half of domestic violence incidents in these studies directly involved drugs and/or alcohol (Mirrlees-Black 1999). Other studies have indicated that, although the abuser may have had alcohol problems, incidents of abuse were often unconnected to the drinking (Frieze and Browne 1989). Critical discussions of the links between substance use and domestic violence (Galvani 2001; Hutchinson 2003) argue that while there are increased vulnerabilities where there is substance use, it should not be inferred that drugs or alcohol *cause* domestic violence. Perpetrators of abuse may become drunk because they want to be violent and their drinking becomes part of their repertoire for establishing a regime of fear and control.

Undermining the mother–child relationship

A particular issue for those working across the areas of child protection and domestic violence is that domestic violence frequently undermines the relationship between mothers and their children (Humphreys *et al.* forthcoming a). The women interviewed by Mullender *et al.* (2002) all believed their parenting had been affected and the study documented the indirect and direct strategies through which this occurred. Women described the ways in which high anxiety and depression undermined their ability to care for their children, and highlighted their preoccupations with trying to control the domestic environment so that the man's needs were prioritised. This could mean that the children's needs for playing, attention and fun were not met, or only met intermittently when he was not around. Other studies have identified the ways in which, either in the short or long term, women have been disabled by the severity of the violence they have experienced, either needing hospitalisation or being temporarily unable to provide physical care (Radford and Hester 2001; Stark and Flitcraft 1996). This research needs to be placed in the context of other research (Holden *et al.* 1998) which shows that parenting can show very significant improvements in the first six months following separation if the abuser's violence is curtailed.

Belittling and insulting a woman in front of her children undermines not only her respect for herself, but also the authority which she needs to parent confidently. Women may also be sexually assaulted and humiliated in front of their children. In Abrahams' (1994) and McGee's (2000) studies, 10 per cent of women interviewed reported that they had been raped with their children present – a disturbing violation of boundaries which seriously distorts the environment in which mothering occurs (not to mention fathering).

There is also controversy about the extent to which women who are being abused themselves are inclined to be more abusive and neglectful of their own children. Some studies suggest that women living with domestic violence are no more likely than other women to abuse and neglect their children (Holden *et al.* 1998), while other research shows that, in households where there is domestic violence, both mothers and fathers are more likely to physically abuse their children (Ross 1996).

The evidence in this area also needs to take into account the mismatch between the needs of women struggling with their own physical and emotional survival and children who are also extremely distressed and showing emotional and behavioural problems which require more, not less, parental involvement. While there is significant evidence to show that both women and children can recover their mental health when they are in safer environments (Holden *et al.* 1998; Wolfe *et al.* 1986), this may not be apparent while the violence, abuse and other compounding problems such as substance use continue.

Other issues such as leaving children in the care of the abusive father, not separating from the abusive parent, and continuing to return to the abusive relationship may also contribute to undermining the relationship between mothers and their children (ChildLine 1997; Laybourn, Brown and Hill 1996).

There are undoubtedly problems in highlighting these issues including the risk of pathologising the mother–child relationship (Radford and Hester 2001). This is not the intention. Rather it should not be assumed that removal of the perpetrator is a 'quick fix' which will immediately remedy the problems. The withdrawal of professionals when it is assumed the child is safe sets the woman up to fail just at the time when she may be in a position to more easily avail herself and her children of help and support. Recovery processes entail assistance not just for individual women or children, but for *the relationship* between them (Humphreys *et al.* forthcoming b). This is an essential aspect of domestic violence intervention which has been marginalised through failures to conceptualise domestic violence as not only an attack on the survivor (usually the mother), but also an assault on her relationship with her children.

Surviving adversity

A balance needs to be achieved between recognising the potential danger and harm to both adult survivors of domestic violence (usually women) and their children on the one hand and acknowledging their strengths and resilience in the face of adversity. Not all domestic violence is the same, and survivors and their children may be very differently affected. Children and young people actively respond to and interpret the environments in which they live (see Chapter 3) and will often find resources, sources of safety and support within their environments which mitigate the impact of domestic violence.

There are many factors which moderate the risks and experiences of children. Several research studies show that in any sample, some children, at least in the short term, show few negative symptoms and have higher levels of competence than comparison groups (Hughes, Graham-Bermann and Gruber 2001).

Children will be affected by the severity of violence with which they are living and by whether they are being directly abused or not (Edleson 1999), as well as by the extent to which their needs have been neglected (Brandon and Lewis 1996). The mother's ability to maintain her parenting abilities under such adverse conditions and mothers who are perceived by their children to be positively supportive are particularly important moderators of the abuse impact (Cox, Kotch and Everson 2003). Resilience may be strongly influenced by the level of family and community support that children experience and this factor is particularly evident for black and minority ethnic children (Mullender *et al.* 2002). The issue for workers is to assess the extent to which women and children have been isolated and stripped of these essential informal supports.

Children whose mothers' mental health is not unduly affected by depression and anxiety also show greater resilience than children whose mothers are suffering these effects of violence (Moore and Pepler 1998). Children may learn very positive aspects of 'survivorship' from those mothers who model assertive and non-violent responses to violence (Peled 1998).

Like their mothers (Holden *et al.* 1998), many children will recover their competence and behavioural functioning once they are in a safer, more secure environment (Wolfe *et al.* 1986). In particular, children who are not continually subjected to post-separation violence (Mertin 1995) and protracted court cases over child contact (Buchanan *et al.* 2001) show a much stronger pattern of recovery.

Conclusion

A significant evidence base now exists on which child protection practitioners need to draw when securing the safety of children who live with domestic violence. Domestic violence is a widespread social problem. This highlights the need for both community-based services which stretch out to all children in need, as well as services and interventions based on individualised assessments for children considered at risk of harm. In making these assessments, it is essential to explore the ways in which children survive in the face of adversity and place this in the context of what is known about the links between child abuse and domestic violence, the risks of post-separation violence, the particular issues which black and minority ethnic children face in relation to international child abduction and forced marriage, and the complex risks associated with substance use and mental health problems which arise in the context of violence and abuse. The risk assessment of the perpetrator is an essential element in this process, which is considered in Chapter 11 and is a missing aspect of this chapter, but one which needs to be recognised and understood in any response made by child protection services in this area.

References

Abrahams, C. (1994) *Hidden Victims: Children and Domestic Violence.* London: NCH Action for Children.

Aris, R., Harrison, C. and Humphreys, C. (2002) *Safety and Child Contact: An Analysis of the Role of Child Contact Centres in the Context of Domestic Violence and Child Welfare Concerns.* London: Lord Chancellor's Department.

Bagshaw, D. and Chung, D. (2000) *Women, Men and Domestic Violence.* Canberra, Australia: Partnerships Against Domestic Violence.

Barnett, O. and Fagan, R. (1993) 'Alcohol use in male spouse abusers and their female partners.' *Journal of Family Violence 8,* 1–25.

Bhugra, D., Desai, M. and Baldwin, D. (1999) 'Attempted suicide in west London, rates across ethnic communities.' *Psychological Medicine 29,* 1125–30.

Brandon, M. and Lewis, A. (1996) 'Significant harm and children's experiences of domestic violence.' *Child and Family Social Work 1,* 33–42.

Buchanan, A., Hunt, J., Bretherton, H. and Bream, V. (2001) *Families in Conflict: Perspectives of Children and Parents on the Family Court Welfare Service.* Bristol: The Policy Press.

Burgess, A., Baker, T., Greening, D., Hartman, C., Burgess, A., Douglas, J. and Halloran, R. (1997) 'Stalking behaviours within domestic violence.' *Journal of Family Violence 12,* 4, 389–403.

Campbell, J., Soeken, K., McFarlane, J. and Parker, B. (1998) 'Risk factors for femicide among pregnant and non-pregnant battered women.' In J. Campbell (ed) *Empowering Survivors of Abuse: Health Care for Battered Women and Their Children.* Thousand Oaks, CA: Sage Publications, pp.90–7.

Campbell, R., Sullivan, C. and Davidson, W. (1995) 'Women who use domestic violence shelters: Changes in depression over time.' *Psychological Women's Quarterly 19,* 237–55.

Cascardi, M., O'Leary, K.D. and Schlee, K. (1999) 'Co-occurrence and correlates of posttraumatic stress disorder and major depression in physically abused women.' *Journal of Family Violence 14,* 227–49.

Cawson, P. (2002) *Child Maltreatment in the Family: The Experience of a National Sample of Young People.* London: NSPCC.

ChildLine (1997) *Beyond the Limit: Children Who Live with Parental Alcohol Misuse.* London: ChildLine.

Cleaver, H., Unell, I. and Aldgate, A. (1999) *Children's Needs – Parenting Capacity: The Impact of Parental Mental Illness, Problem Alcohol and Drug Use, and Domestic Violence on Children's Development.* London: The Stationery Office.

Cox, C., Kotch, J. and Everson, M. (2003) 'A longitudinal study of modifying influences in the relationship between domestic violence and child maltreatment.' *Journal of Family Violence 18,* 1, 5–17.

Davis, K. and Andra, M. (2000) 'Stalking perpetrators and psychological maltreatment of partners: Anger-jealousy, attachment insecurity, need of control and break-up context.' *Violence and Victims 15,* 4, 407–25.

Department of Health (1995) *Messages from Research.* London: HMSO.

Edleson, J. (1999) 'Children witnessing of adult domestic violence.' *Journal of Interpersonal Violence 14,* 839–70.

Farmer, E. and Pollock, S. (1998) *Substitute Care for Sexually Abused and Abusing Children.* Chichester: Wiley.

Frieze, L. and Browne, A. (1989) 'Violence in marriage.' In L. Ohlin and M. Tonry (eds) *Family Violence.* Chicago: University of Chicago Press.

Galvani, S. (2001) 'The role of alcohol in violence against women: Why should we care?' *Practice 13,* 2, 5–20.

Gielen, A., O'Campo, P., Faden, R., Kass, N. and Xue, X. (1994) 'Interpersonal conflict and physical violence during the childbearing year.' *Social Science and Medicine 39,* 781–7.

Gleason, W. (1993) 'Mental disorders in battered women: An empirical study.' *Violence and Victims 8,* 53–68.

Golding, J. (1999) 'Intimate partner violence as a risk factor for mental disorders: A meta analysis.' *Journal of Family Violence 14,* 99–132.

Gorin, S. (2004) *Understanding What Children Say: Children's Experiences of Domestic Violence, Parental Substance Misuse and Parental Health Problems*. London: National Children's Bureau and NSPCC.

Graham-Bermann, S. and Levendosky, A. (1998) 'Traumatic stress symptoms in children of battered women.' *Journal of Interpersonal Violence 13*, 15–25.

Grief, G. and Hegar, R. (1991) 'Parents whose children are abducted by the other parent: Implications for treatment.' *American Journal of Family Therapy 19*, 215–25.

Guy, P. and Harrison, L. (2003) 'Evidence-based social work with people who have substance problems.' In J. Horwath and S. Shardlow (eds) *Making Links Across Specialisms*. Lyme Regis: Russell House Publishing.

Harwin, J. and Forrester, D. (2002) *Parental Substance Misuse and Child Welfare, Executive Interim Report*. London: Nuffield Foundation.

Hendricks, J., Kaplan, T. and Black, D. (1993) *When Father Kills Mother: Guiding Children Through Trauma and Grief*. London: Routledge.

Herman, J. (1992) *Trauma and Recovery*. New York: Basic Books.

Hester, M. and Pearson, C. (1998) *From Periphery to Centre – Domestic Violence in Work with Abused Children*. Bristol: The Policy Press.

Hester, M., Pearson, C. and Harwin, N. (2000) *Making an Impact: A Reader*. London: Jessica Kingsley Publishers.

Holden, G., Stein, J., Retchie, K. and Jouriles, E. (1998) 'Parenting behaviours and beliefs of battered women.' In G. Holden, R. Geffner and E. Jouriles (eds) *Children Exposed to Marital Violence: Theory, Research and Applied Issues*. Washington, DC: American Psychological Association, pp.289–334.

Home Office (2003) *Hidden Harm, Responding to the Needs of Children of Problem Drug Users*. Advisory Council on Misuse of Drugs. London: Home Office.

Hughes, H. (1988) 'Psychological and behavioral correlates of family violence in child witnesses and victims.' *American Journal of Orthopsychiatry 58*, 77–90.

Hughes, H., Graham-Bermann, S. and Gruber, G. (2001) 'Resilience in children exposed to domestic violence.' In S. Graham-Bermann and J. Edleson (eds) *Domestic Violence in the Lives of Children*. Washington, DC: American Psychological Association.

Humphreys, C. (1999) 'Avoidance and confrontation: The practice of social workers in relation to domestic violence and child abuse.' *Journal of Child and Family Social Work 4*, 1, 77–87.

Humphreys, C. (2000) *Challenging Practice: Social Work, Domestic Violence and Child Protection*. Bristol: The Policy Press.

Humphreys, C. and Thiara, R. (2002) *Routes to Safety: Protection Issues Facing Abused Women and Children and the Role of Outreach Services*. Bristol: Women's Aid Publications.

Humphreys, C. and Thiara, R. (2003) 'Domestic violence and mental health: "I call it symptoms of abuse."' *British Journal of Social Work 33*, 2, 209–26.

Humphreys, C., Regan, L., River, D. and Thiara, R.K. (2005) 'Domestic violence and substance use: Tackling complexity.' *British Journal of Social Work 35*, 7, 1–18.

Humphreys, C., Thiara, R.K., Mullender, A. and Skamballis, A. (forthcoming a) 'Talking to my mum.' *Journal of Social Work*.

Humphreys, C., Thiara, R., Mullender, A., and Skamballis, A. (forthcoming b) *Talking About Domestic Abuse: A Photo Activity Workbook to Develop Communication between Mothers and Young People*. London: Jessica Kingsley Publishers.

Hutchinson, I. (2003) 'Substance use and abused women's utilization of the police.' *Journal of Family Violence 18*, 2, 93–106.

Jaffe, P., Wolfe, D. and Wilson, S. (1990) *Children of Battered Women*. Newbury Park, CA: Sage Publications.

Jameison, W. and Hart, L. (1999) *A Handbook for Health and Social Service Professionals Responding to Abuse During Pregnancy*. National Clearinghouse on Family Violence. Ottawa, Canada: Health Canada.

Johnson, H. (1998) 'Rethinking survey research.' In R. Dobash and R. Dobash (eds) *Rethinking Violence Against Women*. London: Sage Publications, pp.23–51.

Jones, L., Hughes, M. and Unterstaller, U. (2001) 'Post-traumatic stress disorder in victims of domestic violence: A review of the research.' *Trauma, Violence and Abuse 2*, 2, 99–119.

Kelly, L. (1994) 'The interconnectedness of domestic violence and child abuse: challenges for research, policy and practice.' In A. Mullender and R. Morley (eds) *Children Living With Domestic Violence.* London: Whiting and Birch.

Kewshaw, C., Budd, T., Kinshott, G., Mattison, J., Mayhew, P. and Myhill, A. (2000) *The 2000 British Crime Survey: England and Wales.* Home Office Statistical Bulletin 18/00. London: Home Office.

Khatkar, H. (2002) *Policy Guidelines and Forced Marriage Project.* Conference Paper, Children and Domestic Violence, Children's Society Annual Conference, West Midlands, March.

Kroll, B. (2004) 'Living with an elephant: growing up with parental substance misuse.' *Child and Family Social Work 9*, 129–40.

Laing, L. (2001) 'Children, young people and domestic violence.' Issue Paper 2, Sydney, Australian Domestic Violence Clearinghouse. Available at www.austdvclearinghouse.unsw.edu.au

Laybourn, A., Brown, J. and Hill, M. (1996) *Hurting on the Inside.* Avebury: Aldershot.

Leonard, K. (2002) 'Alcohol and substance abuse in marital violence and child maltreatment.' In C. Wekerle and A.-M. Wall (eds) *The Violence and Addiction Equation.* London: Routledge.

McClosky, L., Figueredo, A. and Koss, P. (1995) 'The effects of systemic family violence on children's mental health.' *Child Development 66*, 1239–61.

McGee, C. (2000) *Childhood Experiences of Domestic Violence.* London: Jessica Kingsley Publishers.

McLean, D. (1997) 'International child abduction – some recent trends.' *Child and Family Law Quarterly 9*, 386–96.

Mechanic, M., Weaver, T. and Resick, P. (2000) 'Intimate partner violence and stalking behaviour: Exploration of patterns and correlates in a sample of acutely battered women.' *Violence and Victims 15*, 1, 55–72.

Mertin, P. (1995) 'A follow-up study of children from domestic violence.' *Australian Journal of Family Law 9*, 76–85.

Mezey, G. and Bewley, S. (1997) 'Domestic violence and pregnancy.' *British Journal of Obstetrics and Gynaecology 104*, 528–31.

Mirrlees-Black, C. (1999) *Domestic Violence: Findings from a New British Crime Survey Self-Completion Questionnaire.* London: HMSO.

Moore, T. and Pepler, D. (1998) 'Correlates of adjustment in children at risk.' In G. Holden, R. Geffner and E. Jouriles (eds) *Children Exposed to Marital Violence.* Washington, DC: American Psychological Association.

Morrison, K. (2001) 'Predicting violent behaviour in stalkers: A preliminary investigation of Canadian cases in criminal harassment.' *Journal of Forensic Science 46*, 6, 1403–10.

Mullender, A. and Morley, S. (eds) (1994) *Children Living With Domestic Violence.* London: Whiting and Birch.

Mullender, A., Kelly, L., Hague, G., Malos, E. and Iman, U. (2002) *Children's Perspectives on Domestic Violence.* London: Routledge.

O'Keefe, M. (1995) 'Predictors of child abuse in maritally violent families.' *Journal of Interpersonal Violence 10*, 3–25.

Peled, E. (1998) 'The experience of living with violence for preadolescent children of battered women.' *Youth and Society 29*, 395–430.

Plass, P., Finkelhor, D. and Hotaling, G. (1997) 'Risk factors for family abduction: Demographic and family interaction characteristics.' *Journal of Family Violence 12*, 333–48.

Radford, L. and Hester, M. (2001) 'Overcoming mother blaming? Future directions for research on mothering and domestic violence.' In S. Graham-Bermann and J. Edleson (eds) *Domestic Violence in the Lives of Children: The Future of Research, Intervention and Social Policy.* Washington, DC: American Psychological Association.

Richards, L. and Baker, A. (2003) *Findings from the Multi-agency Domestic Violence Murder Reviews in London.* London: Association of Police Officers (ACPO).

Ross, S. (1996) 'Risk of physical abuse to children of spouse abusing parents.' *Child Abuse and Neglect 20*, 589–98.

Rossman, B. (2001) 'Longer term effects of children's exposure to domestic violence.' In S. Graham-Bermann and J. Edleson (eds) *Domestic Violence in the Lives of Children: The Future of Research, Intervention and Social Policy.* Washington, DC: American Psychological Association.

Samas, Y. and Eade, J. (2003) *Community Perceptions of Forced Marriage.* London: Foreign and Commonwealth Office, Community Liaison Unit.

Saunders, H. (2004) *Twenty-Nine Child Homicides: Lessons Still to be Learnt on Domestic Violence and Child Protection.* Bristol: Women's Aid.

Saunders, H. and Humphreys, C. (eds) (2002) *Safe and Sound: A Resource Manual for Working With Children Who Have Experienced Domestic Violence.* Bristol: Women's Aid Federation of England Publications, p.188.

Schornstein, S. (1997) *Domestic Violence and Health Care.* Thousand Oaks, CA: Sage Publications.

Sen, P., Humphreys, C. and Kelly, L. (2003) *Violence Against Women in the UK: CEDAW Thematic Shadow Report.* London: WOMANKIND Worldwide.

Soni-Raleigh, V. (1996) 'Suicide patterns and trends in people of Indian subcontinent and Caribbean Origin in England and Wales.' *Ethnicity and Health 1*, 55–63.

Southall Black Sisters (2001) *Forced Marriage: Interim Report.* London: Southall Black Sisters.

Stanley, N. and Penhale, B. (1999) 'The mental health problems of mothers experiencing the child protection system: Identifying needs and appropriate responses.' *Child Abuse Review 8*, 34–45.

Stanley, N., Penhale, B., Riordan, D., Barbour, R.S. and Holden, S. (2003) *Child Protection and Mental Health Services: Interprofessional Responses to the Needs of Mothers.* Bristol: The Policy Press.

Stark, E. and Flitcraft, A. (1995) 'Killing the beast within: Women battering and female suicidality.' *International Journal of Health Services 25*, 43–64.

Stark, E. and Flitcraft, A. (1996) *Women At Risk: Domestic Violence and Women's Health.* London: Sage Publications.

Sternberg, K., Lamb, M., Greenbaum, C., Dawud. S., Cortes, R., Krispin, O. and Lorey, F. (1993) 'Effects of domestic violence on children's behaviour problems and depression.' *Developmental Psychology 29*, 44–52.

Surtees, P. (1995) 'In the shadow of adversity: The evolution and resolution of anxiety and depressive disorder.' *British Journal of Psychiatry 166*, 583–94.

Walby, S. and Allen, J (2004) *Domestic Violence, Sexual Assault and Stalking: Findings from the British Crime Survey.* Home Office Research Study 276. London: Home Office Research, Development and Statistics Directorate.

Wolfe, D., Zak, L., Wilson, S. and Jaffe, P. (1986) 'Child witnesses to violence between parents: Critical issues in behavioural and social adjustment.' *Journal of Abnormal Child Psychology 14*, 95–104.

Yazdani, A. (1998) *Young Asian Women and Self-Harm: Mental Health Needs Assessment of Young Asian Women in Newham.* London: Newham Innercity Multifund and Newham Asian Women's Project.

Zubretsky, T. (2002) 'Promising directions for helping chemically involved battered women get safe and sober.' In A. Roberts (ed) *Handbook of Domestic Violence Intervention Strategies: Policies, Programs and Legal Remedies.* Oxford: Oxford University Press.

Chapter 2

Multi-Agency and Multi-Disciplinary Work

Barriers and Opportunities

Nicky Stanley and Cathy Humphreys

Introduction

There is no national statutory service in the UK whose principal remit is to protect and support women experiencing domestic violence. The task has been identified and taken on by the voluntary sector and, partly in response to its campaigns, gradually acknowledged as one responsibility among the many shouldered by services such as health, the police, probation and social work. Domestic violence does not fit neatly into statutory family support and child protection services. The focus on the 'paramountcy of the child' in these services means that conflicts arise when there are two victims of the abuse – one of whom is an adult. Hence, there is a potential structural problem which lies at the heart of responding appropriately to the needs of a child living with violence and abuse as well as to those of the adult victim who is usually also the child's mother and primary caregiver. Identifying and overcoming this structural challenge is the key to good practice in work on child protection and domestic violence and takes it beyond the remit of committed individuals who have often attempted to work sensitively and effectively in the area.

This challenge provides the context for this chapter which explores selected aspects of multi-agency and multi-disciplinary working which are relevant to front-line workers and their managers in tackling concerns about children who are living with domestic violence. Workers in this area are required to think about what constitutes good practice in relation to domestic violence, not just good practice in relation to working with children – though of course there are significant overlaps between the two. Not the least of these overlaps is the requirement for multi-agency working.

In the UK, multi-agency local children's safeguarding boards will become a statutory requirement (Children Act 2004, s.13), and new organisational structures such as children's trusts and children's centres will move multi-agency working into the mainstream rather than representing an optional add-on as is frequently the case at present. Discussion of good practice in relation to domestic violence and child protection therefore needs to be directed to a wide range of professionals and agencies who will be working alongside statutory child-care social workers in the future. This chapter will highlight a number of key issues which will become increasingly salient as new service configurations develop in the UK. Such issues include the role of multi-agency domestic violence partnerships, data sharing and referral, the problematic separation of adult and children's services and multi-agency intervention with perpetrators. It will also touch on the more general issue of effective multi-agency and multi-disciplinary work.

Before going any further it may be worthwhile clarifying the terminology we are using. In this we have been helped by the overview by Frost (2005) of front-line working with children which addresses the complex array of language proliferating in the area. The two terms employed here are 'multi-agency working', used to describe work which occurs across and between different agencies, and 'multi-disciplinary working', employed in relation to work between different professionals, some of whom may be co-located within one agency, while others will be working in different organisations. A continuum of work can be identified, with relatively minimal co-operative relationships at one end, moving on to co-ordination of work towards a common goal, through to active collaboration at the other extremity.

Multi-agency working: management and front-line issues

At one level, the necessity for multi-agency working in child protection and family support work area is nowhere more obvious than in the area of domestic violence, where perpetrators of violence need to be challenged, and support and protection for adult and child survivors needs to be delivered. It is not work which can be undertaken by one worker or one agency and frequently requires collaboration with housing, police, education, women and children's voluntary sector organisations, black and minority specialist agencies, health services and probation officers. However, while the need for multi-agency working can appear self-evident, this does not mean that we are entirely uncritical of the concept and this chapter raises a number of issues which need to be addressed if work is to be progressive rather than increasing danger or only experienced as disempowering rather than helpful.

While inquiries into child deaths in the UK, including some such as that into the death of Sukina Hammond (Bridge Child Care Consultancy Services 1991) where domestic violence was a key issue, have emphasised breakdowns in multi-agency communication and collaboration (Reder and Duncan 2004), there is not a great deal of concrete evidence to suggest that multi-agency working has been particularly effective (Corby 2002). There have been few rigorous evaluations; however, one of the more systematic studies (Glisson and Hemmelgarn 1998) undertaken in Tennessee showed that increased inter-organisational co-ordination had a negative effect on service quality and no effect on the outcome of children's improved psycho-social functioning. By contrast, improving the 'organisational climate' measured by low levels of staff conflict, high levels of co-operation, the existence of role clarity and staff being able to exercise personal discretion showed a much greater effect on positive outcomes for children. In the UK context there is, and will continue to be, major re-structuring aimed at increasing multi-agency co-ordination. This may prove an expensive and unhelpful investment unless there is simultaneous attention to improving the 'organisational climate' which can allow multi-disciplinary teams to act effectively in the interests of service users, cutting across vertical hierarchies and bringing decision-making closer to the front-line worker and service users involved (Frost 2005).

Similar reservations exist concerning multi-agency co-ordination in relation to domestic violence. Concerns have been expressed by some writers about the increased surveillance and attendant increase in the power of professionals when agencies develop closely inter-related working practices (Allen 2003). This is borne out by research in the domestic violence arena (Hague, Mullender and Aris 2003) which indicates that the development of more elaborate multi-agency partnership work has not increased the extent to which these partnerships are accountable to survivors of domestic violence. In fact, often the opposite has been true. Greater professionalisation has had the effect of marginalising the voices and the power of the service users to whom these structures should be responsive. In the domestic violence arena there is the added problem that increasing the number of people who know about the whereabouts of a woman and her children escaping domestic violence may only increase the dangers for them. Safety systems need to be tightened in line with the increased knowledge by professionals about the lives of survivors and their children.

On a more positive note, there are excellent examples of multi-agency working in the domestic violence arena which show that policy and practice can change to support survivors and address the issues of social justice (Diamond, Charles and Allen 2004; Hester and Westmarland 2005; Robinson 2003). Work with children which acknowledges and harnesses the knowledge and skills of a range of agencies is more likely to ensure that children's support needs are met (Mullender 2004).

The key question in evaluating the service response is whether it addresses the perpetrator's violence and whether it increases the safety of women and children living with domestic violence as well as responding to the separate needs of children and their mothers. In particular, how the divide is bridged between domestic abuse (usually woman abuse) and child abuse will be a barometer of the success of multi-agency work in this area.

Domestic violence multi-agency forums and partnerships

Inevitably, the top priority is more resources. It is not possible to respond adequately to the linked issues of child abuse and domestic violence without a broad array of community-based services. Every area needs a refuge, an outreach service, groups for children, specialist services which can be accessed for black and minority ethnic women, counselling availability, 24-hour helplines, substance use programmes which acknowledge and address the experiences of domestic violence, a perpetrator programme which meets minimum standards, a supervised contact centre, and an integrated criminal justice response which involves effective co-operation between court support services, police and crown prosecution services. These services need to be accessible to disabled adults and children.

Clearly, many areas fall a long way short of these basic services and hence there is a need for local multi-agency partnerships which have the strategic devel opment of services as a key aspect of their remit. Managers with responsibility for statutory child protection should be well represented at these forums given the very high number of families where domestic violence is an issue within child protection caseloads (Sloan 2004). The UK legislation (Crime and Disorder Act 1998) and guidance (*Developing Domestic Violence Strategies – A Guide for Partnerships*, Home Office 2004) provides the framework for local partnership arrangements through which the domestic violence strategy should be developed. This guidance recommends that partnerships are proactive in working with the proposed local safeguarding boards to establish a shared agenda for children living with domestic violence (p.11).

Without a wide range of community-based services, too many families will be routed into child protection procedures as the only intervention available through which effective action can be taken. Moreover, even where child protection procedures are instituted there will still be a need for a broad range of supportive services. While it is all too easy to blame women for not protecting themselves and their children, where there is domestic violence, it is equally easy to criticise child protection workers (usually social workers) for the inadequacy of their interventions, when in fact they lack sufficient multi-agency backing to respond to families' needs appropriately.

The crucial work of domestic violence forums has been researched by Hague and Malos (1996; Hague 2001). This research makes the point that forums (like all multi-agency working at either operational or strategic level) are only helpful if they improve the breadth of service provision, increase co-ordination between services, improve practice by developing policy and practice guidelines and increased training, alongside an engagement in preventive work. There is little point in a continued 'talking shop' which does not result in actions which improve the direct service to child and adult survivors.

Confidentiality and data-sharing procedures

The complexities of finding a balance between confidentiality (which ensures safety) and data sharing (which can also ensure safety) is undoubtedly a minefield in the area of domestic violence and child abuse. A number of issues need to be disentangled, which include data monitoring, data sharing and referral processes.

Data monitoring refers simply to keeping data/statistics relevant to domestic violence and child abuse in a particular agency and particular area. Systems need to be in place to document the prevalence of reported domestic violence, whether this is within statutory child-care agencies, the court system or refuges, so that there is some possibility of appropriate resources being provided. Not least of these needs is recognising the training needs of the professionals involved and being able to monitor shifts and improvements in practice through the annual collection of benchmark data.

A UK audit (Diamond *et al.* 2004) showed that an agreed definition of domestic violence is the starting point for effective data monitoring: currently, the police are often the primary source of key data. Diamond *et al.* found that only some areas had more effective 'data-capturing systems' that drew data from across agencies and included those working with child abuse.

Data sharing, however, is a more complex process. Studies across different areas of multi-agency working consistently show that agreeing protocols and sharing information about individuals or families is deeply contentious, whether this is in the special needs area (Farmakopoulou 2002), crime prevention (Webb and Vulliamy 2001) or parents with substance use and mental health problems (Kearney and Levin 2000). At the heart of inter-agency problems in domestic violence work lies the need for safety, and tight systems of confidentiality so that women who wish to escape domestic violence do not have their whereabouts inadvertently 'leaked' to the abuser. There is also the added human rights issue of confidential information not being shared with other people without permission.

Such issues have been acknowledged by the Data Protection Act (1998) although there is wide variation as to how this is interpreted between agencies. Approximately two-thirds of partnerships in the UK have, or are in the process of developing, protocols for sharing information (Diamond et al. 2004).

While there is general recognition of the need for 'survivor safety', there are now moves in the UK that will make this more difficult. The proposal to keep a record on every child in the country, which can be shared across agencies, has brought this issue to a head (DfES 2003). The problems in the domestic violence sector involve assuring that data detailed enough to be useful is maintained, while introducing mechanisms which ensure that perpetrators do not have access to their victims.

Currently, many survivors are traced through 'human error' in which court reports, case conference minutes or other documents are inadvertently sent to the perpetrator of abuse. While such errors are not common, they occur on a regular basis and any women's refuge will have recent instances which they can cite. In other circumstances, perpetrators have access via 'friends' in the bureaucracy or in fact are in trusted positions themselves. In the UK, we may now be in danger of legitimising these errors as policy, if any person with 'parental responsibility' (this will include many domestic violence abusers) is allowed access to their child's records, as is currently proposed in some areas. There are similar problems internationally now that the Hague Convention is being used to track not only the perpetrators of violence but also women and children escaping violence (McLean 1997).

Clearly, the emerging use of ICT (information and communication technology) in relation to work with children and families has both opportunities and risks, and as yet the risks of sharing children's records between agencies are not balanced by sufficient safeguards to protect them and their mothers from post-separation violence. The development of such safeguards needs to feature on all multi-agency agendas (Saunders and Barron 2003).

Issues about *referral* are also salient, particularly for statutory child-care agencies. In this context, a number of other issues are pertinent. Guidance in the UK is in the process of changing. However, the current inter-agency guidelines encourage the police to notify social services when they have responded to a domestic violence incident and to make a referral if they have concerns about a child's welfare or safety (Department of Health 1999, p.72). This guidance is a few steps away from the mandatory reporting found in some states of Australia (Waugh and Bonner 2002), and draws a distinction between notification and a clear referral which requires clarification of the concerns.

While these referral policies and guidelines are well intentioned, they are only fruitful if they result in safer and better services for women and children. It requires statutory workers who understand the complex issues of meeting the needs of both the survivor and the child, and enough workers to respond to such referrals. Overwhelming the statutory child and families system with blanket referrals from all organisations when domestic violence is an issue is not helpful and can lead to inappropriate and perfunctory responses. It also needs to be recognised that many women have substantial fears about asking for help because they are worried about their children coming to the notice of child-care social workers (Abrahams 1994; Mullender 1996; Stanley 1997). It is an issue particularly raised in relation to black and minority ethnic women where language, fears of institutional racism, shame and immigration issues may all impact on the compounding nature of their concerns (Batsleer *et al.* 2002; Mullender *et al.* 2002). Survivors will often have experienced being threatened by the perpetrator with social services involvement, and hence there is a particular need for great sensitivity, given the potential for collusion with the perpetrator's threats.

At its worst, referrals from police and other agencies in the UK result in 'cover your back' letters from statutory social workers informing parents that they have come to the notice of social services and that the domestic violence in the household is potentially harmful to their children. Such letters, even when they include information about agencies which might be helpful, reinforce women's worst fears about social work intervention in relation to their children and may therefore close down help-seeking and reinforce the abuser's power and control within the family (Humphreys *et al.* 2001).

Clearly, an important strategic issue (which applies more generally to referrals) is to develop filtering mechanisms for referrals to the statutory agency so that they are able to make an initial assessment about those families who would benefit from an increase in support (section 17 funding for family support, Children Act 1989) and those where there is a risk of significant harm (section 47, Children Act 1989) (Calder, Harold and Howarth 2004). While the UK guidance currently recommends that all children in need should be assessed by social services (Department of Health 1999), it also recommends agreed protocols between agencies about when a referral for a child in need should be made. Again, this is a strategic issue which may involve community-based agencies making initial assessments. It is based on the idea that organisations working with women and/or children, such as health and housing services, may know much more about the risks and the safety mechanisms which are operating within the family (see also Chapter 7). Referral and confidentiality issues can then also be negotiated. These protocols need to be developed and agreed by safeguarding boards. They appear to work best where there is an identified statutory worker with whom the police, voluntary sector, health and housing agencies can consult (Mullender 2004).

The strategic goal for each area/region should be to develop responses across the voluntary and statutory sectors that result in women and children receiving a service which responds to their need for safety as well as resources which reinforce and increase the choices they are able to make. A blanket referral policy in which most domestic violence cases involving children are referred to the statutory agency may in fact increase the danger to children, as the response is flattened out to deal with volume rather than seriousness. Children at real risk of significant harm may then be lost among the 'debris of referrals'.

Separation of services for adults and children

The relationship between children and adult services is a central issue when there is an adult perpetrator (often male), adult victim (usually female) and child victim/s. In the UK, services for children provided by social services, education and health are being brought together under one umbrella – a major multi-agency strategy which is designed to increase co-operation or even collaboration between agencies working with children and young people (Children Act 2004). Within these structures, children 'at risk' should be allocated a lead professional responsible for case management across agencies to provide a range of services tailored to their needs. Moreover, the Home Office guidance (2004) on domestic violence partnerships strongly recommends that children's safeguarding boards provide services for children affected by domestic violence as 'a core part of Boards' children at risk agenda' (p.11) and that work programmes and strategies of domestic violence partnership and local safeguarding boards are aligned. If guidance such as this becomes a reality, there is a possibility that services for children living with domestic violence may improve.

However, there may also be losses unless compensatory mechanisms can be developed, particularly with adult mental health services, community health and substance use services. The evidence in the previous chapter concerning mental health and substance use issues is indicative of the high level of need in these areas. The imperative for mental health services to address the links between women's experience of violence and their mental health through multi-agency working is emphasised by the *Implementation Guidance* on women's mental health (Department of Health 2003). The UK training pack on child protection and mental health (Falkov 1998) is designed to initially bring managers in the two areas together to agree issues of referral, funding and training so that service users do not fall into the cracks between services. This is a particular issue when mental health services have become targeted on 'severe and enduring' mental health issues, and survivors suffering depression, trauma and suicide attempts find it difficult if not impossible in some areas to be assessed for services (Stanley *et al.* 2003). Women suffering depression and trauma reactions may be on the brink of having their children taken into care, yet be unable to find a service which will support their recovery. Referral or support from the local GP to access community-based counselling services may be more appropriate in many of these cases. However, in the UK these services are scarce and, as Davidson *et al.* (2001) note, little is known about the capacity of health services to offer appropriate care and referral to other agencies once domestic violence has been identified. Mapping relevant local counselling services and ensuring health practitioners are aware of their existence is an obvious issue for local partnerships and particularly health agencies within these multi-agency forums to address.

There are also many survivors who are suffering neither mental health nor substance use problems. However, they require a support and advocacy service to assist them with the intense difficulties they face with the emotional chaos of sep-aration, and the logistical hurdles of finding housing, instituting legal proceed-ings, and rebuilding their relationships with their children. In some areas, a small team of domestic violence advocates have been employed to consult on specific cases, develop the strategic issues for the agency, and respond to the survivors involved so that their needs can be addressed without this affecting the focus on the children (Findlater and Kelly 1999). Other areas have developed advocacy services outside the statutory sector, with seconded workers or independent workers responding to the complex needs of survivors. These initiatives provide important avenues through which the needs of adult survivors can be met while the statutory social worker continues to focus on the child. The model clearly fails if services for survivors cannot establish a close working relationship with statu-tory workers and co-ordination and collaboration will be major issues for the lead professional/case manager to address. Joint training, the development of a shared value base, and continued attention to facilitating the relationships between the front-line workers in each service are essential, not marginal, aspects of this work.

Intervention with perpetrators

Nowhere is multi-agency co-operation more important than when working with perpetrators of abuse. The need for civil and criminal proceedings, the issues of safety and violence against workers, the assessment issues, the implications for child protection conferences and the problems of service provision underpin the complexity of work in this area. While Chapters 11 and 12 explore aspects of working with perpetrators, and Chapter 13 addresses the issues of violence against workers, the multi-agency issues need to be raised here.

The central tenet of work in this area is that multi-agency intervention must be effective enough for survivors to believe that they will be safer and more secure outside the relationship than inside it. Domestic violence abusers at the more serious end of the continuum of abuse, where one would expect child protection concerns to be raised, establish a regime of control which typically enforces a belief that they are all-powerful, that any resistance is fruitless, that the violence is the survivor's fault and moreover that 'breaking the rules' and defying the regime of control will result in punishment (Herman 1992). Multi-agency case conferences, whether they are under the umbrella of child protection or criminal justice intervention (domestic abuse multi-agency risk assessment conferences), need to provide convincing evidence to survivors and their children that they are powerful enough to tackle the abuser.

When the relationship between chronic and severe domestic violence and child abuse is considered, the centrality of police involvement in these families is evident. Co-operation between all workers is needed, but police and statutory children and families' workers need to develop a collaboration which may include joint interviewing and evidence gathering if a protective strategy is to evolve. Integrated criminal justice projects in which police, prosecution and domestic violence courts have clear and agreed protocols have also shown an exponential rise in the number of guilty pleas, convictions and participation in perpetrator programmes (Humphreys and Holder 2002; Robinson 2003). The relationship of these domestic violence projects to the protection of children needs to be recognised as these interventions often target the most serious offenders.

While the UK does not allow third parties to take out protection orders as originally proposed in the Family Law Act 1996 (Burton 2003; Humphreys and Kaye 1997), strong encouragement and support for survivors to take out orders needs to be given by workers. Advice needs to recognise that this is a prevention strategy which may not necessarily involve separation, but allows much greater leverage for the police and courts if further incidents of violence occur. Police and prosecution co-operation to make sure that breaches of protection orders are acted upon will increase women's confidence in these forms of multi-agency support and should be facilitated by the implementation of the Domestic Violence, Crime and Victims Act 2004 in the UK.

While work in this area will undoubtedly be enhanced by situating it within a strong legal framework, there are further issues which will need to be tackled in any comprehensive assessment (see Calder *et al.* 2004); these are discussed in depth in Chapter 10. However, there are some basic issues for workers. First, any assessment will need to ensure not only that children are interviewed separately, but that adult carers are also. There are difficulties about the perpetrator either being too close or too distant – an invisible figure in the background perpetrating abuse, but not available for assessment or interview – or ever-present, not allowing a separate assessment to occur. Either scenario is problematic and will need to be carefully negotiated.

Second, workers should not be working alone where there is domestic violence. This is particularly pertinent during assessment. Research with women suggests that one of their greatest concerns is that they will not be believed (Mullender and Hague 2001). Perpetrators are often very plausible and charming. While they constitute a very heterogeneous group, a commonly reported characteristic is their tendency to 'flip' – charming one minute (often in public) and violent and abusive the next (Humphreys and Thiara 2002). Workers may experience the former and find it difficult to conceive of the latter. Survivors and their children are also subjected to both, and their experiences, both positive and negative, may need to be elicited so that the patterns of abuse and the women's and children's vulnerabilities are clarified. This 'check' through the assessment process provided by a second worker is extremely important, and the inclusion of professionals experienced in working with perpetrators is invaluable. The model developing in one area of the UK in which a well-established perpetrator programme contributes to the assessment for statutory children and families' agencies is to be recommended as the way forward for good practice in this area (see Chapter 11). At the very least there needs to be someone in a multi-agency setting trained and experienced in assessment and work with domestic violence perpetrators.

However, parallel or joint assessments will need to be structured by protocols which ensure that the safety of women and children is not compromised. Failure to establish such guidelines from the outset can be damaging both to women and children and to the long-term prospects for multi-agency and multi-professional work (see Bell and Stanley 2005). The same concern for women and children's security needs to underpin child protection conferences when domestic violence is an issue. Ensuring that the case conference does not expose women and children to further or subsequent violence is a responsibility not just for the conference chair and the participating professionals, but also for those who take and distribute conference minutes. This is an area of work which needs to be acknowledged and addressed by local safeguarding boards working in conjunction with domestic violence partnerships.

Assessment is only one aspect of work with perpetrators. Clearly, working with perpetrators is a skill and one which is ideally supported through work on perpetrator programmes which meet minimum standards (see Chapter 11), rather than individual working. The minimum standard guidelines (RESPECT 2004) recommend that a women's support programme runs parallel to any perpetrator programme to provide pro-active outreach to women and children as well as a triangulation of information relevant to the perpetrator's progress. Children's work is now being established alongside these programmes and is a further example of good practice (www.dvip.org).

Conclusions

The issues which need to be addressed by any multi-agency initiative that addresses children's needs in the context of domestic violence are myriad. A number of external injunctions through government guidance actively support different forms of working together across agencies (Department for Education and Skills 2003; Home Office 2004). In the strongly managerial environment which operates in the UK, increasing the number of performance indicators and local public service agreements (LPSA) against which to measure progress as recommended in the Home Office guidance (2004, p.33) would add to the resourcing and (it is hoped) efficiency of multi-agency working. Anything less may end up with the worst of all worlds: injunctions to collaborate without the necessary managerial will and resourcing to make this work in practice – a dangerous scenario when lives and serious crime are involved (Saunders 2005; Walby and Allen 2004).

However, a climate in which workers actively perceive benefit in mutual co-operation as the basis for inter-agency working (Farmakopoulou 2002) is where the most effective partnership arrangements will be found. Creating 'communities of practice' (Wenger 1998) in which the needs of service users are central and where workers trust each other and work towards a set of agreed goals will be where the real tests of multi-agency working lie. At the centre of this work should be the needs of adult and child survivors who experience the multi-agency network around them as empowering their decisions and facilitating steps towards safety and justice.

References

Abrahams, C. (1994) *Hidden Victims: Children and Domestic Violence.* London: NCH Action for Children.

Allen, C. (2003) 'Desperately seeking fusion: on "joined up thinking", "holistic practice" and the new economy of welfare professional power.' *British Journal of Sociology 54,* 287–306.

Batsleer, J., Burnman, E., Chantler, K., McIntosh, H., Pantling, K., Smailes, S. and Warner, S. (2002) *Domestic Violence and Minoritisation: Supporting Women to Independence.* Manchester: Women's Studies Research Centre, Manchester Metropolitan University.

Bell, J. and Stanley, N. (2005) *Tackling Domestic Violence at the Local Level: An Evaluation of the Preston Road Domestic Violence Project.* Hull: University of Hull.

Bridge Child Care Consultancy Services (1991) *Sukina: An Evaluation Report of the Circumstances Leading to Her Death.* London: The Bridge.

Burton, M. (2003) 'Third party applications for protection orders in England and Wales: Service providers' views on implementing Section 60 of the Family Law Act, 1996.' *Social Welfare and Family Law 25,* 2, 137–50.

Calder, M., Harold, G. and Howarth, E. (2004) *Children Living with Domestic Violence: Towards a Framework for Assessment and Intervention.* Lyme Regis: Russell House Publishing.

Corby, B. (2002) 'Inter-professional cooperation and inter-agency coordination.' In K. Wilson and A. James (eds) *The Child Protection Handbook* (2nd edn). London: Baillière Tindall.

Davidson, L.L., King, V., Garcia, J. and Marchant, S. (2001) 'What role can the health services play?' In J. Taylor-Browne (ed) *What Works in Reducing Domestic Violence? A Comprehensive Guide for Professionals.* London: Whiting and Birch.

Department for Education and Skills (DfES) (2003) *Every Child Matters.* London: The Stationery Office.

Department of Health (1999) *Working Together to Safeguard Children.* London: The Stationery Office.

Department of Health (2003) *Women into the Mainstream: Implementation Guidance.* London: The Stationery Office.

Diamond, A., Charles, C. and Allen, T. (2004) *Domestic Violence and Crime and Disorder Reduction Partnerships: Findings from a Self-Completion Questionnaire.* Home Office Online Research Report, No. 56/04. London: Home Office.

Falkov, A. (ed) (1998) *Crossing Bridges: Training Resources for Working with Mentally Ill Parents and Their Children.* Brighton: Pavilion Publishing.

Farmakopoulou, N. (2002) 'What lies underneath? An inter-organisational analysis of collaboration between education and social work.' *British Journal of Social Work 32,* 1051–66.

Findlater, J. and Kelly, S. (1999) 'Reframing child safety in Michigan: Building collaboration among domestic violence, family preservation and child protection services.' *Child Maltreatment 4,* 2, 167–74.

Frost, N. (2005) *Professionalism, Partnership and Joined-Up Thinking: A Research Review of Frontline Working with Children, Research in Practice.* Dartington, Devon: Research in Practice.

Glisson, C. and Hemmelgarn, A. (1998) 'The effects of organisational climate and interorganizational coordination on the quality and outcomes of children's service systems.' *Child Abuse and Neglect 22,* 5, 401–21.

Hague, G. (2001) 'Multi-agency initiatives.' In J. Taylor-Browne (ed) *What Works in Reducing Domestic Violence?* London: Whiting and Birch.

Hague, G. and Malos, E. (1996) *Tackling Domestic Violence: A Guide to Developing Multi-Agency Initiatives.* Bristol: The Policy Press.

Hague, G., Mullender, A. and Aris, R. (2003) *Is Anyone Listening? Accountability and Women Survivors of Domestic Violence.* London: Routledge.

Herman, J. (1992) *Trauma and Recovery.* New York: Basic Books.

Hester, M. and Westmarland, N. (2005) *Tackling Domestic Violence: Effective Interventions and Approaches.* Home Office Research Study 290. London: Home Office Research, Development Statistics Directorate.

Home Office (2004) *Developing Domestic Violence Strategies – A Guide for Partnerships.* London: Violent Crime Unit, Home Office.

Humphreys, C. and Holder, R. (2002) 'An integrated criminal justice response to domestic violence: "It's challenging, but it's not rocket science."' *SAFE, The Domestic Abuse Quarterly 3,* 16–19.

Humphreys, C. and Kaye, M. (1997) 'Third party applications for Protection Orders: Opportunities, ambiguities and traps.' *Journal of Social Welfare and Family Law 19,* 4, 403–21.

Humphreys, C. and Thiara, R. (2002) *Routes to Safety: Protection Issues Facing Abused Women and Children and the Role of Outreach Services.* Bristol: Women's Aid Federation, p.133.

Humphreys, C., Abrahams, H., Hague, G., Hester, M., Lowe, P. and Mullender, A. (2001) 'Domestic violence and child abuse: Developing sensitive policies and guidance.' *Child Abuse Review 10,* 183–97.

Kearney, P. and Levin, E. (2000) *Alcohol, Drug and Mental Health Problems: Working with Families.* London: National Institute of Social Work.

McLean, D. (1997) 'International child abduction – some recent trends.' *Child and Family Law Quarterly 9,* 386–96.

Mullender, A. (1996) *Rethinking Domestic Violence: The Social Work and Probation Response.* London: Routledge.

Mullender, A. (2004) *Tackling Domestic Violence: Providing Support for Children who have Witnessed Domestic Violence.* Home Office Development and Practice Report 33. London: Home Office.

Mullender, A. and Hague, G. (2001) 'Women survivors' views.' In J. Taylor-Browne (ed) *What Works in Reducing Domestic Violence?* London: Whiting and Birch.

Mullender, A., Kelly, L., Hague, G., Malos, E. and Iman, U. (2002) *Children's Perspectives on Domestic Violence.* London: Routledge.

Reder, P. and Duncan, S. (2004) 'From Colwell to Climbie: Inquiring into fatal child abuse.' In N. Stanley and J. Manthorpe (eds) *The Age of the Inquiry: Learning and Blaming in Health and Social Care.* London: Routledge.

RESPECT (2004) *Statement of Principles and Minimum Standards of Practice for Domestic Violence Perpetrator Programmes and Associated Women's Services.* Available at www.respect.uk.net

Robinson, A. (2003) *The Cardiff Women's Safety Unit: A Multi-Agency Approach to Domestic Violence, Final Evaluation Report.* Cardiff: University of Cardiff.

Saunders, H. (2005) *Twenty Nine Child Homicides.* Bristol: Women's Aid.

Saunders, H. and Barron, J. (2003) *Failure to Protect? Domestic Violence and the Experiences of Abused Women and Family Courts.* Bristol: Women's Aid.

Sloan, D. (2004) *Children in Need Census 2003.* Social Factors Survey, Domestic Violence Analysis. Available at www.cheshire.gov.uk

Stanley, N. (1997) 'Domestic violence and child abuse: Developing social work practice.' *Child and Family Social Work 2*, 3, 135–45.

Stanley, N., Penhale, B., Riordan, D., Barbour, R.S. and Holden, S. (2003) *Child Protection and Mental Health Services: Interprofessional Responses to the Needs of Mothers.* Bristol: The Policy Press.

Walby, S. and Allen, J. (2004) *Domestic Violence, Sexual Assault and Stalking: Findings from the British Crime Survey.* Home Office Research Study 276. London: Home Office Research, Development and Statistics Directorate.

Waugh, F. and Bonner, M. (2002) 'Domestic violence and child protection issues in safety planning.' *Child Abuse Review 11*, 5, 282–95.

Webb, R. and Vulliamy, G. (2001) 'Joining up solutions: the rhetoric and practice of inter-agency co-operation.' *Children and Society 15*, 315–32.

Wenger, E. (1998) *Communities of Practice.* Cambridge: Cambridge University Press.

Part Two

Children's Views and Needs

Chapter 3

What Children Tell Us

'He Said He Was Going to Kill Our Mum'

Audrey Mullender

Introduction

It took until 1994 to begin to hear the voices of children speaking directly about domestic violence (Abrahams 1994; Higgins 1994). As in research more generally (Qvortrup 1994), children were not regarded as able to bear reliable witness to their own experience. Parents and professionals had been interviewed in the US and Canada since the 1980s about children living in situations where their mothers were being abused (notably by Jaffe, Wolfe and Wilson 1990), but it took far longer to listen to children.

The first British book on children living with domestic violence (Mullender and Morley 1994) included one chapter of children's own accounts. Later in the same year, a study by NCH Action for Children (Abrahams 1994) featured interviews with seven girls aged between 8 and 17 talking about the abuse they had witnessed and experienced, its effects, their own feelings and understandings, how they had coped and whether anyone had offered them any real help.

Several studies since then have told us more. Violence at home, for a worrying number of children, formed a backdrop to an analysis of calls to ChildLine (Epstein and Keep 1995). Children told ChildLine counsellors either that they felt helpless, anxious and confused or that they were trying to hold the family together or to end the violence. They had called because they could not talk to a frightening father or to a mother they were trying to protect or to anyone outside because the abuse was strictly a family secret. Some who had tried had not been believed, for example at school. Police intervention, where it was mentioned, had not stopped the violence. Few were in touch with social workers (six had actually called to ask to be taken into care) or with refuges.

A national refuge-based study (Hague *et al.* 1996; Mullender *et al.* 1998) included individual and group interviews with children who had recently left violent situations. As well as distress and fear, children revealed their resilience and coping strategies, for example when moving home and school, with the consequent disruptions to their family and friendship networks. Talking about refuges, it seemed that these losses and the further restrictions (overcrowding, younger children being a nuisance, not being able to have friends back because of keeping the location secret) were, for many, outweighed by finally being safe. They liked being with other children and having play facilities and organised activities. Some did not want to leave. In a further refuge-related study (Humphreys 2000), five children all said they would have liked continued contact with a children's programme.

In another small-scale study of the issues and needs of children living with domestic violence in Coventry, 22 children and young people were seen individually or in a group (Hendessi 1997). All had either seen or heard the violence and all had been affected by it emotionally, physically or educationally. They had not felt able to turn for help to either adults or friends. Minority ethnic children faced additional problems, including racial harassment, fear of abduction and the inadequacy of specialist services. All children again had their own coping strategies. The youngest tended to disengage in various ways (playing, hiding, fantasising), while the older ones showed a wider range of symptoms and behaviours, notably truancy among the teenagers.

The two largest studies of children's own experiences of domestic violence conducted in this country to date have been those by McGee (2000) and Mullender *et al.* (2000, 2002), funded respectively by the NSPCC (National Society for the Prevention of Cruelty to Children) and the Economic and Social Research Council (ESRC). By chance, each involved interviews with 54 children. In both, interviewers talked to children about living with direct and indirect abuse, witnessing and overhearing physical, emotional and sexual abuse, and the impacts this had had. Children were also asked about the help they had received. In both studies, experiences of the police were often negative (except where their actions had resulted in safety), and of teachers and social workers variable, whereas refuges were positively regarded by children as having removed them from danger and offered them the chance to talk freely to someone who understood, often for the first time. The Mullender *et al.* (2002) study shows clearly that children found their mothers, in particular, as well as their siblings and friends, and other family members and adults living close to them, to be crucial sources of support – typically far more so than professionals. At their best, adults in authority provided a listening ear and got things sorted. At their worst, they refused to believe children and attributed to naughtiness the effects of sometimes living literally in fear of their lives. It is very hard to reveal the truth when you have been sworn to secrecy by a violent man so this study demonstrates how much further we have to go in listening to children. McGee (2000) also found that children often did not know where to go for help or, if they had heard of ChildLine or other agencies, could not necessarily get to a telephone in safety and privacy. Some children, of differing ages, thought the perpetrator would simply deny whatever they said, even if they could find the words to explain. The Mullender *et al.* (2002) study is also particularly rich in the experiences of black and minority ethnic children, with a whole chapter drawing on interviews with Asian children (see also Imam 1994). Issues for them included the duty not to besmirch their family's honour, the sometimes unmet expectations on paternal family members to provide support, the need to respect a father as an elder even when he was violent, the importance of faith for some, and the links between fear of violence in the home and of racist abuse outside it.

This chapter will draw on three of the above research studies (Hague *et al.* 1996; Humphreys 2000; Mullender *et al.* 2002), and from one or two other stated sources, for direct quotes from children who have lived with domestic violence and who can tell us what it consisted of in their experience, how it overlapped with other forms of abuse, what impact it had on them, and what helped, both in their own efforts and those of other people. The main sources will be referred to throughout as the 'refuge study' (Hague *et al.* 1996), the 'outreach survey' (Humphreys 2000) and the 'ESRC study' (Mullender *et al.* 2002).

What children see and hear – what domestic violence is

Children are witnesses, to a greater or lesser extent, of every aspect of domestic violence against their mothers:

> I've seen him kick and punch, and pull her hair. Once he threw petrol over her. I remember him cutting my mum's lips. (13-year-old girl; outreach survey)

In the Mullender *et al.* (2002) study, persistent and brutal violence had included attempted killings with knives, ropes and poison. Shockingly, pregnancy can be a time of particular risk:

> I remember he kicked my mum in the stomach when she was pregnant. (13-year-old girl; refuge study)

Sadly, it should not surprise us that children have been exposed to such things, because domestic violence is not rare. As many as one in three women can describe having experienced violence in an intimate relationship worse than being grabbed, pushed or shaken, with similar rates across all social and ethnic groupings (Mooney 1994). Although women may also be violent towards men, and there is certainly abuse in same-sex relationships (Island and Letellier 1991; Renzetti 1992), men's abuse of women is historically, statistically and globally the predominant pattern and the one that causes the most fear and physical harm (Mirrlees-Black 1999).

Domestic violence is typically not about one-off incidents of actual violence but a sustained pattern of abusive behaviours and attitudes that may escalate over time. Threatening words and gestures become part of a pervasive atmosphere of fear. Children's drawings show men's clenched fists and women's tears. The intimidation is frequently life-threatening, with something approaching two women a week in England and Wales killed by a partner or ex-partner (see Home Office Crime Statistics, year on year). Strangulation is the most common form of death, with one child producing a graphic picture of a couple silhouetted in a single lit window, the man with his hands round the woman's neck.

Children draw and talk not only about physical but also about verbal and emotional abuse and intimidation, with the abuser undermining the woman until she feels worthless and powerless to escape. Another child drew a picture of a man calling her mother 'stupid' while threatening her with a knife (see Children's Subcommittee of the London Coordinating Committee to End Woman Abuse 1994). Words like the following from children must always be believed and acted upon:

> I felt scared and worried. He said he was going to kill our mum. (13-year-old girl; outreach survey)

Other aspects of domestic violence include inappropriate punishment by violent men – one five-year-old was dragged away from his own birthday party by the hair for becoming over-excited (Mullender *et al.* 2002) – children being directly involved in the domestic violence by being forced to watch, or being used by men to threaten or hurt their partners. Other children (in Mullender *et al.* 2002) could recall rows over money spent on them and even money stolen from them by the perpetrator.

Some children talked about sexual jealousy:

> My mum wasn't even allowed to hang washed clothes outside because he would say she was going out so she could look at other men in the front street. (8-year-old girl; ESRC study)

This adds up to the pattern that has been illustrated by practitioners in Duluth in the form of the 'power and control wheel' (see Figure 3.1). This pattern of behaviour cannot be adequately understood as 'family conflict', or as a phenomenon of 'dysfunctional' or 'dangerous' families (Mullender 1996). It has to be seen as criminal behaviour and as the responsibility of the perpetrator.

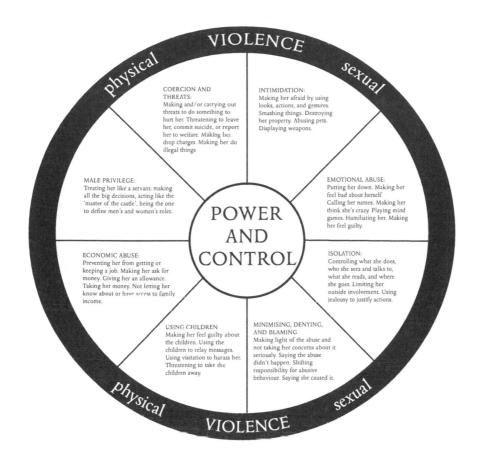

Figure 3.1 Power and control wheel. Source: Pence (1987, p.12). Reproduced by permission of Domestic Abuse and Intervention Project.

Children can grow in this understanding over time. What to a younger one may be:

> all fighting and things like that. I didn't like it. (8-year-old boy; ESRC study)

to an older child, over a number of years, begins to make a different kind of sense:

> it was just one of those things that happened between women and men… I just thought before that…they didn't get along…[but] it got much worse…he just got more vicious. I think it's really life-threatening now, that he's really serious and means to do real harm to us. (13-year-old girl; ESRC study)

Overlap with direct child abuse

Children's accounts make clear the overlap between woman abuse and child abuse:

> He hit my mum, I saw it… My dad hit my sister with a plate and she started bleeding on her head. She was red everywhere. (6-year-old boy; Higgins 1994)

Children who participated in the research studies drawn on in this chapter had also had personal experience of being abused:

> My dad has also hurt me on occasions. He would throw drinks over me and the[n] kick me and punch me in the head but then he would make me stop crying and tell me it didn't hurt. He would tell me it was all my fault and that's why he hit me. (16-year-old; outreach survey)

Other research confirms these double risks (Farmer and Owen 1995; Hester and Pearson 1998; London Borough of Hackney 1993). As many as two out of three child abuse cases may have woman abuse also present so knowledge of one should always be regarded as a reason to look for the other. If an abused woman is in danger, the children may well be also (Bridge Child Care Community Services 1991). Helping an abused woman to be safe is often the best way to make the children safe also, because the woman, once she is out of danger herself, is likely to be far better able to meet their needs (Kelly 1994).

There are also overlaps for children and women in emotional abuse:

> I stood up to him when I was home and he really done my head in all the time. I got just as much abuse as what my mam did. (17-year-old young woman; refuge study)

and in sexual abuse:

> I was raped, you see… Now we're going to court… It was my step-dad who did it. (15-year-old girl; refuge study)

The impact on children of living with domestic violence

Children do know when domestic violence is happening in their households. The majority of children see or overhear it (Abrahams 1994) and almost all see their mothers upset or crying. Mullender *et al.* (2002) found that children knew of incidents of which their parents thought they had been unaware. Living through all this has an impact of its own, beyond that caused by any direct abuse:

> It doesn't just affect the mother – it's the kids… Because they're the ones that have got to see it and hear it. (17-year-old young woman; refuge study)

For children, it is often very frightening:

> I am scared when they fight in the dark. (Children's Subcommittee of the London Coordinating Committee to End Woman Abuse 1994)

and can make them feel guilty:

> I would feel like killing myself because I would think it's my fault, 'cos he drilled it in my head. (17-year-old young woman; refuge study)

These effects can stay with children for some time afterwards and it is one of the roles of refuge children's workers to try and help them make sense of what happened and move on:

> especially I notice, with under-5s, is they can be sitting playing…and then, suddenly…they will say: 'My dad smashed the house up,' or 'My dad had a knife and there was blood'. And then you realise that they have been sitting there and this picture has come into their heads. (Refuge children's worker talking about the value of playwork with the younger residents; refuge study)

A further long-term effect can be to put young people off marriage and relationships:

> [when asked whether, one day, she would like to live with someone and have a family] Never. I don't want to go through what my mum did. (13-year-old girl; refuge study)

The impact domestic violence has depends on the individual child's level of understanding, personality, circumstances, coping strategies and degree of support. There is no one syndrome – children show their distress in as wide a variety of ways as over anything else. The response can be age-related. In the youngest children, for example, one might see sleep disturbances, eating problems, unnatural quietness or clinginess. One mother described how her two-year-old had shown his reactions:

> He was very quiet…he just used to sit… Whenever he saw us arguing, he used to be crying his eyes out all the time. He was 'Mummy, Mummy' and coming to me all the time. (Refuge study)

At any age there can be physical, emotional, psychological and/or behavioural problems, maybe just at home or revealing themselves at school. These may very easily be confused with psychological problems or with physical illness:

> Sometimes I do get bad headaches. (13-year-old boy; ESRC study)

The response in the same child can vary over time and can include opposite behaviours at different times. One young woman described how she had gone from being clingy and withdrawn to acting out (at one time thought of as gendered behaviours specific to girls and boys). Asked what effect her home life had had on her, she said:

> A bad effect. At first, it was – I wouldn't leave my mam, wouldn't leave her anywhere. I was round her all the time. And then, when I was about 14, I used to stay out all the time… Anywhere, just to get out of the house…because I used to make situations worse by answering back. (17-year-old young woman; refuge study)

Similarly, individual children in the same family, despite living through the same events, may each react entirely differently. In one household with three sons (source: refuge study), the eldest physically fought his father, the youngest became very withdrawn, while the middle boy took to staying in his room and developed mental health problems.

One Canadian study showed well over twice the rate of behavioural and psychological problems of other children among those who were living with domestic violence (Wolfe *et al.* 1986). It also showed that some children can recover completely once they are safe and that some appear to have the resilience to survive without particular negative effects. Thus it is important not to see damage, and particularly lasting damage, as inevitable while, at the same time, not underestimating the harm that domestic violence can do to children or the importance of offering realistic help.

Children themselves also talk about the horridness and the unfairness of the losses involved in domestic violence, particularly when there are several moves for practical or safety reasons. School, friends, family, possessions, pets may all have to be left behind:

> I was really upset because I had to leave Thumper behind… I cried and cried. (12-year-old girl, later reconciled with her rabbit; ESRC study)

There are additional issues for black and minority ethnic children who move away from the family and community that constitute their cultural identity:

> You are left without any help or support from the community, if they feel that you have gone against the religion. (16-year-old young woman; ESRC study)

Some practitioners and policy makers take the view that living with domestic violence is itself a form of abuse and should lead to automatic registration on the grounds of emotional abuse. The problem with this kind of response, though, in addition to making blanket assumptions that may not be true for all children in all circumstances, is that it is likely to stop abused women from asking for help for fear of losing their children – a highly counter-productive result.

Why doesn't she leave?

Early on, the woman, and also the children, often believe that the violence is a one-off. The man is typically contrite and he makes promises that it will never happen again:

> Usually he just hits her and...storms out...he just gets so angry... And he feels so bad about it. (13-year-old girl; refuge study)

Both the woman and the children typically still love the man at this point and want the violence to end, not the relationship that they have with him:

> I just wish he would stop and wouldn't get so angry. It's awful. It's so upsetting. (12-year-old boy; refuge study)

After a while, though, it may be the children who see, before their mother, that the violence is not going to stop and that she is in real danger:

> My mum cared for my dad but she was going to get hurt again. I used to see it all. I'd get very upset. (15-year-old boy; ESRC study)

Leaving is not always that easy, not least when either mother or child has an illness or disability:

> We had to be close to a hospital because [my brother] sometimes stopped breathing...they offered us a new place but it was on the fifth floor and I'm scared of heights and my mum's got asthma. So we couldn't move. (12-year-old girl; ESRC study)

And, just sometimes, it is the abuser who leaves rather than the rest of the family:

> Then we came back because Dad was gone, so we just came back and tidied up what he'd messed up and went to bed. (10-year-old girl; ESRC study)

This reminds us that all the emphasis on women leaving violent men perhaps takes the attention away from taking effective action against the perpetrator, as the law increasingly permits. Occupation orders can be applied for under the Family Law Act 1996 part IV and there is now a limited provision in the Children Act 1989 which allows an exclusion order to be taken alongside an interim care order.

Children's own coping strategies

We have gradually come to understand that children are not passive victims of domestic violence but that they are social actors with their own ways of coping:

> We all cope in all sorts of ways. (From group interview with 8- to 13-year-olds; ESRC study)

They also want to be involved:

> It would be better if they let us help. (12-year-old girl; ESRC study)

Of course, there are dangers in intervening directly:

> I have seen my mum be kicked and thrown about. When I tried to help my mum, he pressed and grabbed me. I was angry and I wanted to kick him. (13-year-old girl; outreach survey)

But not everyone has the courage or the ability to intervene:

> I would never stand up to my dad because I've been to[o] scared but on one occasion I pushed my dad to get him off my mum, but she pushed me down to protect me. (16-year-old girl; outreach survey)

After leaving the violence, children still do all they can to help their mothers:

> I help Mum so she doesn't get bad memories. (13-year-old boy; Higgins 1994)

What had helped the most: informal support

It comes through strongly from the ESRC study that children and young people living with domestic violence or its aftermath draw most extensively on informal sources of help. A key finding of the ESRC study was the importance of mothers to children throughout the period of living with the violence and after:

> My mum has helped me the most... I can't really think of anyone else who has really helped me apart from my mum. (13-year-old boy; ESRC study)

Children who are losing all their other support structures, either because the violent man keeps them isolated or because they have had to escape to a refuge, depend heavily on a secure attachment to their mother to help them cope emotionally. A further finding was that, ironically, mothers and children were often trying to protect each other, with mothers unaware how much their children knew:

> But we could hear them arguing them when they were in a separate room. (13-year-old boy; ESRC study)

Children described trying not to let on how much they did know because they thought they were not supposed to talk about it and that their mothers had enough to deal with. This means that it is important to help develop open and honest communication between mothers and their children in contexts of domestic violence (see Chapter 1).

Next after their mothers, children looked to other children, both siblings and friends, for emotional support. In the ESRC study, this was graphically demonstrated by one boy who, at the age of eight, used to climb out of one window and in at another to be with his 13-year-old brother when the violence was happening. The most likely person a child would have told about the violence was a friend. Older girls, in particular, looked for someone who could keep a secret and who would understand:

> My best friend, A, she was having a similar problem. Her mum had run away from her dad's house because he used to beat her up... So we could share what was going on and try to keep each other going. (13-year-old girl; ESRC study)

Sadly, this had not always been possible:

> [My] friend would say 'Isn't it a shame that you've got to be in a refuge', so we said: 'No, not really, it's better than being at home'... They didn't understand... And you couldn't explain. (17-year-old young woman; refuge study)

Recognising how important friends are to young people reminds us that moving around and changing schools to escape the violence destroys children's peer support networks, although many respondents in all three of the studies talked about making new friends in the refuge with others who could understand the past, share the present and build towards the future:

> We look after each other. (10-year-old girl; outreach survey)

After mothers, brothers and sisters, grandmothers were the next most commonly mentioned relatives. Asian children, in particular, had a positive expectation that family members would help; where this did not happen, notably on their father's side for reasons of tradition, it left the woman and her children potentially isolated from their entire family and community.

Sources of formal support

Refuges

Beyond family and friends, children had found refuges to be the most helpful. When asked why women and children go into refuges, one girl replied:

> 'cause they are all getting away from violence. We're all getting away from violence and abuse in here. That's why we are all here. It's good. (11-year-old girl; refuge study)

Children may show a remarkable recovery once they are in a refuge, in terms of a boost to self-esteem and general adjustment:

> We are here to sort ourselves out and get some confidence. (16-year-old girl; outreach survey)

Refuge workers, and children's workers in particular, are seen as offering important support and help. Children most valued a listening ear from someone who understood and was sympathetic:

> She loves the kids. She's the one I've always gone to…she's like a big mother. She's great. (10-year-old boy; refuge study)

Although refuges are by no means perfect – being sometimes overcrowded, noisy and associated with losses and moves in children's lives – most children were full of praise for how it felt to be safe at last:

> You weren't scared of anything. You didn't have to be worried that, like, your dad was going to find you or anything like that. (9-year-old girl; ESRC study)

Children particularly appreciated the 'no violence' rule in the refuge, as an important aspect of helping them feel safe:

> That's good. You shouldn't smack children. It's not fair. (11-year-old girl; refuge study)

> I know that if I saw…anyone else smacking the kids, that used to frighten me because it used to bring back all the memories of seeing my mam getting hit. (17-year-old young woman; refuge study)

Other professionals

Children recalled the police being called frequently to their homes but, once there, doing relatively little that was effective against the abuser. The rather few children in the ESRC study who had had contact with other professionals were typically unsure where they had come from. It was just possible to discern odd references to social workers, court welfare officers, doctors and psychologists. Even then, most, according to the children and young people's accounts, seem to have ignored or skirted round domestic violence as an issue. This made it hard to converse at anything but the most superficial level:

> I used to not know what to say. I used to think I was saying the wrong thing. (15-year-old boy; ESRC study)

The practitioners concerned did not ask what was wrong at home and so were unable to get behind children's health or developmental problems. The children sensed that the adults often did not understand about domestic violence and that it was not safe to talk to them, so they did not fully confide in them. In at least two cases, children had felt forced by the courts into continued contact they had not wanted with the abuser. Having a routine procedure for asking about direct and indirect abuse, in confidence, is essential in all child care, child welfare and child protection contexts if we are actually to arrive at what is best for children. There were other reasons to distrust social workers:

> They threatened that we would be taken into care if she stayed on after he had hit me so badly and hit her. (16-year-old girl; ESRC study)

Given that we have seen how important mothers are to their children where domestic violence is concerned, it would be good to think that social services could work more effectively in partnership with abused women and their children, and Chapter 8 explores this issue.

Some Asian children and young people in the ESRC study additionally feared a racist and inappropriate response from professionals and their agencies:

> Sometimes we have to sort things out in our own way – white people can never really do things in the same way if they don't understand. (16-year-old young woman; ESRC study)

One or two had had bad experiences, for example a lack of confidentiality in a close-knit community. Here again, there are lessons from which we must learn.

Children's services: direct work with children

One key message from listening to children is that we can do far more to offer them continuing help. Refuge children's and outreach workers already undertake a great deal of support of confused and distressed children in relatively informal ways – and they represent a major national resource that is often under-appreci-ated – but other sources of help are decidedly patchy (Humphreys *et al.* 2000).

In the ESRC study, only one child mentioned attending a children's group (Mullender 1994). Yet this kind of resource, which can be run in any children's setting, can do much to help participants come to terms with the violence they have lived with, as well as helping them feel they are not the only ones and that it is okay to talk about the abuse:

> There's all other kids who've been through the same thing...we all do...drawings...about abuse and stuff like that... I can talk to them about...how it happened... We talk about abusing and we have a theme each week...and sometimes they do puppet shows to show us, like, how it happened. (9-year-old girl; ESRC study)

Only two other children out of the 54 in the ESRC study mentioned having had any counselling, one through school and the other through a specialist domestic violence project. Yet young people themselves can see the value of this:

> I think there should be a hell of a lot more done, to talk to them...it's all right [saying]...'Everything's going to be all right'... I think some kids should have counselling... You shouldn't have that sort of strain on a kid. (17-year-old young woman; refuge study)

The purpose of this, according to children, can be to:

> make them feel good about themselves and make them feel it wasn't their fault. (11-year-old girl; ESRC study)

Conclusion

Over the past decade, we have come to understand that it is perfectly possible, provided communication is sensitive and age appropriate, to talk to children and young people about their experiences of living with domestic violence and that they have much to teach us. We no longer think of children as the 'silent witnesses' of domestic violence but as social actors who have their own perceptions and understandings, their own strength and resilience, and their own coping strategies on which to draw. They are involved in their own situations; they have an effect on the circumstances of their own lives. Above all, from their experience of living with it, they can tell us a great deal about domestic violence. They can enable us to understand what helps and what does not, what they want and what they need from us as professionals.

A key message is not to cut across what already exists in their own world when we try to help – not to disrupt the crucial support of their own mothers, family members and friends. The two most important things children ask for are to be safe and to have someone to talk to. We have not done well enough in either of these respects up to now. Let us hope that this book will help us do better.

References

Abrahams, C. (1994) *The Hidden Victims: Children and Domestic Violence.* London: NCH Action for Children.

Bridge Child Care Community Services (1991) *Sukina: An Evaluation Report of the Circumstances Leading to Her Death.* London: Bridge Child Care Community Services.

Children's Subcommittee of the London Coordinating Committee to End Woman Abuse, London, Ontario (1994) 'Make a difference: how to respond to child witnesses of woman abuse.' In A. Mullender and R. Morley (eds) *Children Living with Domestic Violence: Putting Men's Abuse of Women on the Child Care Agenda.* London, Ontario: Whiting and Birch.

Epstein, C. and Keep, G. (1995) 'What children tell ChildLine about domestic violence.' In A. Saunders with C. Epstein, G. Keep and T. Debbonaire (eds) *'It Hurts Me Too': Children's Experiences of Domestic Violence and Refuge Life*. Bristol: Women's Aid Federation of England/ChildLine/NISW.

Farmer, E. and Owen, M. (1995) *Child Protection Practice: Private Risks and Public Remedies*. London: HMSO.

Hague, G., Kelly, L., Malos, E. and Mullender, A. with Debbonaire, T. (1996) *Children, Domestic Violence and Refuges: A Study of Needs and Responses*. Bristol: Women's Aid Federation of England.

Hendessi, M. (1997) *Voices of Children Witnessing Domestic Violence: A Form of Child Abuse*. Coventry: Coventry City Council Domestic Violence Focus Group.

Hester, M. and Pearson, C. (1998) *From Periphery to Centre: Domestic Violence in Work with Abused Children*. Bristol: The Policy Press.

Higgins, G. (1994) 'Children's accounts.' In A. Mullender and R. Morley (eds) *Children Living with Domestic Violence: Putting Men's Abuse of Women on the Child Care Agenda*. London: Whiting and Birch.

Humphreys, C. (2000) *Starting Over: A Consultation with Women and Children from Milton Keynes Women's Aid Outreach Project*. Bristol: Women's Aid Publications.

Humphreys, C., Hester, M., Hague, G., Mullender, A., Abrahams, H. and Lowe, P. (2000) *From Good Intentions to Good Practice: Working with Families Where There is Domestic Violence*. Bristol: The Policy Press.

Imam, U.F. (1994) 'Asian children and domestic violence.' In A. Mullender and R. Morley (eds) *Children Living with Domestic Violence: Putting Men's Abuse of Women on the Child Care Agenda*. London: Whiting and Birch.

Island, D. and Letellier, P. (1991) *Men Who Beat the Men Who Love Them: Battered Gay Men and Domestic Violence*. Binghamton, NY: Harrington Park Press (Haworth).

Jaffe, P.G., Wolfe, D.A. and Wilson, S.K. (1990) *Children of Battered Women*. Newbury Park, CA: Sage Publications.

Kelly, L. (1994) 'The interconnectedness of domestic violence and child abuse: challenges for research, policy and practice.' In A. Mullender and R. Morley (eds) *Children Living with Domestic Violence: Putting Men's Abuse of Women on the Child Care Agenda*. London: Whiting and Birch.

London Borough of Hackney (1993) *The Links Between Domestic Violence and Child Abuse: Developing Services*. London: London Borough of Hackney.

McGee, C. (2000) *Childhood Experiences of Domestic Violence*. London: Jessica Kingsley Publishers.

Mirrlees-Black, C. (1999) *Domestic Violence: Findings from a New British Crime Survey Self-Complete Questionnaire*. Home Office Research Study No. 191. London: Home Office.

Mooney, J. (1994) *The Hidden Figure: Domestic Violence in North London*. London: London Borough of Islington, Police and Crime Prevention Unit (or from Middlesex University, Centre for Criminology).

Mullender, A. (1994) 'Groups for child witnesses of woman abuse: Learning from North America.' In A. Mullender and R. Morley (eds) *Children Living with Domestic Violence: Putting Men's Abuse of Women on the Child Care Agenda*. London: Whiting and Birch.

Mullender, A. (1996) *Rethinking Domestic Violence: The Social Work and Probation Response*. London: Routledge.

Mullender, A. and Morley, R. (eds) (1994) *Children Living with Domestic Violence: Putting Men's Abuse of Women on the Child Care Agenda*. London: Whiting and Birch.

Mullender, A., Debbonaire, T., Hague, G., Kelly, L. and Malos, E. (1998) 'Working with children in women's refuges.' *Child and Family Social Work 3*, 87–98.

Mullender, A., Hague, G., Imam, U., Kelly, L., Malos, E. and Regan, L. (2002) *Children's Perspectives on Domestic Violence*. London: Sage Publications.

Mullender, A., Kelly, L., Hague, G., Malos, E. and Imam, U. (2000) *Children's Needs, Coping Strategies and Understanding of Woman Abuse: End of Award Report Submitted to the ESRC (Award No.: L 129 25 1037)*. Coventry: University of Warwick, Department of Social Policy and Social Work (available from School of Health and Social Studies, University of Warwick, Coventry CV4 7AL).

Pence, E. (1987) *In Our Best Interest: A Process for Personal and Social Change.* Duluth, MN: Minnesota Program Development Inc.

Qvortrup, J. (1994) 'Childhood matters: An introduction.' In J. Qvortrup, M. Bardy, G. Sgritta and H. Wintersberger (eds) *Childhood Matters: Social Theory, Practice and Politics.* Aldershot: Avebury.

Renzetti, C.M. (1992) *Violent Betrayal: Partner Abuse in Lesbian Relationships.* Newbury Park, CA: Sage Publications.

Wolfe, D.A., Zak, L., Wilson, S. and Jaffe, P. (1986) 'Child witnesses to violence between parents: critical issues in behavioural and social adjustment.' *Journal of Abnormal Child Psychology 14,* 1, 95–104.

Chapter 4

Prevention Programmes
for Children and Young People

Jane Ellis, Nicky Stanley and Jo Bell

Introduction

Since the early 1990s, there has been increased awareness and concern about the welfare of children and young people living with domestic violence (Abrahams 1994; Hester, Pearson and Harwin 2000; Mullender and Morley 1994; Stanley 1997), with estimates that a significant proportion of children – between 27 and 60 per cent – experience it in some form (Children and Young People's Unit 2001; Gibbons, Conroy and Bell 1995). Recognition of the widespread nature of the phenomenon has fuelled a move towards undertaking preventive work with general populations of children and young people in schools. This work aims to educate children and young people about domestic violence with the intention of limiting the incidence of violence in younger generations. Such an approach represents a primary prevention strategy and contrasts with previous domestic violence services for children and young people which focused on secondary and tertiary prevention. These were specialist and/or targeted interventions which were confined to addressing the needs of those known to be living with domestic violence.

Primary prevention programmes addressing domestic violence have been delivered and evaluated in North America since the mid-1980s (Burkell and Ellis 1995; Dusenbury *et al.* 1997; Meyer and Stein 2001). In England, such programmes have emerged more recently and several intersecting ideas about children, violence and prevention have underpinned their development: these will be explored in the first section of the chapter. The second section of the chapter reports on a mapping study which reviewed the development of these programmes in England and provides an overview of their key features. The final part of this chapter describes an in-depth evaluation of one such programme, identifying achievements and messages for those designing and delivering similar programmes.

Primary prevention in domestic violence

The dominant model of prevention adopted in England is based on social learning theory (Bandura 1977, 1986), which posits that children learn behaviours, including undesirable ones, when positive outcomes are achieved without eliciting negative sanctions, through which behaviour is reinforced and repeated. Accepted widely in the US, and generally in crime prevention as the 'social development model' (Catalano and Hawkins 1996; Farrington 2000; Hawkins, Catalano and Miller 1992), this is an appealing approach since it suggests that, as behaviours are learned, desirable ones can be acquired in the 'right' environment or undesirable ones already acquired can be un/re-learned. Preventive work based on this approach aims to limit exposure to negative role models and encourage the development of skills. It has a predictive and arguably deterministic element in that services are targeted at those exposed to identified risk factors – with risk rather than need now being the prime means of allocating scarce resources (Kemshall 2002). This model has been widely adopted in England and operationalised through initiatives such as Sure Start, On Track, Children's Fund, Communities That Care and a range of youth justice schemes.

In relation to the primary prevention of domestic violence, this model provides a useful rationale for universal work, since those living with violence can gain support and protection in a potentially non-stigmatising context (Jaffe, Wolfe and Wilson 1990), while simultaneously enabling all children and young people to develop knowledge, skills and attitudes to understand and conduct non-abusive relationships. Developmentally, adolescence, rather than childhood, is regarded as the crucial time to undertake prevention work since it is identified as the period when young people are first venturing into intimate sexual relationships, some of which will be abusive. It is also a time when there is considerable pressure to conform to the social and cultural expectations of gender.

Social learning theory however is not unproblematic since, when applied to explanations of men's violence, it corresponds with the much-rejected 'cycle of violence' theory, which explains domestic violence as an outcome of men having experienced violence in childhood. Undoubtedly, there is empirical evidence showing a relationship between childhood violence and violence in adulthood (Dutton 1995; Hotaling and Sugarman 1986). However, there is no evidence that proves that this is a causal relationship (DfES 2003), nor does the 'cycle of violence' explain the gendered nature of domestic violence or why all boys who experience violence in childhood do not go on to become adult perpetrators. So while feminists and women's organisations have campaigned for and embraced the development of schools programmes, tensions exist since this model of prevention is fundamentally antithetical to feminist explanations of men's violence. This ideological conflict has led to multiple approaches and agendas for programmes with different curriculum content (Gamache and Snapp 1995). Much as in the US, adopting a social learning perspective can lead to an individualistic, ungendered and cognitive-behavioural approach to the work, with programmes focusing on intra- and interpersonal skills rather than (or as well as) addressing systemic, social or cultural knowledges, practices and processes which sanction men's violence.

Tied into this debate is the contested role of schools and teachers in responding to or addressing social issues. Schools as a universal service give access to almost all children and young people and therefore are viewed as a key agency in the delivery of a range of services and as a conduit through which a number of social issues can be addressed (e.g. DfES 2003; Home Office 2004a). They are, on the one hand, positioned as inculcators of societal norms and values and are central in the processes of forming normative gendered identities (Butler 1993; Connell 1993) and so condoning gendered violence (Jaffe et al. 1990; Jones and Mahony 1989). However, schools can also function as agents of social change, so that they can be conceptualised as both sustaining violence and as the starting point for ending it (Harber 2002). This presents challenges and opportunities in establishing and delivering work in schools on gender violence, particularly in the context of the radical shift in educational policy in the UK in the last 20 years which has seen the social justice/equality agenda of the post-war period marginalised by the New Right agenda of competitive individualism, consumerism and notions of the 'responsible citizen'.

Schools, now at arm's length from local education authority (LEA) direction, can opt to address violence with children and young people where they think it is relevant. The introduction of personal, social and health education (PSHE) into the curriculum in England and Wales created opportunities for domestic violence to be addressed alongside such issues as healthy relationships, sex education, bullying, and drugs and alcohol awareness programmes. Within PSHE, the tension inherent between education's potential to both protect and challenge traditional social values has been particularly evident in the debates surrounding sex education (Lewis and Knijn 2002).

However, PSHE lessons have offered opportunities to deliver universal preventive programmes to children and young people. In addition to raising awareness and promoting the development of social and relationship skills, such programmes have the potential to develop and build on the capacity of children and young people to offer one another support. It is increasingly acknowledged (see Chapter 3 by Audrey Mullender; Vincent and Daniel 2004) that children and young people experiencing abuse, relationship problems or domestic violence will often, in the first instance, confide in their peers. Programmes delivered under the umbrella of PSHE have the potential to strengthen the capacity of young people to seek and offer this type of support as well as alerting participants to the existence and means of accessing formal services. However, as the mapping study described below demonstrates, without a coherent national strategy for preventive work on domestic violence with children and young people, development has been localised and fragmented as well as meeting some resistance (James-Hanman 1999; Normandeau, Damant and Rinfret-Raynor 2001).

Mapping programmes in England, Wales and Northen Ireland
Context

A study undertaken in England, Wales and Northern Ireland commissioned by WOMANKIND Worldwide found that, by 2003, programmes were being, or had been, delivered in 102 local authorities (Ellis 2004). Although the spread of programmes was wide, generally the work was better established and further developed in urban areas. This appeared to be related to the availability of funding and/or the presence of individuals or collectives promoting the work rather than the work being mainstreamed or embedded in the school curriculum. Funding was a key factor in determining many aspects of the work. Although the work was financed from numerous sources, almost all funding was short-term, making programmes insecure and potentially unsustainable along with raising a number of organisational and management issues. Six bodies were the principal funders, with the Children's Fund, LEAs and community safety partnerships contributing to around a fifth of all programmes. Seventy per cent of programmes began between 2000 and 2003; this rapid development was directly related to an increase in the availability of Home Office funding and the creation of initiatives such as the Children's Fund with its prevention agenda.

On average, programmes lasted two years, with sustainability being highly dependent not only on the type of funding, but also on the extent to which the work was embedded in the school curriculum or whether it had been developed and supported in a strong multi-agency context. Programmes were initiated through a number of routes, with a range of organisations and individuals promoting the work, although two main patterns emerged from the study. The first of these involved specialist service providers such as Women's Aid or Rape Crisis extending their services to general populations of children and young people; the second entailed work being instigated by multi-agency forums and/or crime partnerships. There were few examples of the work being initiated by schools or LEAs, which contributed to the difficulty in mainstreaming programmes. It was notable that, in areas where the work had been successfully developed and delivered in a multi-agency setting, an education professional was always a central participant.

Programmes were delivered to a range of policy agendas; again this related to funding sources. Where work was funded by community safety partnerships, the Children's Fund or the Home Office, crime reduction/prevention was the principal agenda; however, where schools, LEAs or youth services carried a significant proportion of the costs, personal and social development and rights (children's, women's, human) were the key agendas. The work was almost exclusively delivered as part of the PSHE curriculum and although this is the most obvious and easiest place to accommodate the work, other subject areas such as English, history and citizenship might also offer opportunities. While some programmes did promote a whole-school approach and made clear links to other education initiatives, such as Excellence in Cities, social inclusion and bullying, how and to what extent individual schools embedded the work was unclear.

Content and structure of programmes

The programmes studied varied markedly in length, ranging from one-off 20-minute 'talks' in school assemblies to programmes of unspecified length. The most common length and pattern for programmes was six hours, delivered as six one-hour sessions; the predominance of this model appeared to be determined by resources, understandings of curriculum planning or by what organisations assumed schools would be prepared to take up. There was no evidence that the length of a programme was related to judgements about what children and young people might need or want to learn. Principally there were five key programmes in use. The Sandwell pack, *Violence Free Relationships* (2000), was delivered in four areas and had been used as a basis for a number of others. Several areas intended to adopt the Westminster programme (Debbonaire and WDVF 2002). The *STOP* pack (London Borough of Islington 1994) was used exclusively as a resource to inform new programmes. Leeds reported five current or past programmes, which were heavily used as a foundation for new work in other areas. Work based on *Protective Behaviours* (2004), a personal safety programme, was delivered in five areas. In essence this was an ungendered cognitive-behavioural model of violence and its prevention although, in some of its manifestations, it did address gender issues.

A complex and interlinked set of themes ran through programmes, which reflected the multiple agendas of programmes and competing approaches to the work. Affective, values and skills education along with learning about violence were evident. Some topics aimed at supporting children and young people who were living with violence, while also equipping all participants with knowledge and skills to identify and avoid (as either perpetrator or victim) violent relationships. Least evident were challenges to the cultural norms of schools or activities where children and young people were able to explore their experiences of power/powerlessness in their relationships. Many programmes drew on feminist understandings of violence while others were tentative, using a gender-neutral definition or explaining violence as an outcome of interpersonal conflict rather than locating it in the broader social context.

Most programmes included a breadth of methods that might engage children and young people and match a range of learning styles, although some were more participative and experiential than others. Just over half of the programme packs studied included practice guidance with a range of topics covered to varying degrees. Only four programmes included teaching notes and points for discussion to guide those delivering them, although there were very few comments in any programme on negative responses the material might elicit or how to deal with these should they arise.

Participants

Almost all programmes were delivered in mainstream schools with just over a third also operating in special schools. Just over a third were also delivered in a range of community settings, the most common being young people's centres which increased the possibility of reaching socially excluded groups of children and young people. The majority of programmes were delivered in mixed sex groups, although 41 per cent combined mixed and single sex working in a variety of ways; this enabled programmes to be more responsive to the needs of particular groups and to profit from the advantages of both approaches. The number of children and young people who participated in programmes in a given year ranged from 20 to 7500, with two-thirds of programmes having fewer than 500 participants; mainstreaming or multi-agency working appeared to be a more effective means of gaining access to greater numbers of children and young people. However, given the structure and non-institutionalised nature of most programmes, it can be concluded that the vast majority of children and young people had limited opportunities to address issues of domestic violence through the education system. Where teachers were not involved in delivering the programmes, as was the case with almost half of those studied, the potential for long-term change appeared limited since relatively small numbers of children and young people could be worked with at any one time and there was less likely to be continuity and progression as programmes were mostly delivered once to particular groups of children and young people.

Staff from a number of organisations were involved in delivering the work, although youth workers and staff from women's organisations, predominantly Women's Aid, featured most often. Almost all staff had undertaken specific training on domestic violence where the most common topics addressed were types of abuse and issues of power and control. The least common aspect was managing group dynamics, which suggested that the focus was on knowledge and understanding of issues rather than on skills to facilitate learning. No references were made in the packs to the gender or ethnicity of facilitators or how this might impact on group dynamics and learning.

Evaluating programmes

It was difficult to draw any firm conclusions about the efficacy or impact of the work as very few rigorous evaluations had been conducted or published at the time the mapping exercise was undertaken. Forty-three per cent of programmes had been evaluated in some way. Pre- and post-intervention questionnaires were the most common tool suggested or used in evaluating programmes. In the seven evaluation reports made available for the study, multi-methodological strategies had been employed. All of these evaluations were conducted immediately after the end of the programme; therefore long-term outcomes were unknown. However, all of these programmes had been well received by most children and young people, although in two cases young men in secondary schools were generally less responsive than girls or younger boys. Many adults thought programmes were successful and the approaches to the topic were engaging. Teachers generally thought drama and/or theatre were good ways to deliver PSHE and that programmes raised awareness which enabled young people to think in a more informed way about forming non-abusive relationships. The final section of this chapter reports on one of the few independent programme evaluations undertaken in England and Wales to date and considers the evidence for the achievements and difficulties encountered by such programmes in depth.

A programme evaluation: preventing domestic violence in schools

The Healthy Relationships Schools Programme was designed specifically for delivery to Year 8 pupils, aged 12 or 13, in schools on an inner-city housing estate characterised by high rates of social exclusion. The participating schools were selected by the domestic violence project which designed and implemented the programme. This neighbourhood-based project, which also provided services for women experiencing domestic violence and for perpetrators (Bell and Stanley 2005), was jointly funded and administered by New Deal for Communities, the local health action zone (a government-funded initiative aimed at improving the health of a particular locality, now discontinued) and the probation service. The schools programme emphasised the social learning model discussed above and its design was informed by a number of published programmes.

The programme aimed to help young people recognise domestic violence in order that they might avoid such abuse in future relationships. As the programme title suggested, the focus was on positive behaviour in relationships, although issues of gender, power and inequality were also identified and explored. The main messages were centred on helping young people develop caring and respectful relationships in which their first priority would be to look after their own physical and emotional well-being and to recognise destructive behaviour in their own and their parents' relationships.

The domestic violence project commissioned a local theatre company with experience of theatre-in-education work to write and deliver a drama production and to collaborate with project staff in developing a series of related interactive workshops. The issues in the performance and follow-up workshops were chosen to reflect the PSHE requirements of the National Curriculum which emphasise young people's need to develop social skills, awareness, self-esteem and motivation. The programme was delivered in four schools between 2001 and 2003. The evaluation involved three of these schools and was undertaken by an independent university team using a three-stage survey implemented before, immediately after and one year after the programmes; discussion groups with pupils were also undertaken.

The first workshop was delivered by the theatre company staff immediately following the drama performance. Five subsequent workshops, each lasting an hour, were delivered on a weekly basis by the domestic violence project worker who worked alongside a school nurse and a youth worker, and in some schools the PSHE teacher. One teacher from the school was present at all times to supervise pupils and participate when appropriate.

There were significant variations in the input received by different schools included in the evaluation. Some of these appeared to be determined by the ability of schools to find room for the programme in the timetable. Two schools received the full programme which consisted of the drama performance and subsequent workshop followed by a series of five additional weekly workshops. The other school received an abbreviated package consisting of the drama performance and subsequent workshop only. A total of 150 pupils who attended the play and the workshop which followed it, and 185 pupils who received the full programme package, participated in the evaluation.

In addition, ownership of the programme moved in 2002 from the domestic violence project (which closed prematurely) to a neighbourhood development corporation. This had the effect of shifting the underpinning ideology of the programme away from an explicitly feminist agenda towards a less gendered approach. There were also variations in the gender mix of the staff delivering the programme. While most of the staff were female, in one school a male facilitator was incorporated into the team. This appeared to be significant for the boys participating in the programme.

Increasing awareness and capacity to seek and offer support

The evaluation suggested that the programme had been effective in increasing awareness and understanding of domestic violence among young people in schools in the area. Prior to the programme, the evaluation, in common with Mullender's (2000) survey, identified considerable confusion concerning the nature of domestic violence. Following the programme, pupils in all three schools were more likely to see domestic violence as something that happened in families. The shift was particularly noticeable in the school where awareness of domestic violence was lowest prior to the programme. In this school, where the programme delivered included a more explicit approach to gender issues, the pupils were also more likely to consider that domestic violence was mostly about men bullying women after the programme. However, pupils' understanding of domestic violence increased along this dimension in all schools. Pupils participating in the group discussions described how the programme had changed the way they thought about domestic violence:

> It made my understanding clear. Before this was brought up I didn't even know what it meant. (Year 8 girl)

> I thought it was just one of those things that hardly happens but it showed me that it wasn't. (Year 8 boy)

The evaluation also found that participants had absorbed messages about disclosing domestic violence and seeking help from the programme. The most popular choice of sources of support reported by pupils included friends, parents and other close family members who were trusted. These sources of support were also more likely to be accessible to participants:

> My uncle – I can actually talk to him properly – he would sit and listen. (Year 8 boy)

> Friends, sometimes friends can be more understanding. (Year 8 girl)

A group of girls participating in one of the discussion groups reflected on the value of increased awareness in developing their capacity to offer peer support:

> It made you think that it does happen more often than you think, but people don't tell you.

> It could be happening to someone you talk to but they don't tell you.

> It helps you notice it more – like if someone was going through it you could help them out. (Year 8 girls)

Gender issues

While pupils' responses to questions concerning equality in relationships demonstrated generally positive attitudes and beliefs both before and after the programme, there was evidence of an increasing tolerance towards aggression in females, particularly in the school where the programme delivered carried a more explicitly feminist agenda. The findings here on attitudes towards aggression in relationships highlighted the dangers and difficulties of delivering messages such as 'girl power' and 'we can do it too' to young people at this developmental stage. Future programmes need to address gender issues in an appropriate and sensitive way and be wary of encouraging girls to approve assertive models of behaviour which could encompass violence.

Overall, pupils reported high levels of satisfaction with the programme; they enjoyed learning about domestic violence in a participatory and interactive way. Boys were generally less enthusiastic than girls who reported higher levels of satisfaction with the programme overall. In the main, boys had more enthusiasm for the play than the workshops. Boys were also more positive about the active elements of the workshops than the girls. In the school where a male facilitator had contributed to the delivery of the programme, boys had clearly valued his involvement. At this school, boys were less positive about the play and more positive about the workshops than the boys in the school with comparable programme input. These findings highlight the value of a male role model who can communicate messages about respect and equality in relationships while conveying an image of masculinity acceptable to adolescent boys.

Sustaining change

Data from the third stage of the survey, which could only be completed in one school, indicated that some change was sustained over time. However, there was also evidence that some of the messages and information from the programme had not been retained by pupils one year after the end of the programme. Programmes need to be embedded in the PSHE curriculum if they are to have a long-term impact. One discussion group participant identified the need for such messages to be repeated:

> I would like to have it again in Year 11 so I could keep it in mind – to learn it again in case I forgot. (Year 8 boy)

These girls described the perceived benefits of a more inclusive and ongoing approach to domestic violence prevention in schools:

You learn more – it's more about what you need to know if it does happen.

You need to learn about real life, not just about things to get a job.

I think you learn more. Like the stuff that you learn in school it's not about family or anything.

This is more about what you need to know if anything does happen.

I think you need both sorts of lessons because you need to be educated for different jobs but you also need to learn about real life and what's going on and what could happen to you. (Year 8 girls)

Conclusion

The evidence presented in this chapter indicates that, while domestic violence prevention programmes aimed at young people can have identifiable outcomes, such work remains at the early stages in England and Wales. If these programmes are to have a long-term impact and to provide young people with support throughout the rocky terrain of adolescent relationships, they need to be more fully integrated into schools' curricula: such an approach would ensure mainstream funding for primary prevention in domestic violence. Currently, too many programmes appear to be delivered on a one-off basis to comparatively small groups of young people with no follow-up or reinforcement of key messages.

However, the future ownership of such programmes needs careful consideration. The ideology, design and delivery of preventive programmes clearly make a difference and such matters as the extent to which a programme explicitly addresses gender inequality, the use of theatre/drama elements and the gender of the staff delivering the programmes appear to be significant. The development of extended schools in England and Wales (DfES 2003) may offer more opportunities for such programmes to be delivered through long-term partnerships between schools and voluntary organisations such as Women's Aid but, as noted earlier and demonstrated by the case study included in this chapter, long-term sustainability is not generally a feature of the voluntary sector. The incorporation of domestic violence into the new child protection guidance for schools (DfES 2004), with encouragement to use available resources, suggests some government support for prevention programmes. Likewise, Home Office (2004b) guidance encourages schools and colleges to address domestic violence under the topic of personal safety; however, no additional funding had been identified or made available at the time of writing.

Mainstreaming the work might have the effect of restricting opportunities to explore different models of design and delivery for such programmes. Large-scale evaluation would be helpful in identifying models whose effects are sustainable over time. As this chapter has demonstrated, young people themselves have strong feelings about which learning approaches are most effective and can comment on the relevance and usefulness of preventive programmes. Their views need to be incorporated into any evaluation.

References

Abrahams, C. (1994) *The Hidden Victims: Children and Domestic Violence.* London: NCH Action for Children.

Bandura, A. (1977) *Social Learning Theory.* Englewood Cliffs, NJ: Prentice-Hall.

Bandura, A. (1986) *Social Foundations of Thought and Action.* Englewood Cliffs, NJ: Prentice-Hall.

Bell, J. and Stanley, N. (2005) *Tackling Domestic Violence at the Local Level: An Evaluation of the Preston Road Domestic Violence Project.* Hull: University of Hull.

Burkell, J. and Ellis, K. (1995) *Principles of Effective Anti-Violence Education: A Review of Prevention Literature.* London, Ontario: Centre for Research on Violence Against Women and Children.

Butler, J. (1993) *Bodies That Matter: On the Discursive Limits of Sex.* London: Sage Publications.

Catalano, R. and Hawkins, D. (1996) 'The social development model: A theory of antisocial behaviour.' In D. Hawkins (ed) *Delinquency and Crime: Current Theories.* Cambridge: Cambridge University Press.

Children and Young People's Unit (2001) *Tomorrow's Future. Building a Strategy for Children and Young People.* London: Department for Education and Skills.

Connell, R.W. (1993) *Schools and Social Justice.* Philadelphia, PA: Temple University Press.

Debbonaire, T. and Westminster Domestic Violence Forum (WDVF) (2002) *Domestic Violence Prevention Pack for Schools.* London: WDVF.

Department for Education and Skills (DFES) (2003) *Every Child Matters.* Cmnd 5860. London: The Stationery Office.

Department for Education and Skills (2004) *Safeguarding Children. Child Protection: Guidance About Child Protection Arrangements for the Education Service.* London: DfES.

Dusenbury, L., Falco, M., Lake, A., Brannigan, R. and Bosworth, K. (1997) 'Nine critical elements of promising violence prevention programs.' *Journal of School Health 67,* 10, 409–14.

Dutton, D. (1995) 'Male abusiveness in intimate relationships.' *Clinical Psychology Review 15,* 6, 367–581.

Ellis, J. (2004) *Preventing Violence Against Women and Girls: A study of educational programmes for children and young people.* London: WOMANKIND Worldwide.

Farrington, D. (2000) 'Explaining and preventing crime: The globalisation of knowledge.' Keynote address to the American Society of Criminology 1999, *Criminology 38,* 1, 1–23.

Gamache, D. and Snapp, S. (1995) 'Teach your children well. Elementary schools and violence prevention.' In E. Peled, P. Jaffe and J. Edleson (eds) *Ending the Cycle of Violence. Community Responses to Children of Battered Women.* Thousand Oaks, CA: Sage Publications.

Gibbons, J., Conroy, S. and Bell, C. (1995) *Operating the Child Protection System.* London: HMSO.

Harber, C. (2002) 'Schools as violence: An exploratory overview.' *Educational Review 54,* 1, 7–16.

Hawkins, D., Catalano, R. and Miller, J. (1992) 'Risk and protective factors for alcohol and other drug problems in adolescence and early adulthood: Implications for substance abuse prevention.' *Psychological Bulletin 112,* 1, 64–105.

Hester, M., Pearson, C. and Harwin, N. (2000) *Making an Impact: Children and Domestic Violence: A Reader.* London: Jessica Kingsley Publishers.

Home Office (2004a) *The Role of Education in Enhancing Life Chances and Preventing Offending.* Development and Practice Report 19. London: Home Office.

Home Office (2004b) *Developing Domestic Violence Strategies: A Guide for Partnerships.* London: Home Office Violent Crime Unit.

Hotaling, G.T. and Sugarman, D.B. (1986) 'An analysis of risk markers in husband to wife violence: The current state of knowledge.' *Violence and Victims 1,* 2, 101–24.

Jaffe, P., Wolfe, D. and Wilson, S. (1990) *Children of Battered Women*. Newbury Park, CA: Sage Publications.

James-Hanman, D. (1999) 'Inter-agency work with children and young people.' In N. Harwin, G. Hague and E. Malos (eds) *The Multi-Agency Approach to Domestic Violence: New Opportunities, Old Challenges?* London: Whiting and Birch.

Jones, C. and Mahony, P. (1989) *Learning Our Lines. Sexuality and Social Control in Education*. London: Women's Press.

Kemshall, H. (2002) *Risk, Social Policy and Welfare*. Buckingham: Open University Press.

Lewis, J. and Knijn, T. (2002) 'The politics of sex education policy in England and Wales and the Netherlands since the 1980s.' *Journal of Social Policy 31*, 4, 669–94.

London Borough of Islington (1994) *STOP: Striving to Prevent Domestic Violence – Resource for Working with Children and Young People*. LBI: Women's Equality Unit.

Meyer, H. and Stein, N. (2001) *Relationship Violence Prevention Education in Schools. What's Working, What's Getting in the Way, and What Might Be Some Future Directions*. Paper presented at the 7th International Family Violence Research Conference, Portsmouth, NH.

Mullender, A. (2000) *Reducing Domestic Violence: What Works? Meeting the Needs of Children*. Crime Reduction Research Series. Coventry: University of Warwick.

Mullender, A. and Morley, R. (1994) *Children Living with Domestic Violence: Putting Men's Abuse of Women on the Child Care Agenda*. London: Whiting and Birch.

Normandeau, S., Damant, D. and Rinfret-Raynor, M. (2001) *Program Developers and Program Consumers: Some Important Features of the Diffusion of School-Based Violence Prevention Programs*. Available at www.harbour.sfu.ca/treda/reports/gc205.htm

Protective Behaviours (UK) (2004) Information available at www.protectivebehaviours.co.uk

Sandwell Against Domestic Violence Project (2000) *Violence Free Relationships: Asserting Rights. A Programme for Young People*. Sandwell: SADVP.

Stanley, N. (1997) 'Domestic violence and child abuse: Developing social work practice.' *Child and Family Social Work 2*, 3, 135–45.

Vincent, S. and Daniel, B. (2004) 'An analysis of children's and young people's calls to ChildLine about abuse and neglect: A study for the Scottish child protection review.' *Child Abuse Review 13*, 2, 158–71.

Chapter 5

Listen Louder

Working with Children and Young People

Claire Houghton

Introduction

> Member of Scottish Parliament (MSP): You spoke about feeling more confident once you got to know your child support worker. How did you feel before your support worker came into your life?

> 'Mags' (age 14): I did not know what to do. I had no-one to talk to. All my feelings just crammed up inside me, and sometimes they got the better of me. I do not know what I would do if I did not have a support worker. (Scottish Parliament 2002a, col. 2433)

In November 2002, a young person with experience of domestic abuse and receiving support from Women's Aid broke new ground in representing children and young people experiencing domestic abuse in Scotland. She gave evidence at a Parliamentary Committee in support of a petition demanding more help and support, on behalf of children involved in the Listen Louder campaign, co-ordinated by Scottish Women's Aid. Over the next three years, the Scottish Parliament and Executive began not only to listen but to act on what was said by children and young people, acknowledging them as not only competent but as 'first class' (Scottish Parliament 2002a, col. 2431) witnesses about their own lives, and experts in relation to the services they needed.

The Listen Louder campaign utilised a unique body of skills and knowledge developed through decades of direct work with children surviving domestic abuse: it transposed, enhanced and developed this expertise to empower young people to have a say in service development and engage in the world of politics.

Encouraging and enabling children and young people to express their feelings and views in the 1990s, documenting and publicising their views (Scottish Women's Aid 1995, 1997, 1999) and related research (for example Forman 1991; Mullender and Morley 1994), had been successful in transforming public awareness of the effects of living with domestic abuse on children and young people and of the links between domestic abuse and child abuse. However, despite the inauguration of the Scottish Parliament in 1999 and its early commitments to 'put children first' (First Minister) and make domestic abuse a priority for government, the close network of children's and young people's support workers in Women's Aid (and the young people they worked with) were acutely aware of the continued existence of gaps in their service. They were also aware that many young people could articulate their experiences, needs and views on services, that involvement in research or campaigning with and for their peers could have an intrinsic value, and that the political climate was such that young people's involvement and real influence might be possible. This chapter charts the process, progress and challenges of the Listen Louder campaign: the fertile ground for children's voices to be heard; the multi-faceted layers of young people's participation; the identification of need by young people and the political and organisational influence they achieved.

The context for the campaign

To understand the context to children's voices gaining political prominence, it is important to consider the specifics of the situation in Scotland. That Mags actually gave evidence in person to a committee of the Scottish Parliament is a tribute, not only to her bravery and the support of her peers, and the commitment of children's support workers, but to opportunities that have arisen through devolution. The establishment of the Scottish Parliament radically changed the political context for working with women, children and young people experiencing domestic abuse: many powers relating to domestic abuse (including legislative powers) were devolved from Westminster to Scotland (with notable exceptions of immigration and benefits); the first elections ensured 'high' female representation (37% of MSPs) which immediately made a difference to the way politics in Scotland was being conducted (Breitenbach and Mackay 2001); and a 'power sharing' structure made it more possible for 'the people' to participate in the development, consideration and scrutiny of policy and legislation.

From the onset, parliamentary debates (seven in the first five years were dedicated to violence against women) recognised feminist organisations and in particular Women's Aid as the experts in the field of domestic abuse, who had struggled for decades 'in the face of hostility from other agencies and the public', 'on a shoestring', to support women and their children (Scottish Parliament 2002b, col.

15917). The *National Strategy to Address Domestic Abuse in Scotland* (Scottish Executive 2000a) attained united parliamentary (cross-party) agreement and exemplifies the 'mainstreaming' of the feminist violence against women agenda in Scotland (Breitenbach and Mackay 2001). There is now widespread acceptance of the feminist analysis of abuse, recognising domestic abuse as a gender-based abuse that requires a gender-specific response, which is reflected in the rhetoric of Parliament:

> I accept that no form of violence against anyone – regardless of their gender – should be tolerated. I am saying that domestic violence against women is a manifestation of the structural inequalities in society and that, if we do not address those inequalities, the violence will continue. (Scottish Parliament 2003, col. 3724)

The implementation of the strategy's wide-ranging plan of action will be achieved through an infrastructure consisting of a 'national group' (The National Group to Address Violence Against Women) of eight experts chaired by a Minister, focused working groups covering specific areas of prevention, protection, provision, and multi-agency partnerships in each of the 32 local authority areas. However, the challenge will be to ensure that the feminist organisations that instigated and defined the political agenda are not sidelined and are adequately funded for their vital and expanding services. Nearly £33 million has been allocated up to 2006 to implement the strategy, including refuge development and services development (requiring match funding with local authorities). The next challenge facing the national group is to devise a coherent national funding strategy which addresses the range of services women, children and young people state that they need, and prevention and training services (see Scottish Executive 2004a).

One of the crucial achievements of the National Strategy is that it sets not only the experiences but the rights of children and young people firmly within this feminist discourse: it states that, in accepting the definition of domestic abuse (the mental, emotional, physical, sexual abuse of women by their partner or ex-partner), 'it must be recognised that children are witness and subject to much of this abuse and there is some correlation between domestic abuse and the mental, physical and sexual abuse of children' (Scottish Executive 2000a, p.6); an urgent priority for action is the 'development of a clear understanding of needs' of children and young people (p.20) and, most progressively, it states that children as well as women 'must receive support and services to enable them to identify their needs, make choices and have their needs addressed, as well as to participate in developing services to address their needs in the future' (p.7). Unfortunately, the mainstreaming of children's experiences and rights in the domestic abuse strategy, including the recognition of children's agency in defining services, did not ensure that domestic abuse was mainstreamed into the subsequent reform of children's services.

For Scotland's Children (Scottish Executive 2001) set the agenda for better integrated children's services in Scotland a year after the strategy and failed to reflect (or even reference) the strategy's commitment to identify children and young people experiencing domestic abuse as a particular group that 'requires services to meet their specific needs' (Scottish Executive 2000a, p.7). It did, however, raise issues directly relevant to this group of children and young people such as the lack of a common definition of 'children in need', the lack of integration of policy within the Executive, and the struggle to agree outcomes and targets across departments and agencies. It consolidated a children's rights perspective (following the Children (Scotland) Act 1995 and the ratification of the United Nations Convention on the Rights of the Child), through a framework that viewed the child as an active agent in his or her world with a right to participate in decisions which made an impact on their lives, while recognising that this cultural shift would prove a challenge for adults and adult-led agencies.

A later audit and review of child protection in Scotland (Scottish Executive 2002a) was influential in bringing domestic abuse, the National Strategy, and to a certain extent Women's Aid from the periphery to a more central role in child protection and thereafter children's services. 'At least' a third of child protection cases reviewed involved domestic abuse and the audit's broadened definition of abusive situations clearly included 'domestic abuse (primarily of mothers) which caused the physical or emotional abuse of children' (Scottish Executive 2000a, p.36), both key factors in the recognition of children and young people experiencing domestic abuse as 'children in need'. However, it warns that progress is undermined when increased awareness leads to haphazard, unhelpful practices such as immediately viewing children as in need of 'child protection' and not recognising 'that protecting the mother may be the best way to protect the child/ren' (Scottish Executive 2002a, p.154): its partner report, Growing Support (Scottish Executive 2002b), challenges the key concept of 'parental responsibilities' without any distinction on the grounds of gender (highly relevant to the current review of Family Law) in relation to vulnerable children and further highlights the need to support non-abusing mothers and target abusive men. The review recognised that agencies have major difficulties in helping children in these situations; and that providing for the needs of children experiencing domestic abuse should be a priority for inter-agency planning.

Children and young people's involvement in identifying those needs and consequent local and national action to meet their needs was, and is, the challenge. Since devolution it has been said that the rhetorical battle for children's participation in national policy making has been won across the UK, the problem being how to involve children effectively and meaningfully (Hill et al. 2004). The

Scottish Parliament commissioned guidelines for its committees to improve their consultation with children and young people in relevant aspects of policy making and legislation (Borland *et al.* 2001). The Executive funded a *Re:action Consultation Toolkit* (Save the Children 2001) for those wishing to consult children and young people on policy issues – it was prime time for agencies to match the rhetoric with action for children and young people experiencing domestic abuse (Scottish Women's Aid 2002).

In a country of over five million people (Scotland's Census 2001), approximately two million are women – one in five of whom experience domestic abuse at some point in their lives (Scottish Executive 2000b); one million are children (Scottish Executive 2001), which means that a large number of children live with domestic abuse. Although there is no national prevalence figure available, a small local pilot study highlighted that a third of pupils in one school disclosed (anonymously) that they were living with domestic abuse (Alexander, Macdonald and Paton 2004), laying the ground for a national study.

The scope for the needs of this group of children to be overlooked has been great: traditionally this has been conceptualised as an 'adult' issue, where children have been the 'hidden victims' and women the 'service users'. It has been addressed in the context of a service culture where children were viewed as passive recipients of services rather than citizens with human rights (Scottish Executive 2001). Compounding this, the policy discourses of violence against women, and children and young people (including children's services and child protection), had been separate and disparate, with little influence over each other, and the new (extensive) role of the Executive was a long way from integrated, joined-up working.

Yet children experiencing domestic abuse had not been silent and were frustrated that adults 'ignore me just because I am small'. Their Please Listen (Scottish Women's Aid 1999) postcard campaign elicited responses as early as the first parliamentary debate on domestic abuse:

> The clear message that comes through from the children's comments is that they need services in their own right…the most telling comments are the two words 'please listen'. Listening in itself is not enough. We need to hear the voices of children and act upon them. (Scottish Parliament 1999, col. 191)

At that time, a member of the partnership devising the national strategy had written to the children 'can you shout a bit louder please, us auld yins are a bit deaf': a child's postcard unwittingly gave the ultimate response 'Listen more loudly please'. When neither the domestic abuse, child protection or children's services agenda had led to a significant increase in the number of support workers for children and young people across Scotland by 2002, the Listen Louder campaign for action for children and young people experiencing domestic abuse was born.

The Listen Louder campaign

The Listen Louder campaign involved many children and young people who had experience of domestic abuse, some of whom were living in refuges (safe houses), some had moved on (receiving follow-on support), and others (unfortunately very few) had an outreach support worker in their community. It also involved other young people supporting their campaign against domestic abuse and for support-peers at school, drama groups, drumming and other youth groups. Over three years, children and young people achieved different levels of participation (Hart 1997) when expressing their views, wishes and needs to relevant audiences (Borland et al. 2001) through events, film making, and the first research in Scotland with children experiencing domestic abuse. Participation took a number of different forms:

1. A high profile yearly public event ensured that children, and only children, had access to Ministers of the Scottish Parliament. The event was chaired by young people who very ably ensured that no-one spoke except children and Ministers. Ministers' Question Time, where children from across Scotland devised questions (to be read by themselves or another if it was unsafe to do so), put Ministers on the 'hotspot' in relation to what mattered to young people. Multimedia presentations (spoken word, DVDs, plays) dramatised young people's views through their words, poems, stories, creations relating to abuse, support, prevention and peer support. Due to popular demand, the event/venue itself involved an increasing amount of participation and noisy collective enjoyment for all young people attending.

2. Listen Louder films and DVDs showed participation at its minimum and optimal levels: from a graphic designer donating time to set children's work and views to music (the adults chose Suzanne Vega), to 100 young people's postcards to Parliament set to music chosen by a separate small group of young people (they chose an upbeat and recent dance soundtrack!); a camcorded film by three young women, with background music of traffic, about their outreach support and how support workers should be available to children in every community throughout Scotland (North Ayrshire Women's Aid); young people experiencing domestic abuse and a youth group working together to devise, script, photograph and develop a 'Young People Against Domestic Abuse' DVD (Scottish Women's Aid 2003) aimed at their peers, with music and support from R'n'B star Christina Aguilera, co-ordinated by the young people and their support worker at Dunfermline Women's Aid. Influenced by these

pioneering projects, young people in contact with Women's Aid groups across Scotland were invited to work with the Media Co-op film company and Scottish Women's Aid to create, script, film (parts), edit and develop their own Listen Louder film (Scottish Women's Aid 2004).

3.   Groundbreaking research (commissioned by a working group of the National Group to Address Violence Against Women) examined women and children's experiences, preferences and priorities in relation to refuge provision (Fitzpatrick *et al.* 2003). Women's Aid received funding to undertake and record 11 focus groups (57 children) throughout Scotland in collaboration with the Glasgow University research team, who in their analysis exemplified children as 'co-constructors of knowledge' (Moss 2002, p.6), young people's views figuring largely in their recommendations. When asked for views on the allocation of £6 million of Executive funding for refuge development (£10 million in all), one boy said 'I'd rather tell them myself' (refuge research focus group, unpublished), and so, through Listen Louder events, he (and many other young people) did.

4.   The views expressed by children and young people in this refuge research and through Listen Louder projects – of their experiences of support services and involvement in research/policy-making processes – are integral to current research into their views of best practice (Houghton, forthcoming), which so far has involved a further 44 children and young people in a sequence of focus groups, interviews and workshops (including their production of and launch of the above film based on their own priorities).

Participation of children and young people in the two pieces of research (the 'refuge' and 'best practice' studies) and the creative projects was framed in the light of collective knowledge and experience of support workers, insights from children they had worked with in the past and were working with currently, closely relating and conflating their best practice in supporting children and young people experiencing domestic abuse to best practice in researching with children and young people (see for example Alderson 1995; Mullender *et al.* 2002). Levels of participation varied for many reasons, most especially the time and resources available, but political expediency, especially in relation to funding and policy opportunities, was also significant. The degree of participation was also influenced by matching the nature of activity to its purpose (Sinclair 2004), to children's ideas, and also their abilities, age, and their situation/feelings in relation to domestic abuse: their safety and protection were paramount, not only in relation to protection from the abuser but in ensuring that the process did not cause further harm in any way.

Time was of the essence in numerous ways, including the fact that this might be one of the first times the child had spoken or been listened to, that the pace of the child's disclosure and communication might have meant that a lot of time listening, perhaps on different occasions, would have been preferable (and was often not possible) or that their lives might be such that they were 'vulnerable to disclosing information which they had barely had time to process beforehand' (Curtis *et al.* 2004, p.171). The uncertainty of their lives might result in children feeling too vulnerable or upset suddenly to take part at all; participation might represent an extra pressure and also children might move on soon after taking part (for example due to their housing situation or further abuse). The balance between including children at this difficult time in their lives as 'agents of their own lives...on the basis of who they are, rather than who they will become' (Moss 2002, p.6), while not exploiting them or wasting their time, was important, as was stating clearly that big changes such as building a new refuge would not happen in their time (all children enthusiastically joined in 'to make things better for future children'). It was therefore essential that participation in the research complemented and was part of their ongoing support from their support worker and mother/carer.

Women's Aid developed a culture where each actual act of participation and/or consultation had an intrinsic value (pride and respect in being asked views, enjoyment, peer support) and a reward (trips, vouchers, meals), the reward not being known before participation. Careful framing of activities contributed to challenging and alleviating feelings that children themselves associated with domestic abuse: empowerment could combat feelings of powerlessness; groupwork could alleviate isolation; exploring issues together could address feelings of blame/silence/it's taboo; meeting others your own age who'd 'been through it' could make you feel better (Fitzpatrick *et al.* 2003; Scottish Women's Aid 1994, 1997, 1999, 2004); speaking out and being noisy could break the silence and fear, and be fun!

The continued role of the support worker (pre-, during and post-interaction with the researcher, or presence at an event, or production of a film) was essential, especially in their continuous support of the child/young person according to her/his wishes and needs, but also in ensuring that the principles of respect, rights and role in decision making was reflected through their local approach, so participation was not experienced as a tokenistic or isolated event (Borland *et al.* 2001; Sinclair 2004). While the child was in contact with the campaign their support worker could instantly feed back to young people any national influence achieved, and further relevant opportunities where their voices could be heard and best interests served (Borland *et al.* 2001): Listen Louder events and productions provided fora through which children could access and influence those in power in the short term, long before research reports were completed and put into action.

Listen Louder – achieving change

It is young people's engagement with and access to the highest level of policy makers, and their achievement in changing the face of domestic abuse services in Scotland, that sets this campaign apart. The campaign caught public, agency and media attention. Actual engagement with Ministers effectively brought their portfolios of education and young people (including children's services and child protection), social justice (including violence against women and housing) and health together. It was unprecedented that three Ministers attend a launch and then, when a young person bluntly asked why she was being forced to have contact with her extremely abusive father despite her clear evidence to the court, the Justice Minister in the audience was brought to the stage (and into the frame of responsibility). Margaret Curran MSP (the chair of the National Group and Minister for Social Justice at the time), a leading advocate against violence against women, declared to the young people that Ministers would take action: she invited children to the National Group (a closed meeting held shortly afterwards) where they galvanised commitment to implement the domestic abuse strategy (protection, provision, prevention) with the participation of young people; she immediately dedicated interim funding (£0.5 million in total) to those Women's Aid groups without a children's service 'while longer term solutions are explored' (Scottish Parliament 2002b, col. 15906); all Ministers present made a commitment to the children to improve support, which ensured that the Cabinet Delivery Group for Children finally expressed collective responsibility for action. A group of young people delivered their petition for more support ('we need more help') to Parliament and their representative, Mags, was praised by the convenor as 'as good a petitioner as we have seen' (Scottish Parliament 2002a, col. 2432). She was successful in progressing the 'cause' of young people's participation while achieving unanimous cross-party support and acceptance of the petition (creating champions of children's issues in violence against women debates) and thereby setting into action the committee's powers to scrutinise the work of the Executive.

As a cumulative result of this pressure for cohesive action, a high level working group to devise a strategy for support services for children and young people experiencing domestic abuse was formed, bringing together Scottish Executive leads in child protection, children's services, violence against women, health and the Scottish Children's Reporters Association, NHS Scotland and Scottish Women's Aid. Meanwhile, Ministerial response was such that at each event (or quickly thereafter) children and young people achieved change and witnessed immediate effects of their participation:

1. The Scottish Executive accepted a model for future refuge provision in Scotland which is a small cluster of self-contained family flats with communal space including age-specific rooms: the traditional shared

model is to be phased out. Young people's recommendations (Fitzpatrick *et al.* 2003) were largely taken on board in the second phase of funding for 29 refuge development projects (£10 million in all); however, a major flaw in many new projects is that although there is improved designated space for children there are not age-appropriate spaces. One boy elected to return for the final Listen Louder event and, although delighted with local plans reflecting his views, he challenged the Minister about the partial implementation of recommendations: he was reassured that any future development would take cognisance of all elements of the model and that a template for refuges would be created, with (it was hoped) the involvement of young people.

2. Ministers announced that they would immediately fund a computer in every refuge, moved by the computer-aided expression of feelings/views by young people (pioneering work over the last decade by South Ayrshire Women's Aid culminating in the 'Opinion Zone' CD-ROM launched in early 2005), and also by young people's expressed frustration in terms of homework space, time and lack of internet access.

3. Ministers supported the peer support campaign in Year Two: 'Domestic Abuse is not OK but it's OK to talk about it: support each other'; each pupil in Scotland receiving a postcard (but not as yet adult support should they need it). Young people each year showed that support of their peers (those who had experienced domestic abuse and those who had not) was crucial. Young supporters of the campaign formed peer groups to change attitudes, name abuse for what it is, break down barriers and encourage young people to talk to each other, and aimed their DVD and drama productions at all adults and young people. A recent Minister for Education and Young People, moved by his first experience of Listen Louder in 2004 and specifically by a high-school play on the subject of disclosure, is keen to progress the young people's agenda for education services complementing National Group action to implement *Preventing Domestic Abuse: A National Strategy* (Scottish Executive 2003).

4. Young people continuously detailed the lack of support available through the research, events and films, and identified gaps and needs in relation to services (an increased level and range of support in refuge, when they leave (follow on), plus access to support wherever they live, involving one-to-one and group support, age-appropriate support/activities, helplines, drop-in centres, 24-hour support and outreach support workers). The working group collected and heard their evidence and that of pilot outreach and prevention projects in Ayrshire and commissioned research to map services (Stafford 2003) that confirmed Women's Aid as the provider of direct specialist services in Scotland. The report questioned the ad-hoc, inconsistent, piecemeal

approach to funding across local authorities (approximately £2.1 million in total), which was 'not apparently related to need or population density' (Stafford 2003, p.19). The group made firm recommendations to Ministers to fund the specialist service, as well as progressing work to establish all agencies' responsibility to young people experiencing domestic abuse. It further analysed children's data in relation to the staff they felt necessary to meet children's expressed needs (a minimum of two full-time support workers per refuge to ensure each child receives a quality continuous service, and an outreach support worker in all areas to begin to address the needs of children in the wider community).

5.   At the final Listen Louder event, the First Minister had named support services to young people affected by domestic abuse as a national priority for children's services plans 2005–8; specific guidance relating to the inclusion of services to children experiencing domestic abuse was issued to local authority planners (Scottish Executive 2004b); and the Communities Minister announced £6 million in funding (2006–8) through the Violence Against Women agenda to be focused directly at Women's Aid support services for children and young people experiencing domestic abuse.

Listen Louder – challenges for the future

Children and young people experiencing domestic abuse have successfully challenged the dominant discourse which depicts children and young people as lacking the knowledge, agency or competence to participate in policy debate (Edwards *et al.* 2004). They have transformed the current political climate and the future of domestic abuse services in Scotland, and provided much-needed evidence (Sinclair 2004) that participation can have an impact on major policy and resource decisions. By doing so, they have set adults many challenges:

- Will the participation of young people endure and become embedded in the future delivery, progression and evaluation of policies in which they have actually had influence?

- Will the complexities of domestic abuse be recognised and the link between adults' rights and children's rights, woman protection and child protection, women's services and children's services be central to future reform?

- Will protective and preventive measures enhance and not hinder the provision of services, for example ensuring only safe contact is awarded? Will participative approaches receive adequate funding?

- Can local planning partners 'Listen Louder'? Will they listen to young people's high evaluation of distinct specialist services when mainstreaming, integrating and allocating resources?

- Will we continue to work with children and young people to find ways of enabling those who are still silent to speak, and those who speak to reveal more if they choose, in their own time, in their own way? Will we work with their technological expertise to open new avenues of communication?

- Can we work together to ensure that whoever the child chooses to trust – family, friend, voluntary or statutory worker – that privileged person is supported and enabled to listen and act?

In relation to domestic abuse there are now four 'P's: provision, protection, prevention *and* participation. Once you are invited to 'walk a mile in a kid's shoes' (Scottish Women's Aid 2004), you can never stop.

References

Alderson, P. (1995) *Listening to Children: Children, Ethics and Social Research.* Barkingside: Barnardo's.

Alexander, H., Macdonald, E. and Paton, S. (2004) 'Raising the issue of domestic abuse in school.' *Children and Society,* published online 17 June 2004.

Borland, M., Hill, M., Laybourn, A. and Stafford, A. (2001) *Improving Consultation with Children and Young People in Relevant Aspects of Policy-Making and Legislation in Scotland: Guidelines for Scottish Parliamentary Committees.* Edinburgh: Scottish Parliament.

Breitenbach, E. and Mackay, F. (2001) *Women and Contemporary Scottish Politics: An Anthology.* Edinburgh: Polygon.

Curtis, K., Roberts, H., Copperman, J., Downie, A. and Liabo, K. (2004) '"How come I don't get asked no questions?" Researching "hard to reach" children and teenagers.' *Children and Family Social Work 9,* 167–75.

Edwards, R. and Davis, J., with Participants (2004) Final Seminar of the series Challenging 'Social Inclusion': Perspectives for and from Children and Young People. 'Setting the Agenda: Social Inclusion, Children and Young People.' *Children and Society 18,* 2, 97–105.

Fitzpatrick, S., Lynch, E., Goodlad, R. with Houghton, C. (2003) *Refuges for Women, Children and Young People in Scotland.* Edinburgh: Scottish Executive.

Forman, J. (1991) *Is There a Correlation Between Child Sexual Abuse and Domestic Violence? An Exploratory Study of the Link Between Child Sexual Abuse and Domestic Violence in a Sample of Intrafamilial Child Sexual Abuse Cases.* Glasgow: Women's Support Project.

Hart, R. (1997) *Children's Participation: The Theory and Practice of Involving Young Citizens in Community Development and Environmental Care.* New York: Unicef.

Hill, M., Davis, J., Prout, A., Tisdall, K. (eds) (2004) 'Moving the participation agenda forward.' *Children and Society 18,* 2, 77–96.

Houghton, C. (forthcoming) *'I Can Speak For Myself, You Don't Have To': Children and Young People Experiencing Domestic Abuse – Their Views of Good Practice* (working title only). Coventry: University of Warwick.

Moss, P. (2002) *From Children's Services to Children's Spaces.* Paper presented at seminar 1 of the ESRC Seminar Series Challenging 'Social Inclusion'. Perspectives for and from Children and Young People. Edinburgh: University of Edinburgh.

Mullender, A. and Morley, R. (1994) *Children Living with Domestic Violence: Putting Men's Abuse of Women on the Child Care Agenda.* London: Whiting and Birch.

Mullender, A., Hague, G., Imam, U., Kelly, L., Malos, E. and Regan, R. (2002) *Children's Perspectives on Domestic Violence.* London: Sage Publications.

Save the Children (2001) *Re:action Consultation Toolkit: A Practical Toolkit for Consulting Children and Young People on Policy Issues.* Edinburgh: Save the Children Programme.

Scottish Executive (2000a) *National Strategy to Address Domestic Abuse in Scotland.* Edinburgh: Scottish Executive.

Scottish Executive (2000b) *Domestic Abuse Recorded by the Police in Scotland 1 April–31 December 1999.* Statistical Bulletin: Criminal Justice Series Bulletin CrJ/2000/5. Edinburgh: Scottish Executive.

Scottish Executive (2001) *For Scotland's Children.* Edinburgh: Scottish Executive.

Scottish Executive (2002a) *It's Everyone's Job to Make Sure I'm Alright: Report of the Child Protection Audit and Review.* Edinburgh: Scottish Executive.

Scottish Executive (2002b) *Growing Support: A Review of Services for Vulnerable Families with Very Young Children.* Edinburgh: Scottish Executive.

Scottish Executive (2003) *Preventing Domestic Abuse: A National Strategy.* Edinburgh: Scottish Executive.

Scottish Executive (2004a) *Domestic Abuse: A National Training Strategy.* Edinburgh: Scottish Executive.

Scottish Executive (2004b) *Children and Young People Experiencing Domestic Abuse: Guidance Note for Planners.* Edinburgh: Scottish Executive.

Scottish Parliament (1999) *Official Report: Session 1999–2000.* Vol. 02 No. 02. 2 September 1999. Debates: Domestic Violence. Edinburgh: Scottish Parliament.

Scottish Parliament (2002a) *Public Petitions Committee Official Report: Session 1.* 19 November 2002. New Petitions: Domestic Abuse (Support) (PE560). Edinburgh: Scottish Parliament.

Scottish Parliament (2002b) *Official Report: Session 1.* 28 November 2002. Debates: Domestic Abuse. Edinburgh: Scottish Parliament.

Scottish Parliament (2003) *Official Report: Session 2.* 27 November 2003. Debates: Violence Against Women. Edinburgh: Scottish Parliament.

Scottish Women's Aid (1994) *Welcome and Hello Magazines.* Edinburgh: Scottish Women's Aid.

Scottish Women's Aid (1995) *Children: Equality and Respect: Children and Young People's Experiences of Domestic Abuse.* Edinburgh: Scottish Women's Aid.

Scottish Women's Aid (1997) *Young People Say.* Edinburgh: Scottish Women's Aid.

Scottish Women's Aid (1999) *Young People's Aid.* Edinburgh: Scottish Women's Aid.

Scottish Women's Aid (2002) *Listen Louder: Prevention, Protection, Participation, Provision.* Edinburgh: Scottish Women's Aid.

Scottish Women's Aid (2003) *Young People Against Domestic Abuse DVD.* Edinburgh: Scottish Women's Aid.

Scottish Women's Aid (2004) *Listen Louder Film.* Glasgow: Media Co-op.

Sinclair, R. (2004) 'Participation in practice: Making it meaningful, effective, sustainable.' *Children and Society 18,* 2, 106–18.

Stafford, A. (2003) *Mapping Support Services to Children and Young People Experiencing Domestic Abuse in Scotland.* Edinburgh: Scottish Executive.

Part Three

Protecting Women
and Children

Chapter 6

Asking About Domestic Violence – Implications for Practice

Marianne Hester

Introduction

Asking about domestic violence (or routine enquiry) by professionals working in child protection, health and other social care settings can enable women, and sometimes children, to disclose their experiences of domestic violence so that they may be given the appropriate support or be referred to other agencies (Hester and Westmarland 2005). It is an approach that has developed mainly in the health-care field and flows from the recognition that women may be more likely to disclose domestic violence to a health-care professional than to other agencies such as the police (Davidson *et al.* 2000, 2001). This chapter looks at the findings from some of the only research to date in the UK involving routine enquiry by social workers and other child protection professionals. It indicates how use of routine enquiry, when coupled with training on awareness of domestic violence and how to ask about domestic violence, plus inventories or other 'tools' to help systematic enquiry, may improve practice with mothers and children living in circumstances of domestic violence. The emphasis on initial service responses to women and children complements the account in the following chapter by Jan Breckenridge and Claire Ralfs of an Australian framework which aims to develop front-line workers' responses to domestic violence. The studies examined here focused on an NSPCC team between 1996 and 1998 – 'the NSPCC study' (Hester and Pearson 1998) – and on health visitors and social care staff between 2001 and 2003 – 'the Home Office study' (Hester and Westmarland 2005).

The NSPCC study

The NSPCC study was carried out in close co-operation between researchers from the University of Bristol, led by the author, and an NSPCC team (Hester and Pearson 1998), and funded by a grant from the Joseph Rowntree Foundation. A 'reflective practitioner' action research approach to evaluation was used (Everitt *et al.* 1992; Shakespeare, Atkinson and French 1993). The NSPCC team had as their main area of work ongoing preventive and recovery work with children. They had previously found that engaging with the issue of domestic violence in their work led to positive outcomes for women and their children. However, the team were unsure how to incorporate domestic violence as a consistent issue, and were also unsure as child-care professionals how to work with needs that they had previously considered the domain of those working with adults.

In order to introduce the issue of domestic violence into the work of the team two main approaches were adopted:

1. The use of team meetings to discuss definitions of domestic violence, and to examine the incorporation of domestic violence through 're-framing' of past and current cases.

2. The development of a simple monitoring scheme for domestic violence to be applied across the team's work and to allow systematic and routine enquiry.

Interviews with staff and analysis of case files were carried out to ascertain and chart any changes concerning the practice of the team following the implementation of routine enquiry. Some observation of practice was carried out to help aid understanding of the practice of the team in greater depth, and a limited survey of survey users' views was carried out.

Three separate periods over the 2.5 years included in the research were examined to ascertain possible changes, with particular focus on the first two years, as follows:

*   period A – the 12 months before the onset of the research project
*   period B – the first 12 months of the project
*   period C – the six-month period following on from period B.

Together, periods A and B constituted the main case file research period, as they involved systematic and detailed analysis of all case files. In period C, only those cases identified by the team as involving domestic violence were analysed. During the main period of the research, the overall number of referrals to the team was 267 (131 in period A and 136 in period B). Of these, 111 cases were accepted for service by the team (59 in period A and 52 in period B). The focus of the team's work was on children who had experienced abuse, and three-quarters of the cases accepted for service involved sexual abuse. There was social services involvement in relation to less than three-quarters of the children (72.9%) in cases accepted for service in period A and less than half of the children (48.9%) in cases accepted for service in period B. A small number of these children and their mothers were also, or had been, staying at a refuge.

The majority of the children in the cases accepted for service (where known) were girls. A range of adults was identified as subjects of the request for service, although mothers and their children predominated as service users.

Identifying domestic violence

Various studies have shown women are unlikely to disclose domestic violence unless they can be assured that the reaction will be positive – that is, not woman-blaming, and not punitive as in taking children into care (see e.g. Hester, Pearson and Radford 1997; Hester and Radford 1996). Good practice consists of *asking* all women routinely about domestic violence in *every* case. The very fact of asking about domestic violence conveys an important message to women and children that practitioners are aware of its existence and relevance, thus possibly facilitating disclosure (Hester and Pearson 1998).

The use of a monitoring scheme for domestic violence was thought to be an easy method for the NSPCC team to apply routine enquiry. It would allow domestic violence as an issue to be introduced into the team's work in a systematic way, thus not making any particular individual feel singled out; could help to increase awareness in the team of what domestic violence entailed; and could enable disclosure of domestic violence by children and/or their carers or referrers. Both this study, the Home Office study discussed in this chapter, and other research has found that it is important that the approach used fits well with the existing practice of the professionals concerned (Hester and Westmarland 2005). As most of the work of the team concerned recovery and counselling, and the use of client-led approaches, there was often an emphasis on 'listening' to clients rather than on any systematic asking of questions. Initially, we had thought that a monitoring form, with a set of questions about possible experiences related to domestic violence, could be used in conjunction with current intake and referral procedures. However, after discussion with the team and some observation of team practice, it was decided that a multi-stage monitoring approach should be adopted so that disclosure of domestic violence might occur at any stage in the practice process, and from service users or referrers. Thus, the scheme adopted involved a form to be completed at the referral stage of every case, and after every subsequent contact with service users.

The form consisted of a set of questions related to violence and abuse in the adult's relationship, and a set of questions regarding any impact on the child resulting from this. In practice, the monitoring process was used most frequently with the adults. It was not always possible to ask about domestic violence, and there were occasions when workers felt it was especially inappropriate or unsafe to raise the issue of domestic violence. This included instances where the family was seen together and the male partner, in particular, was present.

There were also concerns about the appropriateness of using the monitoring forms with children to raise domestic violence issues. This approach did not necessarily 'fit' very easily with the client-led emphasis of the team, and could feel overly intrusive, especially as domestic violence was not usually the presenting issue for the child. Yet, in practice, asking children about domestic violence was positive. One 11-year-old girl who was receiving therapeutic work from the NSPCC in connection with physical abuse from her father, when asked about the context of domestic violence (gross physical, sexual and emotional abuse of the mother) within which she had lived, wrote that she found it both upsetting and frightening to talk about because of the potential dangers of disclosure: 'I thought if I tell someone then they go and tell someone and they will come and hurt me.'

Clearly, disclosing information about the violence to her mother seemed even more dangerous than disclosing and talking about the direct abuse to herself. However, being enabled to talk about the domestic violence in a safe context, which included a safe location away from the violent man for her mother and herself, proved very positive.

Overall, the monitoring scheme was found to be useful, and had a very clear impact, with the incidence of domestic violence in cases accepted for service by the team rising from one-third to nearly two-thirds as a result of routinely asking about domestic violence in every case (virtually always violence against the mother by her male partner). While the research resulted in a small increase in referrals involving domestic violence, mostly the rise was due to instances of domestic violence becoming acknowledged and recognised where they had previously been hidden. With regard to disclosure, domestic violence was mostly disclosed by the abused woman, although children, referrers and others also provided evidence of domestic violence. During the period of the research, the amount of disclosure from children remained unchanged, while there was a marked increase in disclosure from abused women themselves and from referrers. The former can be explained by the fact that women were being asked specifically about experiences of domestic violence as a result of the monitoring process. The latter was probably due to the fact that knowledge about the project locally led to an increase in referrals concerning domestic violence.

LINKS BETWEEN DOMESTIC VIOLENCE AND CHILD ABUSE

It also became apparent that, in the cases where domestic violence was identified, the perpetrator of the domestic violence and the abuser of the child(ren) were likely to be the same individual, usually the child's natural father. Moreover, there was much evidence of the generally abusive impact on children, both 'indirect' and 'direct', of living in circumstances of domestic violence.

Analysis of the case files indicated that, of the sexual abuse cases, over half involved domestic violence. With regard to the perpetrator, in over half (53%) of the child sexual abuse cases the abusers were the children's fathers or father figures. This rose to over two-thirds (69%) in instances where domestic violence was also identified. In other words, fathers or father figures were even more likely than other men to be sexually abusive to their children where these same men were also violent and abusive to the mothers (see also Brandon and Lewis 1996; Farmer and Owen 1995; Forman 1995; Goddard and Hiller 1993; Humphreys 1997).

For the team, being made aware of these patterns in the cases they dealt with was important in relation to their practice. Such evidence helped team members to work more realistically with children and their carers where domestic violence was also a part of their experience. Realising that for some children their abuser was also violent towards the mothers, and vice versa, led to greater understanding of the abusive dynamics experienced by the children concerned. It also meant that, in the few instances where mothers contacted the NSPCC regarding support for their children who had lived in circumstances of domestic violence, team members became more open to the possibility that the children had been directly abused in addition to witnessing violence to their mothers. Case files in the final period of the research – period C – indicated that, as a consequence, there was work with children on this wider range of abusive experiences. For example, in one case accepted by the team in period C, the presenting issue for the child, as reported by the mother, was the need to explore issues relating to the domestic violence the child had witnessed (rather than child sexual or physical abuse as in earlier cases). Exploring these issues then led to the discovery of the direct physical and sexual abuse of the child by her father:

> Mrs Blue discussed that Lily [daughter aged 11] had witnessed the violence towards her mum. She [Lily] was threatened verbally and physically and was assaulted physically and verbally by her father... Lily has told [mum] that she doesn't love her dad, but pretended to, to stop him from hurting Mrs Blue... Lily has nightmares, cannot handle aggression in any form...cannot bear anyone to touch her.

Addressing the violence in this way, therefore, led to a greater awareness of the issues for the child in coping with the impact of both the direct abuse and the indirect abuse associated with living in the context of domestic violence. It also led to a greater awareness of the dynamics of the relationship between Lily and her mother, leading to more effective intervention with them both.

Implementation

In the team's recovery work, a variety of practice approaches were drawn upon, such as play therapy, drama therapy, art therapy and family therapy, with an emphasis on integration and on the process being client-led. The main focus of all the work undertaken was the abuse of the child, and this included focusing on a range of areas, such as self-esteem work, 'keeping safe' work, looking at 'muddles', or exploring anxieties/feelings/difficulties through play and art. However, the work of the whole team was increasingly carried out within a 'systemic' framework, whatever the approach used by the individual members of staff.

The team did not adopt a 'classic' family therapy approach since it was considered to omit notions of power and gender, and consequently to lack a dynamic understanding of the family (see MacLeod and Saraga 1988, 1991). However, team members were interested in the application of what they termed a 'systemic' approach, which they saw as allowing them to examine the context for the child who had been abused – such as the individual(s) involved, and the significant relationships for the child. They were concerned that the particular focus on the child in their work was leading to a simplistic pathologising of children as victims, whereby the child was being perceived in practice as needing 'rescuing' and needing 'treatment' as if ill. Instead, they were wanting to enable children to be safe through incorporating and understanding the children's contexts and relationships, and by working in conjunction with the caring adults as well as the children themselves. Where the team was concerned, this change in approach enabled them, and the service users, to decide when to see children individually, when to see children and their parent(s) (or other carers/adults), or perhaps to only see the parent. Previously they had always tended to see the child alone.

Based on this 'systemic' approach, the team increasingly moved towards an approach that supported both mothers and their children in domestic violence cases. This placed the support and protection – and therefore recovery – of the child within a context where the key carer (the mother) was also supported. As one team member explained:

> If a child has been abused, it's what happens next in terms of the help, of an acceptance from particular key carers...that will determine the outcome in terms of the child's recovery... So, therefore, if we can work with women as well as children, carers as well as children, taking account of domestic violence...of the power dynamics around, and the frequency with which men abuse women we know about just in a factual way, then I think that we can start to create with those carers safer environments for them and their children. (Interview with team member)

The Home Office study

The Home Office study formed part of the Government's Crime Reduction Programme, which included the funding of a number of projects across England and Wales aimed at tackling violence against women in relation to domestic violence, rape and sexual assault or prostitution (Hester and Westmarland 2004, 2005; Kelly, Lovett and Regan 2005; Regan, Lovett and Kelly 2004a, 2004b; Skinner and Taylor 2005). The projects were evaluated by independent teams of researchers. The study discussed here draws on the evaluation, carried out by the author, of one of the projects. The project, Suffolk Tools for Practitioners, had as a specific aim to enable the disclosure of domestic violence (Hester and Westmarland 2005).

The Suffolk Tools for Practitioners (Suffolk TfP) project set out to develop a range of 'tools' or interventions combined with training, so that practitioners might respond to survivors of domestic violence in a manner that kept safety at the centre: using routine enquiry questions (or 'screening' – the term used by the project) for service users generally so that they might disclose domestic violence, followed by crisis or safety planning with those found to be experiencing domestic violence. The project was developed with the support of agencies and organisations across Suffolk under the auspices of the County Domestic Violence Forum. The project set up an initial pilot in the district of Waveney, a semi-rural location with Lowestoft as the largest town. The discussion that follows is based on evaluation data from the pilot area over a two-year period, and relates to routine enquiry used by health visitors and social care services staff.

The ideas underpinning the initial development of the tools were related to the approach developed in Duluth, Minnesota, which has at its centre the safety and empowerment of victims as well as accountability of perpetrators. The materials included the Duluth power and control and equality wheels (Pence 1999; see Figure 3.1, p.57). A guidance manual was produced explaining how professionals should use the tools and providing examples of usage, safety implications and confidentiality. Safety planning and crisis planning booklets and a directory of Suffolk agencies were also produced. The tools were implemented by health visitors and social care staff (and to a more limited extent also by Women's Aid outreach workers and probation workers).

It was expected that, prior to the implementation of the tools, practitioners would attend training on both domestic violence awareness and good practice (one day) and use of tools training (two days – how to ask about domestic violence, and develop safety and crisis plans with service users). Sixty-nine individuals from 22 agencies were trained as a result. However, practitioners could not always attend, indicating the difficulties associated with training staff working in under-resourced and highly pressured areas of work. The training was consequently reduced to two days for some groups. In social care services, turnover of staff also meant that individuals who had more recently joined the team received separate training.

Review sessions with the practitioners and the project staff took place in the first one to two months following implementation of the tools. These looked in detail at instances where any tools had been used, and used these 'case studies' to draw lessons and to relate the experiences back to the issues outlined in the training sessions.

In interviews (n=30) during year one and at the end of the evaluation, practitioners involved in the project talked about the important grounding they had obtained from the training. It had given them an insight into the control aspects of domestic violence, and greater understanding of its impacts and implications. They described how this had been crucial to the increased confidence they now felt in asking about and dealing with situations of domestic violence. The health visitors in particular (n=17) stressed that the length, depth and intensity of the training had been necessary to equip them to use the tools with confidence. The review sessions were seen as a crucial part of this.

> If I hadn't had as much [training], I don't think I would have had the confidence to tackle the issues. (Interview with health visitor)

Health visitors

Health visitors found it easier to incorporate asking about domestic violence into their routine work than did social care services staff. The focus by health visitors on mothers, together with their prior experience of using systematic inventories and questions such as the Edinburgh Post-Natal Depression Scale, facilitated the introduction of routine enquiry. Routine enquiry also fitted with the early intervention strategy they were expected to adopt. Interviews towards the end of the evaluation period (n=20) indicated that the health visitors had developed their own ways of asking about domestic violence, usually at the ante-natal visit and at the six-week visit.

Also, they had learned to be more careful about following up with questions if women brought up previous rather than current incidents of domestic violence or other abuse.

> At one point, we were just doing a lot…say if you had half a dozen visits in the day you might be asking each of those half a dozen if it was appropriate. But the one thing I found was when I was being that conscientious…you uncovered so much, which is good, but mentally you just got to the point where you thought, 'Oh dear. I don't think I can ask this. What am I going to uncover?'… But we were asking a lot of people in a lot of different circumstances. And I think we were quite amazed at what was coming out. Because not only was domestic

violence coming out, you'd be uncovering things, maybe child abuse to them when they were young. (Interview with health visitor)

The health visitors interviewed in year one welcomed having the safety planning tool and booklet to use with women in the instances where domestic violence was disclosed. It provided them with something concrete to give women and made them feel better prepared. One service user who was interviewed commented that the safety booklet was very useful and straightforward and that she 'liked the wheel' and the 'good stuff about keeping me and the kids safe without going over the top'. Such views continued to be expressed in the year two interviews, and the proportion of service users with whom safety planning was used doubled across the project period – from 8 per cent (11/136) in year one to 19 per cent (14/74) in year two.

As the health visitors became more proficient and confident in the use of the tools, the number of domestic violence incidents identified also increased. The actual number of disclosures doubled from 12 to 24, despite fewer women being asked. The proportion of domestic violence identified was more than three times greater in year two – with 11 per cent (12/112) of women asked in year one disclosing domestic violence and 38 per cent (24/64) of those asked in year two.

By the end of the evaluation period, interviews with the health visitors indicated that they had shifted their practice from woman blaming to empowering women, by understanding the dynamics of domestic violence and in particular why women 'do not just leave'. The tools which they (and social care staff – see below) found particularly useful by the end of the evaluation were the Duluth wheels, both the power and control and the equality wheels. The wheels were considered valuable in showing the nature and dynamics of domestic violence, and practitioners were able to use the wheels directly with women to help them identify that they were in abusive relationships, as well as enabling early intervention and prevention.

> You know there's one case I had recently…a case conference was called because there's an injured child. And we believe it was a violent stepfather. And she denied everything. And it was very good when we went to case conference and in two weeks she actually got rid of him and she said there was a couple of things that made her realise. One was the equality [wheel]. I had asked her, 'You look at this. Where do you fit in?' And she said, 'It suddenly became clear to me.' And that was very positive. She was able to identify herself in that relationship. I mean she's taken the wheel and said, 'I'm going to use that for future partners.' (Interview with health visitor)

Other practitioners in the locality who were interviewed during year one and again at the end of the evaluation period confirmed the positive change in health visitors' practice that had resulted from their involvement in the project. This included the ability of health visitors to enable disclosure where other agencies were unable to do so, to empower mothers, and improved multi-agency working. For instance, in one situation, where domestic violence was suspected, the child was found to be sitting in a pile of glass and social care services became involved. The mother did not trust social care services but allowed the health visitor to use the tools with her (specifically the screening questions and Duluth wheels). Following this intervention, there were (according to the head of child protection) no repeat incidents of domestic violence and the mother had also understood the dangers to the child.

Social care services

As with the health visitors, the social workers and family support staff interviewed at the end of the evaluation period (n=13) reported feeling more confident in dealing with instances involving domestic violence. The child protection links, especially between the police, health visitors and social care, were also seen as important to this:

> We've tightened the circle when we get the police enquiries that come through from the child protection team... Where the uniform responding officer's been there, and there's a child that's been in the house, then we discuss straight away, have a strategy meeting. If the family aren't known to us then we'll make contact with them or write out to them. And also if there's a health visitor, arrange for a letter to the health visitor so you've got the information exchanged and the loops all closed up...it's really positive because we're all sending a consistent message out... And it just sends out a very clear message to families and agencies alike...and perpetrators. (Interview with senior social worker)

Social care staff interviewed provided numerous examples of how their practice and approach to cases involving domestic violence had changed. They had systematised the use of routine enquiry by incorporating this into the initial assessment. The number of individuals with whom the tools were used had increased by a third (from 23 to 36), and the number of disclosures had more than trebled – from 11 in year one to 34 in year two.

One of the social workers interviewed talked about how pleasantly surprised she was that people responded quite openly when asked about domestic violence. The extent of domestic violence was also greater than she had anticipated:

> And I actually think that people are more, are more open to discussing it than I initially thought they would. I think because you raise it, they are actually more open to talk about it than I thought they perhaps would be... There's a lot more domestic violence than I was aware of. It's one of the things that struck me. (Interview with social worker)

As in the case of the health visitors, by the end of the evaluation the social workers outlined the way their practice had shifted towards empowering women experiencing domestic violence. The Duluth power and control and equality wheels were again important. They found that empowerment could be achieved, for instance, through naming the violence and identifying how it worked by reference to the power and control wheel. This was found to give back some control to the woman who had been abused:

> Because you're bringing it all out in the open, it almost seems to give them back a little bit of what they've lost… I suppose it is control of their lives. I suppose it is the power that their partner had over them. Because they are able to identify with what it is that's been going on, and also because they've got a name for it as well. (Interview with social worker)

In some instances, the tools had helped them in what otherwise appeared to be intractable situations. The senior social worker explained how in serious cases they had achieved good results:

> We complete an initial assessment and we manage to get the victims being empowered to actually make self-referrals to the Police Domestic Violence Unit, which a month or two before they were not going to be able to do it because they lacked the confidence. And that has happened a lot. (Interview with senior social worker)

Conclusion

Where the NSPCC team were concerned, there was a change from seeing domestic violence usually as a separate issue from children and child abuse, to seeing domestic violence as a possibly central issue for children, and as a part of their abusive experiences. Thinking about both child abuse and domestic violence had allowed the team to reflect more thoroughly on their use of particular approaches, largely because many of the underlying dynamics and issues were the same or overlapped. Both domestic violence and child abuse involve one person (often the same individual) exerting power and control over another. The team felt that routinely asking about domestic violence had been very important to this shift in their practice. Overall, the project had enabled the team to incorporate domestic violence as part of the picture in working with abused children and their families, leading to much greater emphasis on safety and more effective work with both women and children. Effective practice included working with mothers and children together to explore their experiences of living with domestic violence.

Where the Suffolk health visitors and social care services' staff were concerned, routine enquiry had become an integral aspect of their work, and they felt their practice was both more effective and rewarding as a result. At the heart of the application of routine enquiry was the use of the Duluth power and control and equality wheels, which helped women to assess their own experiences and relationships and define them as abusive. This approach enabled successful disclosure and safer outcomes and in very diverse situations. For instance, it enabled initial disclosure and early intervention by health visitors, while allowing social care staff to deal with particularly intractable cases. Like the NSPCC staff, the Suffolk health visitors and social care services' staff were able to do much more effective and safety-oriented work with women and children as a result.

Overall, in both the NSPCC and Home Office studies, there were clear indications of positive changes in practice by the professionals concerned, with increase in disclosure of domestic violence as well as greater focus on safety of both the women and children concerned. Aspects that were found to be centrally important included:

- in-depth training in both awareness of and how to ask about domestic violence

- ongoing discussion and reflection about the instances of domestic violence that were being revealed

- incorporating routine enquiry by building on existing practice

- linking understanding of domestic violence and child abuse in ways that did not blame mothers

- working with both mothers and children together

- enabling disclosure and increasing empowerment of women by use of the Duluth power and control and equality wheels.

Other services seeking to incorporate routine enquiry into their practice should consider using these key features of the approach as the basis for building services which promote women's and children's disclosure of domestic violence.

References

Brandon, M. and Lewis, A. (1996) 'Significant harm and children's experiences of domestic violence.' *Child and Family Social Work 1*, 1, 33–42.

Davidson, L., King, V., Garcia, J. and Marchant, S. (2000) *Reducing Domestic Violence...What Works? Health Services.* Home Office Briefing Note. London: Home Office.

Davidson, L., King, V., Garcia, J. and Marchant, S. (2001) 'What role can the health services play?' In J. Taylor-Browne (ed) *What Works in Reducing Domestic Violence?* London: Whiting and Birch.

Everitt, A., Hardiker, P., Littlewood, J. and Mullender, A. (1992) *Applied Research for Better Practice.* Basingstoke: Macmillan.

Farmer, E. and Owen, M. (1995) *Child Protection Practice: Private Risks and Public Remedies.* London: HMSO.

Forman, J. (1995) *Is There a Correlation Between Child Sexual Abuse and Domestic Violence? An Exploratory Study of the Links Between Child Sexual Abuse and Domestic Violence in a Sample of Intrafamilial Child Sexual Abuse Cases.* Glasgow: Women's Support Project.

Goddard, C. and Hiller, P. (1993) 'Child sexual abuse: assault in a violent context.' *Australian Journal of Social Issues 28*, 1, 20–33.

Hester, M. and Pearson, C. (1998) *From Periphery to Centre: Domestic Violence in Work with Abused Children.* Bristol: The Policy Press.

Hester, M. and Radford, L. (1996) *Domestic Violence and Child Contact Arrangements in England and Denmark.* Bristol: The Policy Press.

Hester, M. and Westmarland, N. (2004) *Tackling Street Prostitution: Towards an Holistic Approach.* Home Office Research Study 279. London: Home Office.

Hester, M. and Westmarland, N. (2005) *Tackling Domestic Violence: Effective Interventions and Approaches.* Home Office Research Study 290. London: Home Office.

Hester, M., Pearson, C. and Radford, L. (1997) *Domestic Violence: A National Survey of Court Welfare and Voluntary Sector Mediation Practice.* Bristol: The Policy Press.

Humphreys, C. (1997) *Case Planning Issues Where Domestic Violence Occurs in the Context of Child Protection.* Coventry: University of Warwick.

Kelly, L., Lovett, J. and Regan, L. (2005) *A Gap or a Chasm? Attrition in Reported Rape Cases.* Home Office Research Study 293. London: Home Office.

MacLeod, M. and Saraga, E. (1988) 'Challenging the orthodoxy: towards a feminist theory and practice.' *Feminist Review 28*, 16–55.

MacLeod, M. and Saraga, E. (1991) 'Clearing a path through the undergrowth: a feminist reading of recent literature on child sexual abuse.' In P. Carter, T. Jeffs and M.K. Smith (eds) *Social Work and Social Welfare Yearbook: 3.* Buckingham: Open University Press.

Pence, E. (1999) 'Some thoughts on philosophy.' In M. Shepard and E. Pence (eds) *Co-ordinating Community Responses to Domestic Violence: Lessons from Duluth and Beyond.* Thousand Oaks, CA: Sage Publications.

Regan, L., Lovett, J. and Kelly, L. (2004a) *Forensic Nursing: An Option for Improving Responses to Reported Rape and Sexual Assault.* Home Office Online Research report no. 28/04. London: Home Office.

Regan, L., Lovett, J. and Kelly, L. (2004b) *Forensic Nursing: An Option for Improving Responses to Reported Rape and Sexual Assault.* Home Office Development and Practice Report, No. 31. London: Home Office.

Shakespeare, P., Atkinson, T. and French, S. (eds) (1993) *Reflecting on Research Practice.* Buckingham: Open University Press.

Skinner, T. and Taylor, H. (2005) *Providing Counselling, Support and Information to Survivors of Rape: An Evaluation of the 'STAR' Young Person's Project.* Home Office Online Research report no. 51/04. London: Home Office.

Chapter 7

'Point of Contact' Front-Line Workers Responding to Children Living with Domestic Violence

Jan Breckenridge and Claire Ralfs

Introduction

The particular focus of this chapter will be on the development of a Response Framework for front-line workers and the presentation of its potential application in practice settings. In 1997, the Australian government funded and endorsed the programme, Partnerships Against Domestic Violence (PADV). This was an initiative between the Commonwealth states and territories of Australia, which had the aim of working collaboratively towards the common goal of preventing domestic violence across Australia. The research described in this chapter is one of a number of projects funded by the Partnerships Scheme in phase two (PADVII) of the programme which began in 2002. PADVII focused on the priority areas of community education and further interventions with children who live with violence. Specifically, this project concerned itself with the second of these priority areas: responding to children who live with family and domestic violence (FDV).

The project developed comprehensive training materials and resources and a Front-Line Response Framework was developed for front-line workers who have contact with children living with and/or experiencing family and domestic violence. The work described here therefore provides a useful model of comparison with the initiatives described by Marianne Hester in the previous chapter. The project was completed in early 2004 with the evaluation of an extensive trial of both the training and the framework in various agencies and across different professional groups throughout Australia. A consortium of agencies offering special-ist knowledge in this area undertook parts one and two of the project:

- Relationships Australia South Australia (RASA), as the lead agency in the consortium, was responsible for the contract management, consultancy, resource development and implementation.

- The Centre for Gender Related Violence Studies, University of New South Wales, was responsible for the development of a framework for the overall evaluation of the project.

- Family Transitions was responsible for the literature review and establishing the research foundations of the project.

The context of the Front-Line Response Framework

The term *front-line response* will be used in this chapter to refer to the *non-therapeutic* engagement with children or people who live with family and domestic violence. Front-line engagements do not have a responsibility for healing or for the 'resolu-tion' of the problem of family and domestic violence *per se*. Nevertheless, the reality is that front-line workers will very likely, in the course of their professional work, need to interact with children in such situations. With this in mind, the project focused on the potential importance of the role of these workers at the 'point of contact' with children. Accordingly, the goal of the project was to strengthen workers' awareness of their responsibilities towards children living with domestic violence and to enhance their work in contexts where responses may formerly have been absent, minimal or unreflective. Hence, the Front-Line Response Framework was designed to address an identified gap in research, policy and practice regarding effective responses by front-line workers to children experiencing family and domestic violence.

For the purpose of this project there were nine relevant front-line groups. These were:

- the police
- general practitioners
- statutory child welfare/protection workers
- child support workers in agencies funded by the Supported Accommodation Assistance Program (SAAP) such as refuges
- child care and out of school care workers
- family court counsellors and magistrates
- kindergarten, preschool and primary school teaching staff
- maternal and child health nurses
- contact centre workers.

Issues relating to the needs of children from indigenous, culturally and linguistically diverse backgrounds (termed 'CALD'), children living in rural and remote locations and children with disabilities were included within the project objectives.

Why respond directly to children?

The identification of the inadequate responses offered to children living with family and domestic violence is not surprising, given that children's experience of family and domestic violence has been until recently largely absent from public and professional discussions (McIntosh 2002). McIntosh argues that children, including very young infants, respond to exposure to domestic violence with symptoms akin to post-traumatic stress disorder. She compares the trauma of children who are exposed to family and domestic violence to that experienced by children who have been directly assaulted (p.10). McIntosh's research focuses on trauma in all its manifestations, claiming that it impacts directly on children's development because it harms their ability to regulate their emotional life, and thus sets up patterns of relating to others in restricted and self-limiting ways. McIntosh further argues that the experience of children witnessing their father's abuse of their mother is one of horror, and this does psychological harm to the developing child. Arguably, there is now consensus in the literature that children are not simply passive onlookers, as was previously thought; however, the ways in which they may express the effects of the violence can be many and varied (see Graham-Bermann and Levendosky 1998; James 1994; Laing 2000).

Despite the effects of domestic violence, recovery from the ensuing trauma is certainly possible and depends essentially on two factors. The first is an environment that immediately provides safety and security for the child. The environment also needs to foster the child's resilience and this is primarily achieved via the child's attachment to significant people with whom they have contact (Rutter 1999). In this context alone, resilience becomes an extremely important concept. It is important to note here that the concept of resilience refers to a quality or attribute that is supported and developed (or not) through the kinds of interaction and communication that children experience in their social world. It is not useful to see resilience as a set of individual characteristics or 'natural' abilities, without reference to the structural and environmental factors that construct it and the strategies that can be deployed to enhance it. The kind of response front-line workers make to children can also potentially function as a resource that children can draw on in the future to develop their own positive and respectful ways of interacting and relating to others.

The second major factor is the development within the child of a 'narrative' of the experience that is coherent, undistorted, and does not self-pathologise or blame non-offending others (Gorell Barnes 1999; Papadopoulos and Byng-Hall 1997). The capacity of children to relate a coherent, undistorted narrative of what occurred, and their experience of it, may take some time and some work. Fragments of the narrative, including disassociated emotions such as aggression, may present in many contexts in the child's life and need to be thoughtfully responded to by adults who are dealing with the child.

Clearly front-line workers have a significant role to play in the achievement of both of these vital factors in their contact with children. It is absolutely necessary for children to have an authentic and supportive connection with whomever they come into contact with, particularly at the time of first disclosure and in times of crisis.

The front-line response to children

Until the last few years, the needs of children living in situations of domestic violence were for the most part left unattended. McIntosh's (2002) challenge to the work of early researchers who spoke of children as either 'witnesses' or 'observers' of domestic violence remains legitimate. The implication of such labels has been, and is, that these children were unaffected by the violence in the home. An unintended consequence of this was that the child protection issues that were inevitably part of these situations were often ignored. In part, this reflects the theoretical and practice split between domestic violence and child protection, which has and still does exist in Australia. So much so that child protection services have not considered, until very recently, that exposure to family and domestic violence constitutes an 'at-risk' situation for children, and indeed domestic violence has only recently been made a notifiable risk factor by legislation in all Australian states and territories except Western Australia (AIHW 2003).

Equally, family and domestic violence workers, for the most part, have also neglected the needs of children (Irwin and Wilkinson 1997; Smith, O'Connor and Berthelsen 1996). This practice derives from the belief that responses in situations of family and domestic violence need only focus on the mother, and that this was sufficient in itself to address children's needs. While mothers have often been appropriately seen as the conduit for responding to the children, an unintended consequence of this practice is that they are held responsible for the outcomes for their children. Thus, mothers are frequently blamed for any perceived negative outcome. When workers have a blaming or judgemental attitude towards mothers, they are unlikely to listen to them attentively, and therefore may fail to work collaboratively with them on what should be a joint concern, namely meeting the needs of the children (Breckenridge 1999; Fraser 1999). The overt and tacit censure of mothers persists, despite the finding that whether they remain with the perpetrator or not, overwhelmingly women do what they can to protect themselves and their children (Fraser 1999; Irwin and Wilkinson 1997; Levendosky and Graham-Bermann 2001).

To some extent, interaction with children through the mother has been seen as correct practice – where interactions took place at all. However, this restricted strategy might also have been a symptom of workers' fears about how to respond to children. A kind of 'do nothing' approach has also been perpetuated by the observation that often, at face value, children seemed unaffected by the violence because they are observed to be asymptomatic or not obviously traumatised. This notion is challenged by research evidence that shows that when children are exposed to or live with violence, they too are directly affected by it (McIntosh 2002; Mullender *et al.* 2002).

The challenges for this project have been twofold. The first has been to develop a context where front-line workers begin to feel, and act on, a responsibility towards children, despite the conceptual separation of child protection issues and family and domestic violence. The second and perhaps more difficult challenge has been to develop sensitive child-focused front-line intervention strategies that acknowledge the centrality and importance of the mother–child relationship and do not function to negate it.

The consultation process with the field

The Front-Line Response Framework and the accompanying best practice strategies were developed in response to an extensive consultation process with workers from a wide variety of organisations. Consultations took place with representatives from over 60 agencies in five states and territories across Australia. The semi-structured interview schedules provided rich, in-depth qualitative data concerning emerging practice in the field. Workers primarily reported their anxieties about whether responses could be effective and whether there was potential for their actions to increase rather than reduce the trauma experienced by the children (Breckenridge and Ralfs 2002). Workers' anxieties regarding their direct interaction with children appeared to be underpinned by a second key trend which was that none of the groups identified working with these children as a core part of their main professional role. The interviews also clearly highlighted the issue of limited resources and pressures that most front-line workers experience as another barrier to achieving effective responses. Such findings are consistent with the work of Bagshaw and Chung (2000) who found that workers identified limited resources and scant knowledge of domestic violence as barriers to intervention. An unintended consequence of these barriers in practice has been for workers to mostly engage with their primary work roles and to ignore this group of children and their needs.

One finding which was of particular interest to the project team was that the idea of a non-therapeutic response to children was unfamiliar to most of the worker groups with many front-line workers conceptualising a response to children as routinely consisting of a referral for therapy or counselling, regardless of their individual needs and preferences. Clearly this project responded to a timely issue – non-therapeutic front-line responses to children living with family and domestic violence.

Developing a front-line response framework

The consultation with front-line workers provided the fundamental underpinning of the framework that was developed. As such, the model is informed by workers' views, thereby providing a more authentic set of strategies for their front-line responses. The project team deliberately chose the term 'children living with family and domestic violence' to reflect a consensus that assumptions about the effects of violence on children should be avoided. The team has strongly advocated the view that children are competent and capable, and need to be listened to, respected and empowered, but has equally argued that it is important to acknowledge that children are in need of care and protection and must be kept safe from violence. Negotiating the fine line between empowerment and the protection of children has been the principal challenge for the development of the Front-Line Response Framework, as it is for those professionals who have contact with children, including, of course, front-line workers.

In order to achieve this balance, professionals need to:

- be aware of the effects of family and domestic violence on children

- have some understanding of the social context of family and domestic violence

- be thoughtful, present and coherent in responding to children, whatever their context.

To incorporate the above factors in a front-line response was not inherently complex. The project team contends that a very simple response can be highly effective and that the ways in which front-line workers respond to children are very important. In the vast majority of cases where front-line workers engage with children, there is a need to think and behave helpfully in a child-focused way. This can mean responding to parents in terms of a shared focus on the child, but not responding to the child separately. Or it can mean responding primarily to the child with or without the parent(s) present. It is equally important that the front-line response is understood as part of an overall system of social support and that it is not assumed to be a therapeutic or counselling role. This is not to imply, of course, that effective counselling and therapeutic responses are not relevant or part of the social support framework. They are not, however, within the scope of the front-line responses that the framework addresses. For the most part this particular practice focus will require some thoughtfulness, but this does not contradict the assertion that responses may be both simple and straightforward. Helpfulness in many contexts could simply mean a single meaningful interaction with a child. What is important is that the worker has some understanding of what is appropriate to the specific situation.

Using the framework

Figure 7.1 and the accompanying notes seek to clarify the preparations and actions required for workers to provide effective front-line responses. As discussed previously, the research suggests that children are likely to display a range of responses to violence in their family. Consequently, it makes sense to deal with specific situations and the individuals involved within an over-arching framework. The project team came to believe that, rather than being prescriptive about how front-line workers ought to engage, workers would provide more constructive responses if they were able to respond flexibly and contextually to different situations.

It is equally important to note the roles and briefs of different workers who are in the front line of response. Therefore, it may be the case that some professional groups will focus on one step rather than another, or omit a particular step altogether. The steps are designed to represent a coherent conceptual framework of the understandings involved in deciding upon an appropriate response to a child or children.

The steps outlined in Figure 7.1 are expanded in the following pages and are illustrated with examples from practice situations. As with all models, there is not an unproblematic linear progression from one step to the next. There is overlap between the various steps and the same questions may have to be asked more than once in different stages of the response. An underlying assumption of the framework is that there are four fundamental skill areas involved in responding effectively to children who live with family and domestic violence:

1. An ability to communicate with children as individuals in their own right and an awareness that some children do not communicate verbally.

2. An ability to respond respectfully to non-offending parents or other adults involved, particularly if raising sensitive issues about children and/or domestic violence.

3. An ability to communicate respectfully with an 'offending' parent or other adult, where appropriate.

4.   An ability to compile and use appropriately other resources for the child(ren), parent/s and family members, and for themselves as workers.

The framework does not suggest that first response workers are responsible for making a formal assessment or diagnosis of the child and/or family situation. Rather, the framework provides a working outline of the steps and associated questions that may be useful for workers to consider when faced with a situation of a child living with family and domestic violence. In this sense workers are asked to make an assessment of the situation in ways that encourage them to think about *their* involvement and actions in a considered way.

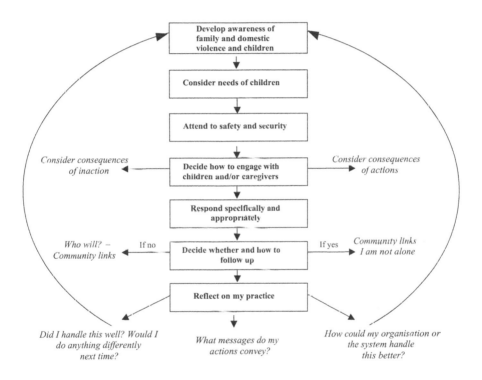

Figure 7.1 Framework for responding to children living with family and domestic violence

The response framework: a step-by-step guide

Step 1: Develop awareness of family and domestic violence and children

It is only recently that researchers have acknowledged that when children are exposed to or live with violence, they too are directly affected by the violence.

When translated into practice, this understanding requires front-line workers to recognise that family and domestic violence does directly affect children and as such it is necessary to consider how to respond to children living in situations such as this. When workers fail to notice children's experiences of domestic violence, the result is further isolation and increased trauma for the child.

A useful starting point for workers where domestic violence is not their core responsibility is to become aware of children and their situations and at the same time become familiar with the various ways in which domestic violence manifests (for example, types of violence and common patterns of violence) as well as the continuum of possible short- and long-term effects that family and domestic violence may have on children. Different children can display a range of reactions to family and domestic violence and have different needs. Younger children may be less able to articulate an understanding of the situation. Children with communication difficulties such as autism and Asperger's syndrome may not be verbal at all and children with cerebral palsy may need to use augmented communication such as compic boards.

As the previous chapter in this book also suggested, when workers access more comprehensive information regarding child development and domestic violence they are more able to assess the context of children who live with family and domestic violence, including the opportunities for response and the limitations of such responses. Such information also facilitates role clarification and an opportunity to consider organisational requirements prior to an intervention.

Step 2: Consider and notice the needs of children

Once a front-line worker understands the various ways in which family and domestic violence is manifested, the different ways children may consequently behave and the role they may take, a further consideration is crucial. It is important not to assume that the child(ren) are unaffected just because they appear to be 'coping'. Children can be traumatised without this being apparent. Children need to be able to speak about their experience, if they so choose, in ways that are affirming of themselves and their significant others. Children who disclose information about the violence need to be believed unless there is evidence to the contrary, and they need to be supported if they are to develop resilience.

These strategies are not suggesting that front-line workers 'assess' or 'diagnose' the child and the family. Rather, workers need only assess the situation to determine how they most appropriately respond. Any assessment must be underpinned by knowledge of the dynamics of domestic and family violence and the ways in which adult and child victims might respond both long term and when in crisis. For example, police officers are often frustrated when women and children fail to disclose abuse and appear to 'protect' the offender. Unless workers are aware of the intense fear that women and children experience and the threats offenders make should they disclose, they might tend towards 'blaming' the victims and fail to intervene. In Australia, police training has attempted to integrate a comprehensive knowledge of the dynamics of domestic violence such that police officers no longer place the responsibility on the victim to take out an apprehended violence order or disclose the violence for intervention to occur. Rather, police take action on their own assessment that violence has occurred and can remove the offender from the home and take out an apprehended violence order on behalf of the victim(s).

Step 3: Attend to safety

Safety is a crucial issue to consider for any front-line worker who is faced with family and domestic violence. Safety includes physical and psychological/emotional dimensions. The child needs not only to be safe, but also to feel safe as no other work can constructively happen until the child is in a safe situation. A range of people may represent and offer safety to children, and workers need to be able to ascertain who they are and how to contact them.

It is critically important to realise that a child needs to be safe after a worker leaves the situation and that any intervention should leave the child in a position of greater safety than before the contact occurred. It is important for workers then to identify what is, or might be, unsafe for the child(ren) and why and when this is most likely to happen. For example, if a child discloses at school, it is important that teachers and principals make sure that statutory authorities are informed and involved before the offender is aware of the disclosure and removes the child.

It is equally important that workers recognise and attend to their own physical and professional safety, and that they are aware that there may be a tension between organisational or professional obligations and the child's need for safety. These are not necessarily compatible and this needs to be assessed carefully. Workers may, in fact, need to continue to attend to safety issues if they have an ongoing relationship with the child and/or either parent. Family and domestic violence workers implement a number of safety measures when involved in ongoing work including not using their second name, not phoning or distributing written information identifying the service or indicating that disclosure has taken place while women remain with the offender. Such strategies may be useful for front-line workers to consider.

Step 4: Decide how to engage with children and/or caregivers

It is often difficult for front-line workers to decide if, how, or when they engage with children and other adults in situations of family and domestic violence. In making such decisions, workers must consider the consequences of both actions and inaction. At times, children and their families may not welcome a worker's interest and involvement. However, there will be occasions where worker contact is vitally important to those living with domestic violence.

Front-line workers must initially decide on the engagement that is appropriate for the particular child(ren) and their significant carers/parents. Mandatory reporting of domestic violence to statutory departments constitutes only one kind of professional response to children and domestic violence. For some front-line workers, there might not be a direct engagement with the child initially. However, this does not preclude a later engagement. In either event, workers need to be child inclusive. Appropriate and sensitive intervention requires workers to be realistic about their role and not to 'rush in' with solutions and set up false expectations of further contact where it is not appropriate. Practice underpinned by respect will be noticed and appreciated by children and constitutes a positive intervention in itself.

Step 5: Respond specifically and appropriately

There is no one perfect outcome in situations of family and domestic violence. Front-line workers can only respond appropriately if they are aware of the specific aspects of the situation. Awareness of these specific details ensures that workers are more likely to make appropriate referrals and not fall into the trap of labelling or stereotyping the child and their family. It is important to recognise that a variety of factors, including age, socio-economic status, ability/disability, location, ethnicity, indigenous or other cultural identity, all affect children and their experience of family and domestic violence. On the other hand, children should not be defined solely in terms of these differences. For example, children with communication difficulties may still be useful sources of information about supportive family and friends.

To ensure that intervention is specific to the context at hand, workers need to know where to obtain information regarding available and relevant local services, including culturally specific services and workers. This information should also include an awareness of the gaps in services so that workers can convey realistic information and support. As part of Step 1, workers may need to ensure that organisations compile information, which they can easily access in crisis situations. A further step may involve the development of active working relationships with key personnel from key local services. Supportive relationships with other agencies and workers may allow front-line workers to better negotiate how to proceed with key people where relevant, including child(ren), context and special needs.

Step 6: Decide whether and how to follow up

A one-off response will rarely be adequate. A follow-up response by the same worker or organisation or a referral agency will usually be required. It may well be that the front-line worker is the best person to have ongoing contact with the child and/or their family. For example, family support workers are often the first group of front-line workers who become aware of domestic violence occurring within a family. The strength of this supportive relationship and the direct contact such workers have with children will often place workers in an excellent position to provide longer-term support.

However, ongoing contact does not mean that a worker has to be strongly engaged with the child or family. Responses may be significant to the child even if they are quite subtle or minimal or do not deal with the domestic violence at all. This is not to suggest that workers ignore the situation after the crisis, but rather, that there is a need to be realistic about ongoing contact with the children and their family, if ongoing contact is appropriate. For example, a teacher who was involved in the initial disclosure may not need to be involved in any follow-up concerning the domestic violence. Nevertheless, the teacher may be well placed to notice the knowledge and skills the child(ren) used in contributing to a variety of situations and may share these observations with the child(ren) where appropriate. Alternatively, a teacher or family support worker or early childhood worker may be in an excellent position to continue to notice the effects of family and domestic violence and provide this information to other professionals.

If a front-line worker is not the best person to follow the situation up – for example, it is not part of their organisational role – then they will need to consider individuals and/or organisations in the community that are appropriate and inform the family about any other form of action they might take. Workers will therefore need to consider ways to communicate appropriately about their availability (or lack of availability) to child(ren), and colleagues where relevant.

Step 7: Reflect on practice

Critically reflecting on one's practice is a crucial element of good practice and one that allows a worker to consider what they and their organisation did well or could have done better. It is important to remember that actions convey a message about what a worker thinks about family and domestic violence. For example, did a worker allow the child(ren) and the parents to express their feelings and experiences so that that they would have felt heard and believed? The consideration of issues such as this directly feeds back into Step 1 and is part of an ongoing development of a worker's awareness of family and domestic violence.

Front-line workers need to remember that there are no perfect solutions. The quality of a worker's responses can be limited if they expect to solve things totally on their own. Further, the role of the front-line worker has only recently been recognised as one that can make a difference to children living with domestic violence at the levels of systems/sectors, organisations as well as with individual workers. It is helpful to consider how these layers intersect and how they may support or inhibit good practice. Continuous monitoring and improvement are required at all three levels. Therefore workers need to reflect on both their own practice and the ways in which their organisation or the system handled the situation, in order to enhance future interventions.

Conclusion

The Front-Line Response Framework was developed by integrating the solid base of information generated by consultations with the most current professional thinking about appropriate strategies to meet the needs of children who are living with family and domestic violence. The framework articulates key concepts and generates questions, which can be appropriately utilised by individual workers in their front-line role as presented but importantly are also taken up in the training materials developed alongside the framework and in the delivery of training programmes. The training materials are comprised of ten comprehensive booklets, including topics such as legal issues, direct work with children, diversity issues, values exercises and detailed information regarding the incidence, dynamics and effects of domestic violence on children. Together they provide a coherent set of materials that are specifically tailored to enhance front-line workers' awareness and understanding of issues surrounding family and domestic violence and its impact on children, and to develop strategies to respond effectively. In this approach, the Response Framework charts new and significant territory and signals a turning point in delivering a strategic community response to an endemic public problem.

References

Australian Institute of Health and Welfare (AIHW) (2003) *Child Protection Australia 2001–02*. AIHW cat. no. CWS 20. Canberra: AIHW (Child Welfare Series no. 32).

Bagshaw, D. and Chung, D. (2000) 'Reshaping responses to domestic violence: The needs of children and young people.' Paper presented at the National Forum *The Way Forward: Children, Young People and Domestic Violence*, Melbourne.

Breckenridge, J. (1999) 'Subjugation and silences: The role of the professions in silencing victims of sexual and domestic violence.' In J. Breckenridge and L. Laing (eds) *Challenging Silence: Innovative Responses to Sexual and Domestic Violence*. St. Leonards: Allen and Unwin.

Breckenridge, J. and Ralfs, C. (2002) *Point of Contact – Consultation and Issues Report*. Unpublished report held by the Office for the Status of Women, Department of Prime Minister and Cabinet, Canberra.

Fraser, H. (1999) 'Considering the needs of children who are exposed to domestic violence: A feminist perspective for practitioners.' *Women Against Violence 6*, July, 34–40.

Gorell Barnes, G. (1999) 'Operationalizing the uncertain: Some clinical reflections.' *Journal of Family Therapy 21*, 2, 145–53.

Graham-Bermann, S.A. and Levendosky, A.A. (1998) 'Traumatic stress symptoms in children of battered women.' *Journal of Interpersonal Violence 14*, 111–28.

Irwin, J. and Wilkinson, M. (1997) 'Women, children and domestic violence.' *Women Against Violence 3*, 15–22.

James, N. (1994) 'Domestic violence: A history of arrest policies and a survey of modern laws.' *Family Law Quarterly 28*, 3, 509 -20.

Laing, L. (2000) 'Children, young people and domestic violence.' *Issue Paper 2*. Sydney: Australian Domestic and Family Violence Clearinghouse.

Levendosky, A.A. and Graham-Bermann, S.A. (2001) 'Parenting in battered women: The effects of domestic violence on women and their children.' *Journal of Family Violence 10*, 2, 171–92.

McIntosh, J. (2002) 'Thought in the face of violence: A child's need.' *Child Abuse and Neglect 26*, 229–41.

Mullender, M., Hague, G., Imam, U., Kelly, L., Malos, E. and Regan, L. (2002) *Children's Perspectives on Domestic Violence*. London: Sage Publications.

Papadopoulos, R. and Byng-Hall, J. (eds) (1997) *Multiple Voices: Narrative in Systemic Family Psychotherapy*. London: Duckworth.

Rutter, M. (1999) 'Resilience concepts and findings: Implications for family therapy.' *Journal of Family Therapy 21*, 2, 119–44.

Smith, J., O'Connor, I. and Berthelsen, D. (1996) 'The effects of witnessing domestic violence on young children's psycho-social adjustment.' *Australian Social Work 49*, 4, 3–10.

Chapter 8

Using Research to Develop Practice in Child Protection and Child Care

Elaine Farmer

Introduction

Historical analyses show that when women have a strong voice, as in the late Victorian and early Edwardian eras, the effect of their campaigns is a greater awareness of and a tougher response to male violence and child abuse (Farmer and Owen 1998; Gordon 1989; Jeffreys 1985; Parker 1995). When the voices of campaigning women are more muted, male violence tends to disappear from sight and societal concerns focus on neglect by mothers. In recent times, feminist activists have worked hard to bring the issues of domestic violence and child sexual abuse to public attention, and since the early 1990s there has been an increasing awareness of the link between domestic violence and child abuse more generally. As a result of active lobbying, changes in legislation, increased research, research overviews and training initiatives (see for example Hester, Pearson and Harwin 2000; Humphreys 2000), domestic violence has been placed firmly on the social work agenda. Undoubtedly, practice has improved. However, there are always continuing challenges to practice, and in this chapter I will draw out some of these and suggest other issues that have received rather less attention.

Case management in child protection

Research has shown that between a fifth and two-thirds of children known to be abused are also living in circumstances of domestic violence (Hester *et al.* 2000). In our study of children placed on the child protection register (Farmer and Owen 1995) 52 per cent of the cases involved domestic violence but half of this was not known to participants at the initial child protection case conference. This was partly because questions about this subject were not a routine part of investigations and partly because mothers caught up in the child protection process feared that the revelation of such violence might lead to the child's removal. Indeed, Gibbons and her colleagues (1995) have shown that this fear was not unfounded. More recently, Brandon and her colleagues (1999) found domestic violence in 47 per cent of cases of children assessed as suffering or likely to suffer significant harm, reducing to 32 per cent one year later. Thus, the incidence of domestic violence in cases of child maltreatment is high. We would expect that practitioners would now routinely ask for this information in child protection cases, although Humphreys (2000) has shown that professionals who do know about incidents of domestic violence sometimes fail to share this information at child protection conferences.

Child protection case conferences

What difference does the presence of domestic violence make to case management? Our study of child protection case conferences (Farmer and Owen 1995) showed that when domestic violence was mentioned at the initial case conference the registration rate was only marginally higher (63%) than when it was not (61%), suggesting that it was not regarded as significantly affecting risk to children, even though it was spread across the full range of households and categories of abuse. Yet, when we analysed the outcomes of the cases of children on the child protection register, we found that most of the children with the worst outcomes at the 20-month follow-up (23% of the 44 cases) were living in families where there was continuing violence by the man towards his female partner. Sometimes there was also serious violence among the children in the family. It should also be noted that, occasionally, the threatening presence of a violent man, or the view that the agencies would be unable to effect change, led to decisions not to register children (see also Miller and Fisher 1992).

The question of whether the mother could protect the child was considered at 60 per cent of the initial case conferences in our study, while the issue of whether the father figure could protect the child was considered in only 19 per cent of those cases where there was a father figure in the family. Clearly expectations are placed on women that are very different from those placed on men. Relying on women to protect their children from violent and abusive partners is clearly a flawed policy. It may not even be one in which professionals believe. At no point in our study did social workers apparently discuss with mothers how far they had been successful in protecting their children, with a view to strengthening that protection if it proved inadequate. But when women who live with violent men are clearly unable to protect themselves, the chances of their being in a position to protect their children may be remote (Kelly 1994; O'Hara 1994).

Child protection interventions

In our child protection study (Farmer and Owen 1998) in cases of sexual abuse, domestic violence had been evident at the time of the abuse in two-fifths of the cases. Among the 29 cases of physical abuse, neglect and emotional abuse, there was a higher rate (59%) of concurrent violence in the family (17 cases). This was usually a man's violence towards his female partner, but in two cases parents were violent towards each other, in one case the woman was violent towards the man, and in another there was violence among the older children and between them and their mother.

In a third of the cases of physical abuse, neglect and emotional abuse, domestic violence was a significant feature of the family situation after registration but was not addressed by professionals either in relation to the power imbalance within the family, the risks to the mother and children, or in relation to whether the mother was able to protect the children. In addition, only occasionally was the fact that a child was witnessing violence to the mother noted as unsatisfactory and in only two instances was concern expressed about the possible effects on the child (Jaffe, Wolfe and Kaye 1990; McGee 2000; Mullender and Morley 1994).

At the time of the study, professionals responded to violence towards women and violence towards children quite differently and the connections between the two were not well recognised. Increasingly, research evidence had shown that men who assault their female partners often also abuse their children and the importance of the link between domestic violence and child abuse was explicitly brought out in the report on Sukina Hammond's death (Bridge Child Care Consultancy Service 1991) and has also featured in other inquiries into child deaths.

Another reason for the lack of professional attention to issues of domestic violence was that, even when father figures were known to have physically abused a child, the focus of professionals usually moved away from them and onto the mother. In all cases, once attention focused on mothers, the issues around which the work revolved were not the abuse itself but more general concerns about child care. This shift of focus from men to women allowed men's violence to their wives or partners to disappear from sight. It also left women in the position of trying to regulate the actions of their partners. Mothers frequently tried to protect their children from their violent or unpredictable partners and they sometimes attempted to use the child protection registration as a deterrent to these men, for example by taking every bruise for inspection to the doctor.

How was it that the risks posed by men who had already physically harmed their children were given no attention? How had this occurred? In some cases, this deflection away from work with men was assisted by the men themselves who ensured that they were out during social work visits or who refused to engage in discussions with the worker about the child. Moreover, since these father figures were often known to be violent men, they could be intimidating to professionals, many of whom were female.

An analysis of the cases of physical abuse by men in our study shows that there were three principal processes by which attention was deflected away from these men and onto their female partners. One occurred when the social worker considered the father figure to be a serious risk to the child and tried to arrange for him to move out. If no charges had been brought by the police, workers could only try to put pressure on mothers to exclude their partner. If this was unsuccessful, workers might concentrate their attention *faute de mieux* on the mothers and on general child-care issues. The mother's opposition to the worker's initial strategy was unlikely to form the basis for a trusting relationship and, in many of these cases, the mothers were withholding information about the man's continuing violence to them and their children.

A second process, which was observed in two cases, was when a male social worker became strongly identified with the father's view of the family situation, taking on his viewpoint that the children were disobedient, and did not take action when the children were physically abused. The father's abuse was reconstructed as discipline, albeit occasionally excessive. Intervention was, again, general support by means of financial and material help, and a reliance on the mother to 'protect' the child. The latter strategy was unrealistic if the man was known to be physically violent towards his wife.

The third process occurred where, either because the man denied causing the child's injury or because, in the absence of any direct evidence, it was unclear which parent had abused the child, the worker focused on some other area of family difficulty. In one such case the father, having admitted the abuse of his baby son and his drink problem under police interrogation, subsequently denied both. In this case, the worker made the focus of the work the father's past history of separations. This approach seemed to represent a 'safe' area for them both but failed to address the risks posed by this father to his child. After the case was de-registered, the father re-abused his baby son.

This absence of a clear focus on the source of risk to children is important because, in such situations, child protection registration or any form of supervision is unlikely to be effective. This has been a theme in a number of inquiries into child deaths, such as those concerning Jasmine Beckford and Tyra Henry (London Borough of Brent 1985; London Borough of Lambeth 1987). Indeed, in a child protection system developed and then driven by child deaths, most of which were committed by men, it is a paradox that attempts at regulation are unrelentingly directed at women.

Child protection reviews

The shift of focus away from men tended to occur early on in intervention and it occurred in *all* the cases of physical abuse by men in which the child and abuser had not been separated. In the highly proceduralised child protection system, it might be thought that the lack of attention to male abusers would be called to account at review meetings. However, we found that once a pattern of case management had been established it was usually endorsed at subsequent reviews, even when it was clearly deficient. For example, the child protection plan at the initial conference recognised the fact that a father figure had been physically abusive in 86 per cent of relevant cases. However, the subsequent shift away from dealing with the implications of this recognition in all these cases was not challenged at the subsequent reviews, with one exception, even when there was evidence of continuing risks to the children (Farmer 1999).

The match of social worker and parents

We also found that the match between social workers and parents was a particularly important issue for black and minority ethnic parents, especially in relation to how much domestic violence came to light. Certainly, the difficult experience of involvement in the child protection system was amplified for black and minority ethnic families where the lack of understanding of the child protection system was greater and was further complicated by their fear of state intervention and previous experiences of racism (Owen and Farmer 1996). For women who need help to leave violent relationships there is also often the fear of rejection by their own communities (Imam 1994; Rai and Ravi 1997). Yet in our study, many black and minority ethnic parents and their children, whose first contact with social services were over child protection matters, very much needed help and services. We found that mothers were most satisfied and children made best progress when the worker was matched along the dimensions of race, ethnic grouping and also gender. However, if this was not possible, then gender was sometimes more important to mothers than race and ethnicity, principally because some mothers, especially those who were Asian, would not confide important issues such as domestic violence to a male worker. Such issues need to be borne in mind when cases are allocated.

Child protection outcomes

As we have seen, most of the children on the child protection register with the worst outcomes at the 20-month follow-up (23% of the 44 cases) were living in families where there was continuing violence by the man towards his female partner, sometimes accompanied by serious violence among the children in the family. In all these cases, despite continuing concerns about child abuse, children remained at home with the alleged abuser present and any work provided was directed at the mothers. Since in all these families it was the father figure who presented risks to the children, the impact of work with the mothers was limited. The social workers in these cases often disregarded violence between the adults, treating it as beyond their control. Nonetheless, children were emotionally distressed by witnessing violence between their parents, and they were at risk from violence themselves, either as a result of the male carer's aggression or through being caught up in violent incidents.

Adolescents with backgrounds of domestic violence

Adolescents who have been subject to child protection investigations and have suffered violence from parents or siblings have been shown as sometimes held as partly to blame, using the argument that the parent was trying to discipline a behaviourally difficult young person. Certainly, they and their parents receive little service (Farmer and Owen 1995). The child protection system may not have a lot to offer adolescents who show difficult behaviour and other services are sparse (Sinclair, Garnett and Berridge 1995), so that if problems persist young people may enter the looked-after system.

In two studies of looked-after children (Farmer and Pollock 1998; Farmer, Moyers and Lipscombe 2004) it has been found that 38 per cent of children entering foster or residential care have backgrounds of domestic violence. In one of these (Farmer and Pollock 1998), this rose to 55 per cent of children with backgrounds of domestic violence in an interview sub-sample of looked-after sexually abused and/or abusing adolescents whose problems were at the more severe end of the spectrum. It is interesting that research suggests that domestic violence may play an important part in the development of sexually abusing behaviour. A study by Skuse and his colleagues (1996) found that four key variables discriminated sexually abusing boys from those who had only suffered sexual abuse and a comparison group of anti-social boys. These were: the experience of intrafamilial violence, witnessing intrafamilial violence, feeling rejected by the family, and discontinuity of care. Similarly, Awad and Saunders (1991) have suggested that physical violence is more common in the backgrounds of young sex offenders than sexual abuse. Kellogg and Menard (2003) investigated a sample of 164 children aged 7–19 who were attending a sexual abuse clinic, and found significant levels of domestic violence and physical abuse in a majority of these children's homes. They suggested that safety plans for sexually abused children should always include screening for family violence.

In still more recent research on children looked after by kin or unrelated foster carers (Farmer and Moyers 2005) we have found that over half (52%) of the children in both types of placement had backgrounds of domestic violence. Since the prevalence of such violence is unlikely to have changed from our earlier studies, this rise in the proportion of looked-after children known to have experienced domestic violence may suggest an increased awareness and more screening of violence by practitioners. In addition, in this study, one in five of the looked-after children in both kinds of placement have experienced violence from their siblings or been violent towards a sibling or both. Interestingly, one in five of these looked-after children had also experienced violence from other adults or had witnessed such violence. It may be important to discover how far children have experienced domestic violence only from their father figures with or without reciprocal violence from the mothers or how far they have experienced more extensive violence from other children and/or other adults in the home (see also Goddard and Hiller 1993; Stanley and Goddard 2002).

Further analyses of the links between backgrounds of domestic violence and other factors in this research on kinship care (Farmer and Moyers 2005) showed that there was no relationship between the levels of behavioural and emotional problems of the children in the placement and their previous experience of domestic violence. However, greater improvement in school attendance was evident for children from violent backgrounds once in kin or unrelated care than for other children. This may be because their attendance had previously been affected by violence in the home. Other research has shown double the rate of absence from school for children from violent homes (Montminy-Danna 1997). When in their placements, the children's educational performance overall showed little relationship to their previous experiences, except that rather more children with violent backgrounds performed well below their ability (see also Hilberman and Munson 1977; Montminy-Danna 1997).

One interesting finding in the kinship care study is that children with backgrounds of domestic violence were much more likely to be close to a sibling than to any of the carers' children. The reverse was true for other children. Similarly, there was more tension between children with violent backgrounds and the carers' children than was the case for children without this background. This might reflect greater difficulty in peer relationships or an impaired ability to trust (see Hague *et al.* 1996). On the whole, the outcomes of children with violent backgrounds were very similar to those without these experiences in this study, although slightly more children who had experienced domestic violence showed either improvements or deterioration in their behaviour over the course of the placement.

Of course, children are affected not only by their prior experiences of violence but, for some, these continue even when they are looked after away from home. In our recent study of adolescents in foster care (Farmer *et al.* 2004; Moyers, Farmer and Lipscombe, forthcoming) some aspect of contact was problematic for the great majority of the young people in the study and many were preoccupied with trying to get their needs met by ambivalent, rejecting or violent parents. We found that almost two-thirds (63%, 43) of the young people in the study had contact with someone that was detrimental to them but very little was done to alter this. Some young people returned time and again to see parents who physically abused or rejected them and legal arrangements did not always protect young people who were determined to keep in contact with family members. For example, the court had banned Danny's stepfather from having any contact with him, but Danny (aged 15) desperately wanted to see his mother and made many visits to her at home. He suffered numerous beatings from his stepfather as a consequence and his foster mother said:

> [He] found difficulty in understanding why his birth mother continually rejected him. [Her] partner continually threatened and physically abused him [and he] found it difficult to express his feelings. Little professional help was offered to assist him in coming to terms with this.

We concluded that boundaries more often needed to be placed around contact with young people and that more work with parents might be useful to help them to negotiate meaningful contact with their children. There is also a real need for work with young people to help them to integrate the reality of parental rejection and ambivalence in ways which allow them to move on and make use of other more sustaining relationships.

Adolescents who show violent behaviour

Young people who grow up witnessing or experiencing violence may resort to violent behaviour themselves as may those with poor impulse control. Much less attention has been paid to violence by children than to domestic violence by adults. Yet, adolescents who show violent behaviour are likely to be at risk of continuing that behaviour as adults. In our recent study of fostered adolescents (Farmer *et al.* 2004) over half (56%) of the 68 young people in the sample had shown violent or aggressive behaviour towards others before their placement, with 3 per cent having a history of cruelty to animals. We are also noting the severe violence that some young people mete out to their mothers, a phenomenon that has as yet attracted little attention. Young people who had shown aggressive behaviour before their foster placement had significantly more placement breakdowns.

During the placements which were followed up for one year, 28 per cent (19) of the young people were physically aggressive to other children or adults. Ben, for example, twice brutally attacked the foster carers' eight-year-old son, hitting and kicking him. Ben also threw stones at the other children and became aggressive towards the foster carers. Of these 19 young people, the risk presented by the violent behaviour of 14 had increased during the course of the placement, for four the risk had decreased and for one the risk had stayed the same. The presence of aggressive behaviour did not significantly relate to the likelihood of placement breakdown. However, on our other outcome measure of the quality of the placement or success (that is, the placement went well or resulted in a planned and appropriate move as opposed to disrupting or continuing unhappily) adolescents who were violent had fewer successful placements, with only a quarter (26%) of the young people who were physically aggressive experiencing successful placements compared with over half (55%) of those who were not (p=0.03).

Young people who had previously been excluded from school were more likely than others to be physically aggressive (p=0.02). Of course, some of these young people may have been excluded from school precisely because they had shown aggressive or violent behaviour.

Moreover, we found that when foster carers did not like the young person at the beginning of the placement they parented them less well (Lipscombe *et al.* 2003, 2004). Carers were more likely to show a decrease in liking by follow-up towards young people who were physically aggressive to others or who had an adverse impact on other children in the household (sometimes because of their violence to other children), which may relate in part to the carers' need to protect their own or other fostered children. When carers did not like young people they showed them less warmth and engagement, became less sensitive to them and provided less intervention for their needs. Furthermore, if the carers began or continued to dislike the young person over the course of the placement, the likelihood of placement breakdown increased. Thus, through these routes, violent behaviour by young people significantly increases the risk of placement breakdown, leading to placement instability which itself has an adverse effect on young people's behavioural and emotional adjustment. In spite of this, once children are in care there is little evidence of interventions or direct work with them to help them to understand and modify their violent behaviour.

It is also worth noting that in our two current studies, in one of which we are examining children placed with kin and in the other children returned to their parents from care, it is clear that children are often left too long in or returned too quickly to family situations often including domestic violence that are highly damaging to them (see also Ward *et al.* 2004). By the time children enter the looked-after system, their problems are often quite entrenched.

Conclusion

Research on case management in child protection shows the importance of a clear disaggregation of the sources of risk to children. Maltreatment caused by a father figure, a mother, a sibling or a combination of family members raises different issues and requires differentiated practice. The increasing recognition of the link between domestic violence and child abuse (Abrahams 1994; Ball 1996; Bowker, Arbitell and McFerron 1988; Browne 1993; Edleson 1999; Farmer and Owen 1995; Goddard and Hiller 1993; Hester *et al.* 2000; Hughes, Parkinson and Vargo 1989; Mullender 1996, 1997) provides potential for a greater emphasis on the inequalities in power within families, and this does provide the starting point for a review of child protection practice.

In child protection work, much might be gained if more attention were paid to asking women about their own strategies for protecting their children (Boushel 1994) and attempts made to assist mothers to strengthen these (Boushel and Farmer 1996; Boushel and Lebacq 1992). Many women will gain by being linked to agencies such as Women's Aid which focus on women and their needs.

Child protection practice in relation to men who physically abuse requires that assessments of parenting always include an assessment of the father figure in the family and the question should be raised in workers' minds that there may be male violence to the mother when physical or sexual abuse to a child is discovered. More ideas about motivating and working with men need to be developed and assessed for effectiveness. Such work may need to be separated from work with mothers. It may require the deployment of male workers or joint work by a male and female worker; locations outside the home may need to be found and groupwork initiated. Social workers need training on dealing with situations of domestic violence (Humphreys 1999; Mullender 1997), including work on getting men to confront and acknowledge their violent behaviour, its sources and consequences (Kelly, Burton and Regan 1997; Pence and Paymar 1990), and women and children need parallel support. Training for professionals needs to address these issues as well as worker safety (Hamner and Statham 1988). Indeed, it has been cogently argued that there is insufficient emphasis on the impact on workers and on their practice of violence and threats from users (Stanley and Goddard 2002; see also Chapter 13 in this book). Child protection reviews should also routinely check whether the workers involved are addressing the family member who presents the major risk to the child. Of course all this requires a legislative and policing context that acknowledges and acts on issues of domestic violence (Parkinson and Humphreys 1998).

It is also important to note that where children are experiencing serious adversities such as domestic violence, parental substance or alcohol misuse, children are sometimes left in such circumstances for too long before they are removed. Between 38 per cent and 52 per cent of children becoming looked after have had backgrounds of domestic violence and a considerable proportion of adolescents in foster care (two-thirds in our study) continue to experience domestic violence, abuse and rejection from their parents during contact visits. More proactive work is needed in relation to contact for looked-after adolescents and especially work with young people to help them to process and come to terms with parental rejection (Farmer *et al.* 2004; Moyers *et al.* forthcoming).

Once in care, a significant minority of adolescents are violent towards their carers and towards other children in the placement, as well as in their school settings. Young people showing violent behaviour have poorer placement outcomes than other children. If these difficulties are to be managed effectively, there is an urgent need to develop more ways of working directly with young people on their violent behaviour as well as on the issues in their backgrounds that feed into and maintain their anger.

References

Abrahams, C. (1994) *The Hidden Victims: Children and Domestic Violence.* London: NCH Action for Children.

Awad, G. and Saunders, E. (1991) 'Male adolescent sexual assaulters: Clinical observations.' *Journal of Interpersonal Violence 6*, 446–60.

Ball, M. (1996) *Domestic Violence and Social Care: A Report on Conferences Held by the Social Services Inspectorate in London and Leeds.* Spring 1995. London: Social Services Inspectorate.

Boushel, M. (1994) 'The protective environment of children: Towards a framework for anti-oppressive, cross-cultural and cross-national understanding.' *British Journal of Social Work 24*, 173–90.

Boushel, M. and Farmer, E. (1996) 'Work with families where children are at risk: Control and/or empowerment?' In P. Parsloe (ed) *Pathways to Empowerment.* Birmingham: Venture Press.

Boushel, M. and Lebacq, M. (1992) 'Towards empowerment in child protection work.' *Children and Society 6*, 1, 38–50.

Bowker, L., Arbitell, M. and McFerron, J.R. (1988) 'On the relationship between wife beating and child abuse.' In K. Yllo and M. Bograd (eds) *Feminist Perspectives on Wife Abuse.* London: Sage Publications.

Brandon, M., Thoburn, J., Lewis, A. and Way, A. (1999) *Safeguarding Children with the Children Act 1989.* London: The Stationery Office.

Bridge Child Care Consultancy Service (1991) *Sukina: An Evaluation Report of the Circumstances Leading to Her Death.* London: Bridge Child Care Consultancy Service.

Browne, K.D. (1993) 'Violence in the family and its links to child abuse.' In C.J. Hobbs and J.M. Wynne (eds) *Bailliere's Clinical Paediatrics: Child Abuse.* London: Bailliere Tindall.

Edleson, J. (1999) 'Children witnessing of adult domestic violence.' *Journal of Interpersonal Violence 14*, 8, 839–70.

Farmer, E. (1999) 'Holes in the safety net: The strengths and weaknesses of child protection procedures.' *Child and Family Social Work 4*, 4, 293–302.

Farmer, E. and Moyers, S. (2005) *Children Placed with Relatives or Friends: Placement Patterns and Outcomes.* Report to the Department for Education and Skills. Bristol: University of Bristol.

Farmer, E. and Owen, M. (1995) *Child Protection Practice: Private Risks and Public Remedies*. London: HMSO.

Farmer, E. and Owen, M. (1998) 'Gender and the child protection process.' *British Journal of Social Work* 28, 4, 545–64.

Farmer, E. and Pollock, S. (1998) *Sexually Abused and Abusing Children in Substitute Care*. Chichester: Wiley.

Farmer, E., Moyers, S. and Lipscombe, J. (2004) *Fostering Adolescents*. London: Jessica Kingsley Publishers.

Gibbons, J., Conroy, S. and Bell, C. (1995) *Operating the Child Protection System: A Study of Child Protection Practice in English Local Authorities*. London: HMSO.

Goddard, C. and Hiller, P. (1993) 'Child sexual abuse: Assault in a violent context.' *Australian Journal of Social Issues 28*, 20–33.

Gordon, L. (1989) *Heroes of Their Own Lives*. London: Virago.

Hague, G., Kelly, L., Malos, E. and Mullender, A. with Debbonaire, T. (1996) *Children, Domestic Violence and Refuges: A Study of Needs and Responses*. Bristol: Women's Aid Federation (England).

Hamner, J. and Statham, D. (1988) *Women and Social Work: Towards a Woman Centred Practice*. Basingstoke: Macmillan.

Hester, M., Pearson, C. and Harwin, N. (2000) *Making an Impact: A Reader*. London: Jessica Kingsley Publishers.

Hilberman, E. and Munson, K. (1977) 'Sixty battered women.' *Victimology 2*, 460–70.

Hughes, M., Parkinson, D. and Vargo, M. (1989) 'Witnessing spouse abuse and experiencing physical abuse: A double whammy?' *Journal of Family Violence 4*, 2, 197–209.

Humphreys, C. (1999) 'Social work practice in relation to domestic violence and child abuse.' *Child and Family Social Work 4*, 77–87.

Humphreys, C. (2000) *Social Work, Domestic Violence and Child Protection: Challenging Practice*. Bristol: The Policy Press.

Imam, U. (1994) 'Asian children and domestic violence.' In A. Mullender and R. Morley (eds) *Children Living with Domestic Violence*. London: Whiting and Birch.

Jaffe, P., Wolfe, D. and Kaye, S. (1990) *Children of Battered Women*. London: Sage Publications.

Jeffreys, S. (1985) *The Spinster and Her Enemies: Feminism and Sexuality 1880–1930*. London: Pandora.

Kellogg, N.D. and Menard, S.W. (2003) 'Violence among family members of children and adolescents evaluated for sexual abuse.' *Child Abuse and Neglect 27*, 12, 1367–76.

Kelly, L. (1994) 'The interconnectedness of domestic violence and child abuse: challenges for research, policy and practice.' In A. Mullender and R. Morley (eds) *Children Living with Domestic Violence: Putting Men's Abuse of Women on the Child Care Agenda*. London: Whiting and Birch.

Kelly, L., Burton, S. and Regan, L. (1997) *Supporting Women and Challenging Men: An Evaluation of a Programme for Violent Men*. York: Joseph Rowntree Foundation.

Lipscombe, J., Farmer, E. and Moyers, S. (2003) 'Parenting fostered adolescents: Skills and strategies.' *Child and Family Social Work 8*, 4, 243–55.

Lipscombe, J., Moyers, S. and Farmer, E. (2004) 'What changes in "parenting" approaches occur over the course of adolescent foster care placements?' *Child and Family Social Work 9*, 347–57.

London Borough of Brent (1985) *A Child in Trust. The Report of the Panel of Inquiry into the Circumstances Surrounding the Death of Jasmine Beckford*. London: London Borough of Brent.

London Borough of Lambeth (1987) *Whose Child? The Report of the Panel Appointed to Inquire into the Death of Tyra Henry*. London: London Borough of Lambeth.

McGee, C. (2000) *Childhood Experiences of Domestic Violence*. London: Jessica Kingsley Publishers.

Miller, L.B. and Fisher, T. (1992) 'Some obstacles to the effective investigation and registration of children at risk: Issues gleaned from a worker's perspective.' *Journal of Social Work Practice 6*, 2, 129–40.

Montminy-Danna, M. (1997) *A Comparative Study of School Performance of Children Who Witness Family Violence and their Non-Reporting Agemates*. MSW, unpublished.

Moyers, S., Farmer, E. and Lipscombe, J. (forthcoming) 'Contact with family members and its impact on adolescents and their foster placements.' *British Journal of Social Work*.

Mullender, A. (1996) *Rethinking Domestic Violence: The Social Work and Probation Response.* London: Routledge.

Mullender, A. (1997) 'Domestic violence and social work.' *Critical Social Policy 50,* 17, 1, 53–78.

Mullender, A. and Morley R. (1994) *Children Living with Domestic Violence.* London: Whiting and Birch.

O'Hara, M. (1994) 'Child deaths in contexts of domestic violence: implications for professional practice.' In A. Mullender and R. Morley (eds) *Children Living with Domestic Violence: Putting Men's Abuse of Women on the Child Care Agenda.* London: Whiting and Birch.

Owen, M. and Farmer, E. (1996) 'Child protection in a multi-racial context.' *Policy and Politics 24,* 3, 299–313.

Parker, R. (1995) 'A brief history of child protection.' In E. Farmer and M. Owen (eds) *Child Protection Practice: Private Risks and Public Remedies.* London: HMSO.

Parkinson, P. and Humphreys, C. (1998) 'Children who witness domestic violence: The implications for children.' *Child and Family Law Quarterly 10,* 147–59.

Pence, E. and Paymar, M. (1990) *Power and Control: Tactics of Men Who Batter. An Educational Curriculum.* Duluth, Minnesota, USA: Minnesota Program Development Inc. (revised edition).

Rai, D. and Ravi, T. (1997) *Re-defining Spaces: The Needs of Black Women and Children in Refuge Support Services and Black Workers in Women's Aid.* Bristol: Women's Aid Federation of England.

Sinclair, R., Garnett, L. and Berridge, D. (1995) *Social Work and Assessment with Adolescents.* London: National Children's Bureau.

Skuse, D., Bentovim, A., Hodges, J., Stevenson, J., Andreou, C., Lanyado, M., Williams, B., New, M. and McMillan, D. (1996) *The Influence of Early Experience of Sexual Abuse on the Formation of Sexual Preferences During Adolescence.* Report to the Department of Health. London: Behavioural Sciences Unit, Institute of Child Health.

Stanley, J. and Goddard, C. (2002) *In the Firing Line: Violence and Power in Child Protection Work.* Chichester: Wiley.

Ward, H., Holmes, L., Soper, J. and Olsen, R. (2004) *Costs and Consequences of Different Types of Child Care Provision.* Report to the Department for Education and Skills. Loughborough: Loughborough University.

Chapter 9

Damned If You Do and Damned If You Don't?

The Contradictions Between Private and Public Law

Christine Harrison

Introduction

The Children Act 1989 in England and Wales aspired to provide a unified legal framework for making decisions about children's welfare (Cretney, Masson and Bailey-Harris 2003), with the same principles applying across the spheres of private law (dealing with matters of children's residence and contact after parental separation) and public law (including issues of significant harm and child protection). An overarching checklist established the child's welfare as paramount in all proceedings and implied consistent treatment of issues affecting children's development and well-being, whenever concerns arise. Before the Act's implementation, it was argued that domestic violence was not adequately addressed in the primary or accompanying secondary legislation. A plethora of concerns has persisted that, despite its intentions, this failure of the Children Act 1989 to address the impact of domestic violence has compromised children's welfare and women's safety (Hester and Radford 1996; Radford, Sayer and AMICA 1999; Saunders and Barron 2003). Nor is it considered that these have been adequately acknowledged by the Children Act 2004 and other recent legal and policy changes, which are thought insufficient to prevent children from being harmed during contact with abusive parents (Saunders 2004).

Questions about recognising the impact of domestic violence on women and children apply in different ways to public and private law proceedings under the Children Act 1989. Where the former is concerned, it is accepted that awareness and practice have improved, but that the child protection system may have concentrated more on women's ability to protect than on the responsibilities of the perpetrator (Jaffe, Lemon and Poisson 2003). In private law, determining arrangements for child contact following parental separation (or where parents have never lived together) in the context of domestic violence has proved contentious (Aris, Harrison and Humphreys 2002). Here, an anxiety has been that issues falling within the definition of significant harm and child protection procedures in the public law sphere are disregarded or viewed as less serious when raised within the private law arena – that a double standard applies through which a pro-contact philosophy displaces child protection. Such is the degree of division between discourses of child contact and child protection that it has been described as child welfare on 'two different planets' (Eriksson and Hester 2001, p.787), a phenomenon widely noted in other jurisdictions (Jaffe *et al.* 2003). This surfaces in divergent professional practices when similar issues of child welfare arise in different spheres, with grave implications for women and children (Kaye, Stubbs and Tolmie 2003).

Earlier chapters have demonstrated how domestic violence remains a significant child welfare issue beyond parental separation, with often severe and enduring consequences for children. This chapter applies a closer focus on how domestic violence has been regarded within private law to highlight the centrality of child protection and child safety to contact arrangements following parental separation. It begins by setting out the legal framework in England and Wales and discusses the key concepts used within legislation and guidance, such as need, harm, and safety for children and women. Against this background, the role and purpose of child contact centre provision is evaluated. Finally, it argues that adopting within child contact services the same definitions of safety and approaches to risk used within domestic violence services (see Chapter 11) would more explicitly recognise child protection issues and better meet the needs of children and women. This area continues to be the subject of legal reform and new policy guidance, and the potential impact of these will be noted. The chapter draws on research about child contact centres, conducted for the Lord Chancellor's Department (now the Department for Constitutional Affairs) between 2001 and 2002 (Aris *et al.* 2002).

Gendered terminology is used to reflect the dominant pattern of domestic violence and of post-separation parenting. Women comprise by far the majority of victims/survivors of domestic violence and those affected by post-separation violence, and are also the majority of resident parents. It is acknowledged that women can perpetrate domestic violence and that this also occurs in same sex relationships, raising the same issues of safety for children and adult survivors.

Private or public? The legal context

While the Children Act 1989 and initial accompanying guidance were silent on the issue of domestic violence (Saunders 2001), it is directly relevant to proceedings initiated in two specific areas. The first of these is in applications for contact or, indeed, residence. When parents separate, or have never lived together, and fail to reach agreement about arrangements for children's care, with or without the assistance of mediation services, then parents with parental responsibility[1] may apply to the family court under section 8 of the Children Act 1989 to determine matters of residence (previously custody) and contact (previously access). This constitutes a minority of separating parents (Maclean and Eekelaar 1997), but their categorisation as 'high conflict' may have disguised the relevance of domestic violence, considered to be a central factor in many instances (Buchanan et al. 2001; Jaffe et al. 2003).

When evaluating how the family court responds to such situations, it has been argued that the law embodies a presumption in favour of contact that underestimates the negative impact of domestic violence on children (Busch and Robertson 2000). There has been a number of significant legal, policy and practice changes in the area of child contact. A series of Court of Appeal decisions, an Experts' Report (Sturge and Glaser 2000) and guidelines on child contact where there is domestic violence (Lord Chancellor's Department 2001) all highlighted the implications for child contact of domestic violence. Although these reflect a desire to recognise the impact of domestic violence when making decisions about child contact, their effectiveness is open to question. In 2002, 61,356 applications for contact led to the making of a contact order, and only 518 (less than 1%) were refused (Judicial Statistics for England). Given what is known about levels of domestic violence, including after separation, this proportion of refusals is perplexing. It raises issues about what contact arrangements are being made, how safe these are for women and children, and the role played by child contact centres. Recent legal reform has included the introduction of 'gateway' forms to ensure that courts are aware of issues of domestic violence at the earliest point in proceedings, but, other than the extension of the definition of significant harm (see further below), the government is not convinced that further reform of primary legislation is necessary (Her Majesty's Government 2005). A decision has been made, however, that new measures for the enforcement of contact orders will be drafted during the 2005 parliamentary session.

The second area relates to child protection inquiries initiated under public law when serious concerns about children's safety and well-being arise. The threshold for inquiries hinges on the concept of significant harm, or risk of significant harm, defined in section 47 of the Children Act 1989. For children in these circumstances, the local authority has a duty to ascertain what further intervention is required, which may include further stages in child protection or court procedures, but can also include services for children in need and their families. Relevant guidance (secondary legislation) includes *Working Together to Safeguard Children* (Department of Health 1999) (which sets out the parameters for local authority inter-agency child protection procedures) and the *Framework for the Assessment of Children in Need and their Families* (Department of Health 2000). An amendment to the meaning of harm (made through section 120 of the Adoption and Children Act 2002) took effect in January 2005 and includes 'impairment suffered from seeing or hearing the ill treatment of another'. This is a major acknowledgement of the significance of domestic violence as a child protection concern. How this is interpreted and applied will be crucial if it is to benefit women and children, rather than to increase a focus on women's failure to protect (Saunders 2004).

Another anomaly relates to children's representation and the appointment of guardians. In public law proceedings, a child is automatically a party and a children's guardian will be appointed by the Child and Family Court Advisory and Support Service (CAFCASS). This is not necessarily the case in private law proceedings. Here, the court can request a welfare report from a children and family reporter, to inform the court of the child's wishes and to make a recommendation about what is considered to be in the child's interest. Only if the court orders that a child becomes a party to proceedings will a solicitor and children's guardian be appointed to represent and advocate on behalf of the child.

Need, harm and safety: child protection and child contact

A growing literature highlights the inter-connections between violence towards women and child abuse (Brown *et al.* 2001; Hume 2003; James 1994). This is evidenced by literature from the domestic violence field, and more recently from research about child protection. A number of dimensions highlight an urgent need to bridge the division described by Eriksson and Hester (2001):

- Violence often begins or escalates during pregnancy (BMA 1998; Mezey and Bewley 1997), making it a dual attack on the mother and on the foetus (Kelly 1994). Even before birth, domestic violence can be a form of child abuse.

- Living with the direct and indirect impact of domestic violence is known to have serious consequences for children's health and well-being (Mullender and Morley 1994; Mullender *et al.* 2002).

- Where there is domestic violence there is frequently also child abuse: the more severe the domestic violence, the more likely the co-occurrence (Edleson 1999; Parkinson and Humphreys 1998).

- Domestic violence is directed towards the child's carer, including attacks on women holding babies (Kaye *et al.* 2003), and often intended to undermine parenting and the mother–child relationship (Bancroft and Silverman 2002).

- The incidence of post-separation violence is high and both women and children are at greater risk of violence at this time (Humphreys and Thiara 2004), with particularly adverse consequences for children (Sturge and Glaser 2000).

- There is growing concern about maternal and child deaths (Saunders 2004) and levels of abduction through child contact (Kilsby 2001).

- Black and minority ethnic women and children face the same issues, but additional social, economic and cultural barriers to reporting violence or finding help (Rai and Thiara 1997).

- When child protection procedures are implemented and child protection conferences convened, domestic violence is known to be present in the majority of cases, and is a key factor in decisions about registration (Sloan 2003).

There can be little doubt that, whether being considered in the area of private or public law, children affected by domestic violence are children in need as defined by the Children Act 1989 (Saunders 2004) and they may be the subject of significant harm and subject to child protection procedures. There is considerable evidence that violence is significant in a sizeable proportion of cases being dealt with in private law, as in public law, proceedings, but that these are less likely to be identified as child protection issues (Brown *et al.* 2001; Buchanan *et al.* 2001). If post-separation violence is neglected, then risk and safety issues for children and women may not be systematically assessed and it could be argued that children may experience a judicial failure to protect (Saunders 2004).

It is against this background that the use of child contact centres must be evaluated, since they are likely to remain pivotal where arrangements for contact in contentious situations are being considered by the family court (Her Majesty's Government 2005).

The role of child contact centres

In response to anxieties about separation and the loss of fathers from children's lives, there was rapid growth in child contact centres from the mid-1980s (Furniss 2000; NACCC 1994). The vast majority of these are supported centres, which provide a neutral meeting place for non-resident parents and children. They are inappropriate where there has been domestic violence because they offer low levels of vigilance. In these situations, the higher levels of vigilance in supervised centres are needed, or no or indirect contact may be more appropriate. Supervised provision is limited and unevenly distributed across the country.

Supported centres are predominantly voluntary provision providing a short-term service based on assumptions about the constructive role that men can play in children's lives and the perceived need to encourage contact. These ideas are very different from those underpinning domestic violence services, or child protection interventions, which emphasise the need to prioritise the safety of children and women. In the contentious area of child contact when there has been domestic violence, contact centres have come to occupy an increasingly ambiguous position (Aris *et al.* 2002). As the judicial process of determining contact has appropriated supported centres, their original aims have been overridden. Research had indicated that supported centres had been accepting referrals where there was a history of male violence (Furniss 1998, 2000) and a large proportion of non-resident fathers using child contact centres are men with a history of domestic violence (Aris *et al.* 2002).

The child contact centre research

This study, funded by the Lord Chancellor's Department, was undertaken by a team at the University of Warwick. The study considered the role of supported and supervised contact centres and identified associated safety issues which could contribute to further policy developments. A multi-methodological approach was adopted, which included:

- a policy questionnaire to all contact centres affiliated to the National Association of Child Contact Centres (86 returns representing a 43% response rate)

- questionnaires and interviews with 70 resident mothers and 35 non-resident fathers, 21 children, 34 referrers (mostly court welfare officers, now known as CAFCASS officers) and 27 contact centre staff from six contact centres (three offering supported, one supervised and two both supported and supervised provision) in two family proceedings jurisdictions.

While the access point for the study was supported and supervised contact centres, insight was gained about the longer-term legal and welfare processes involved in arranging contact and the implications for women and children. This illustrated an array of problems emanating from the use of supported child contact centres when there was a history of domestic violence. It showed how in private law proceedings, the significance of domestic violence, including after separation, and issues of safety and protection which in public law might have been interpreted as constituting significant harm, were minimised. No single act was responsible, but rather at successive points in the process the impact of domestic abuse remained unrecognised or was dismissed as irrelevant. This pushed child safety from the foreground to the margins, leaving some children and women in a powerless position.

Structural factors, like lack of funding and uneven distribution of services, undoubtedly contributed to difficulties in ensuring that contact in a centre was safe and appropriate. At the same time, it appeared that a number of hegemonic ideas about domestic violence were implicated in the marginalisation of safety considerations. Four central themes were identified that permeated the child contact process. These are discussed below and comprise: contested evidence, mother blaming, perceiving children's needs as invariably served by contact and varying levels of safety.

Contested evidence

> They wasn't listening. This guy's hit me. They didn't seem to listen to me, until I went to find the facts and then they listened to me, which is even worse. It's like you have to prove yourself not to be a liar before anyone listens to you... (Mother attending a supported centre)

Difficulty in authenticating domestic violence to the standard required for judicial intervention or convincing to professionals is well established (Humphreys and Holder 2002). Creating a situation where the victim is disbelieved is a known strategy of perpetrators and their minimisation of violence and its impact is documented (Harrison, Mullender and Thiara 2002). The combination of these two factors – difficulties in producing evidence deemed sufficient and the denial and minimisation of perpetrators – created profound difficulties for women in the contact centre research. Eighty-six per cent of the 70 participating resident mothers said that their experience of sometimes severe violence was the main reason for using a centre and the threat of abduction had been experienced by 65 per cent of mothers; 24 per cent reported child abuse and 17 per cent said their ex-partner had convictions for violence. Not only was domestic violence difficult for women to authenticate, but even where there were convictions for violence, men maintained there had been false allegations and continued to deny its relevance to child contact:

> My ex-wife lied and suggested I might abduct the child... It is unfounded. (Father, supported centre)

Interviews with referrers and centre staff showed they held varying views about what they considered adequate evidence of domestic violence. Despite increased awareness about domestic violence and acknowledged difficulties in collating evidence, referrers and contact centre staff characteristically established high thresholds for what they considered compelling evidence. Verbal accounts of violence tended not to be given credence and, faced with situations where women described violence that was denied by men, referrers and contact staff often saw no alternative but to view this as 'one person's word against another'. The belief that women made spurious allegations was also influential. The issue was not whether domestic violence was known about, but rather hinged on the assessment different professionals and centre staff made about the nature of the evidence and whether it was an issue that should affect arrangements for child contact. Referrers and contact centre staff struggled to integrate their knowledge about domestic violence within their practices, or to resolve dilemmas in favour of women (Dalton 1999). Threats of abduction, for example, were very alarming to women, but often regarded as requiring only low levels of vigilance by referrers.

Even incontrovertible evidence of violence, such as convictions or injunctions, was not always regarded as necessitating higher levels of vigilance and supervision, and did not preclude judges ordering contact, solicitors referring or contact centre staff accepting such families at supported centres. This occurred even when it was acknowledged that levels of vigilance available were not adequate for the safety issues posed.

Significantly, while 86 per cent of the 70 participating resident mothers cited violence as the reason for attending a centre, only 25 per cent were attending a supervised child contact centre. The majority of mothers, despite often serious violence, were attending supported centres offering low levels of vigilance and several fathers using centres had served long custodial sentences, including some for attempted murder or grievous bodily harm. Over 60 per cent of mothers described violence continuing through the contact process. This included comments and threats made during contact, notes passed through children, and feeling intimidated on the way to and from contact:

> He's nasty, verbally abusive through the children. He'll say things to the children and they'll come back and tell me…even though the contact centre is public, it is not public enough. (Mother, supported contact)

Despite past violence being the strongest predictor of future violence, the research indicated that when men were plausible, and evidence of violence was contested, then even proven histories were sometimes disregarded by courts, professionals and contact centres.

Mother blaming

> I haven't got a prison record, I'm not a drug user, I've never been violent and yet I'm looked at as if I'm implacably hostile, because I don't feel happy with my child seeing his father. (Mother whose ex-partner had served a custodial sentence for domestic violence using supported contact centre)

Despite awareness of inter-connections between domestic violence, child abuse and child protection, aspects of child welfare law continue to be applied in separate and sometimes contradictory ways. Within public law, there is recognition that male violence towards women may cause significant harm to children (Brandon and Lewis 1996); when violent men remain in the family, social work intervention may lead to child protection procedures being invoked. Women are often the focus of attention, their ability to protect a central aspect of the assessment process (Calder, Harold and Howarth 2004; Edleson 1999). Women who cannot leave, or who are unable to effect the removal of their violent partner, may face the threat of removal of children to the care system.

When women and children find the courage to escape violence or to have their violent partner removed, the period post-separation is known to hold more acute dangers (Wilson and Daly 2002). While, prior to leaving, the test of their ability to prioritise their children's protection is either to leave or evict their violent partner, whether or not they have the necessary personal resources, in the context of private law, they are expected to put their children's interests first by promoting contact with violent fathers.

A perhaps inevitable corollary of the difficulty in providing evidence deemed convincing by professionals and contact centre staff was that women described experiencing a pervasive disbelief, and the view that they made allegations in order to sabotage contact arrangements. Women's perceptions that they were not believed left them in an weak position when negotiating child contact. Where contact had previously been difficult, or where there was a likelihood of this being court-ordered, a centre was seen as a safer option than other forms of contact, and offered some relief from the anxiety of unsupervised arrangements:

> I've found it much better for me because I don't have any contact with him at all. (Mother, supervised centre)

Others indicated that they felt either coerced or compromised into arrangements that they did not believe were adequate in terms of their own or their children's safety and well-being:

> I worried about not being safe and the children were afraid of him as well. He went to a solicitor. I felt pressured, so I said, 'Go on', and came to the centre. (Mother, supported centre)

Despite their own fears, women were essential to contact happening. The majority of children using centres were young and many were babies. Some had never been in the care of their father. The security of their mother being nearby was important, and mothers, even in supervised settings, were frequently called upon to pacify distressed children, or to help with practical tasks like nappy changing. Being available for their children often brought women into direct contact with men with convictions for violence against them and in some instances made women blame themselves and feel that in some way they had let their children down:

> I feel that I have failed her because I don't feel that I can protect her. (Mother, supervised centre)

This context of mother blaming, where either mothers have not produced acceptable evidence or men have refused to accept substantiated evidence of domestic violence, laid the ground for women's fears to be ignored and for men to be rehabilitated. Women could be construed as obstructive, implacably hostile, if their fears were misunderstood and they were believed deliberately to be constructing barriers to child contact:

> I have felt under scrutiny as a mother – from my GP, the paediatrician, CWO and contact centre. It is a very uncomfortable situation to be in, particularly when your only concern is your child. They turn it round to make it that the mothers are the bad people in it. The abuser doesn't have to prove themselves right or wrong. They go to court and lie. Then they say that it must be the mother. (Mother, supervised centre)

While the numbers of black and minority women using contact centres in the study varied across the two sites they were disproportionately high. Constituting 49 per cent of the whole sample, in one individual centre they comprised 60 per cent and in another 84 per cent of mothers. The implications for those who did not speak English as a first language, or who were asylum seekers, were particularly serious.

Tensions became acute when moving on was raised. While fathers viewed contact at a centre as unnecessarily restrictive and invariably saw no problem with unsupervised contact, resident mothers did not want to lose the relative safety that even supported centres afforded. When a history of domestic violence remained unknown or became obscured, when men were charming, women's real anxieties about contact and moving on could make them appear more hostile. Interviews with referrers and contact centre staff confirmed women's views that they were disbelieved or thought deliberately obstructive:

> They sit there and they are constantly slagging the fathers off. Mothers are just
> horrible to them. Sometimes I think that it is like a witches' coven. (Worker, sup-
> ported contact centre)

The reverse of the mother-blaming coin was that little evidence of safe parenting
was required by professionals for fathering to be restored, sometimes leading to
an attenuation of agreed levels of supervision:

> Once children start coming here, I just make my own decisions about what
> supervision is needed. (Co-ordinator, supervised centre)

Perceiving children's needs as invariably served by contact

> I believe that we have to earn the right to be a parent. Domestic violence has
> implications for the child. They are putting the father's right to see his child
> before the child. We should be protecting the innocent, not supporting the man
> who has already proven he has been violent. (Mother, supported centre)

In private law, women's responsibilities for promoting contact depend on professionals and others conceptually disaggregating what is often euphemistically
described as 'conflict between parents' from the needs and interests of children.
This approach means that domestic violence may not be regarded as a child protection issue before or significant to women's safety after separation; correspond-
ingly, men's potential to be good fathers may be evaluated without reference to
their responsibility for violence (NAFCC 2004). This tendency to divorce men's
violence from children's well-being reinforces a model of parental separation
predicated on the concept of loss, of an actual or symbolic relationship with a
father (Bradshaw *et al.* 1999). In part, this reflects a belief that a positive sense of
identity is dependent on contact with the non-resident father. Where the absence
of men from children's lives is associated with a range of social problems, but the
significance of domestic violence is underestimated, this also allows a 'contact at
any cost' philosophy to flourish.

There are few studies of children's perspectives on child contact arrangements made in the context of domestic violence, although their views about
contact and safety are crucial. Some children in the contact centre study were
positive about contact. They described the loss felt when their parents separated
and their pleasure in having contact at the centre. Others expressed ambivalence,
reluctance and in some cases opposition:

> I wish it [contact] never happened at all. (11-year-old girl, supervised contact)

For some children, contact in a centre was better than previous arrangements,
because they felt these had been more harrowing. For a significant minority of

children, one-third of the 21 children who participated, contact was neither positive nor safe. From reports from centre staff, mothers and the observations of researchers, it appeared that the highest levels of anxiety and insecurity affected children whose family history was characterised by domestic violence and there were some situations in which children whose circumstances were indicative of the poorest outcomes (Buchanan *et al.* 2001) were having contact. These situations raised concerns about the manner and extent to which children's views were being elicited and taken into account when contact arrangements were being established. Children were the least likely to be interviewed or consulted about contact, pre-occupations were primarily with parents. In only a small minority of cases had there been detailed assessments based on sustained involvement with children. Once either a voluntary or court-ordered contact was in place, often there was no adult, professional or otherwise, with a specific responsibility to monitor or assess the impact of contact arrangements on children, or to seek their views.

There was evidence of children being placed in double jeopardy. First, they experienced the marginalisation of their perspectives that is characteristic of the divorce field, and the difficulties of sensitising private law processes (Smart 2002). This was exacerbated by the ways in which their mothers were viewed. Although the concepts of 'parental alienation' and 'implacable hostility' are substantially challenged by the weight of research evidence (Brown *et al.* 2001; see also Chapter 10 in this book), they could be used to preclude taking into account the impact on children of domestic violence. When contact is considered invariably beneficial, this can lead to a selective approach to children – who may be believed if they say they want contact, but overridden if they do not. In some instances, children were observed clearly expressing their views and demonstrating their distress, but were ignored. A supervised centre co-ordinator commented about a 12-year-old young man who had been objecting to contact for some time: 'We really must start listening to what he is saying.'

Dominant attitudes about women formed a barrier to attending to children's voices and misconstrued the relationship between women and children. When it was assumed that women were unreliable in knowing their children's needs and interests, not the least consequence was that an important source of support and recovery was ignored, leaving women and children powerless and isolated:

> I feel so helpless that we can't do anything for my daughter. If there was any stopping contact then I would because my children are suffering, but I have no choice. The children have been so disrupted. (Mother attending supported centre whose children had experienced physical and sexual abuse)

Varying levels of safety

A key finding of the study was that integrating knowledge about domestic violence and its impact on women and children could prove problematic for contact centre staff and referrers whose practices were also informed by longer-term professional and personal assumptions that contact is in a child's best interests. Such assumptions also shaped views about safety features and practices within contact centres. Discussions with centre staff and referrers revealed disparities in definitions, purposes and levels of vigilance and safety features expected of supervised and supported centres, as well as regarding the roles of staff and volunteers in centres. For example, supervision of contact is vital to safety, but, in the majority of supported centres, this took the form of observation from a distance. In relation to supervised provision, nearly a third of referrers did not consider a ratio of one staff member to a family to be a basic requirement. The most common safety feature was the use of staggered arrival and departure times (used by 85% of centres responding to the questionnaire), yet less than half the centres had separate entrances and exits, which undermined effectiveness and caused major anxiety to women. There were also different expectations between referrers and centre staff about how active staff should be in facilitating or supporting contact. This was seen as the role of staff by 88 per cent of referrers, but only 60 per cent of staff agreed, the remainder seeing themselves only as having a presence.

Limited supervised provision led 63 per cent of referrers in the sample to comment that they had made referrals to supported centres based on availability, rather than on their assessment of the level of vigilance commensurate with the risk and safety issues involved. A range of features is required to support safety. Under-funded supported centres were not established to deal with issues of domestic violence and were understandably often unable to meet necessary safety standards. Both referrers and centre staff considered that supported centres were being used inappropriately, and not for the purposes for which they were originally developed.

Information sharing, active questioning and assessment are critical practices in heightening professional awareness, planning for safety and ensuring appropriate levels of vigilance (Humphreys and Harrison 2003). Although they require careful implementation and adequate training and support for workers, in the child protection arena they are important strategic elements that have contributed to increased levels of disclosure (Hester and Pearson 1998). While referrers said they routinely screened for domestic violence, contact centre co-ordinators felt that this information was not always conveyed to them, and could emerge when arrangements were in place and families were already attending centres that did not have the appropriate safety features or staffing levels. Practices also varied, in terms of how active centres were in seeking information that might be essential to ensure the safety of children and women. Almost half of the 86 centres responding to the questionnaire did not ask direct questions on their referral form about domestic violence. Over three-quarters of all centres and half of supervised centres did not screen through interview. Over half of all centres and a quarter of supervised centres did not undertake a safety or risk assessment even when domestic violence was identified.

A number of structural and organisational factors were identified that compromised attention to domestic violence and undermined the development of safety practices. These included the pressure of referrals on centres that were voluntary provision without paid or qualified staff and with few resources to install even the most basic safety features. Ambiguity about thresholds, inadequate and variable safety features and inconsistent safety practices systematically weakened attention to safety, distorted operational definitions, and led to overconfidence that some support was preferable to no contact. Supported provision was being used when supervised would be more appropriate and supervised when no contact would be indicated. The research found that the terms 'supervised' and 'supported' did not have clear, shared meaning among the professionals, centre staff and parents involved. Some supervised centres surveyed had fewer safety features than other supported centres, confusing referrers and mothers about the levels of vigilance available.

Conclusions

Since this study was completed a number of developments have been initiated to enhance the provision of child contact services, including increased funding for supervised centres, a common referral form, definitions of and standards for supported and supervised provision and a change programme under the auspices of the National Association of Child Contact Centres to enable centres to acquire accredited status. These are welcome developments, but the themes illustrated above demonstrate the influence of the deeply embedded ideas and values that will also need to be challenged (Dalton 1999).

In the period post-separation, these themes appear to come to the fore with great force and to separate discourses about child contact from those about child protection (Humphreys and Harrison 2003). As a consequence, women who may be assessed in terms of their ability, or failure, to protect children in public law are viewed as being implacably hostile in the private law arena. Once a father is no longer in the household, it may be assumed that domestic violence no longer happens, that it is no longer relevant, or that it did not happen, or was not serious, in the first place. When child contact displaced child protection, safety and recovery were compromised, the concept of significant harm in the Children Act

1989 was undermined, and the Act's intentions to ensure consistent treatment of children in all child welfare legal interventions were confounded.

A failure fully to take account of the relevance and impact of domestic violence, and the ease with which histories disappear and men are perceived to be rehabilitated, carries a number of implications for determining contact arrangements. These include a propensity for referrals to be inappropriately made to supported centres in the belief that some supervision is better than no contact. It can also lead to an attenuation of arrangements for supervision when contact is underway. Since both supported and supervised provision are limited and are considered short-term provision, undue pressure can be placed on women to move on to (even) less support or supervision. In the child contact centre research, professionals consistently judged arrangements that women and children did not consider safe to be so. Women's fears and lack of credibility led to them agreeing to arrangements that were not safe for them or that they felt were detrimental to their children's interests.

The evidence of this chapter, and others in this volume, suggests that understandings about the ways in which violent men operate, about the impact of violence on women and children, and the definitions of safety adopted within domestic violence interventions should underpin arrangements for child contact. Strong evidence exists for privileging safety in all contact proceedings and arrangements, and adopting the approach taken by domestic violence intervention services. This prioritises the recovery of children and women, and includes the absence of any harassment or intimidation; optimising support for recovery and amelioration of harm; recognising that there may be a relationship between children's recovery and their mother's recovery and allowing time and space for this. Ethnic diversity and the need for culturally appropriate services also needs to be acknowledged. Crucial to this shift in conceptualising contact is the recognition that it can be used to further abuse and impede recovery (Jaffe and Geffner 1998; Wyndham 1998). Safe child contact is contingent upon careful and thorough risk and safety assessments whenever there are allegations of domestic violence. Increasing child contact provision may be counterproductive without at the same time a willingness to base this on the framework for safety adopted within domestic violence interventions.

Note

1. The Children Act 1989 (as amended by the Adoption and Children Act 2002) adopts the concept of parental responsibility, which embodies duties as well as rights. Some parents automatically have parental responsibility, while others can acquire this. Parents having parental responsibility include mothers, a mother's husband at the time of the birth and an unmarried father registered as the child's father since 1 December 2003. In other circumstances, fathers can acquire parental responsibility through a written agree-

ment with a mother (parental responsibility agreement) or through an order of the court (parental responsibility order). People other than parents sometimes acquire parental responsibility, for example where a residence order has been made, or where a care order is made to the local authority. It is the case that a number of people can share parental responsibility for a child. Where parental responsibility is conferred at birth, it will only be extinguished through adoption, which vests all the rights, duties and responsibilities in the adoptive parents. Where parental responsibility has been acquired through an order, it ceases only when another order to this effect is made.

References

Aris, R., Harrison, C. and Humphreys, C. (2002) *Safety and Child Contact: An Analysis of the Role of Child Contact Centres in the Context of Domestic Violence and Child Welfare Concerns.* London: Lord Chancellor's Department.

Bancroft, L. and Silverman, J.G. (2002) *The Batterer As Parent: Addressing the Impact of Domestic Violence on Family Dynamics.* Thousand Oaks, CA: Sage Publications.

Bradshaw, J., Stimson, C., Williams, J. and Skinner, C. (1999) *Absent Fathers.* London: Routledge.

Brandon, M. and Lewis, A. (1996) 'Significant harm and children: Experiences of domestic violence.' *Child and Family Social Work 1,* 33–42.

British Medical Association (BMA) (1998) *Domestic Violence: A Health Care Issue?* London: British Medical Association.

Brown, T., Sheehan, R., Frederico, F. and Hewitt, L. (2001) *Resolving Family Violence to Children: The Evaluation of the Project Magellan.* Melbourne: Monash University.

Buchanan, A., Hunt, J., Bretherton, H. and Bream, V. (2001) *Families in Conflict: Perspectives of Children and Parents in the Family Court Welfare Service.* Bristol: The Policy Press.

Busch, R. and Robertson, N. (2000) 'Innovative approaches to child custody and domestic violence in New Zealand: The effects of law reform on the discourses of battering.' *Journal of Aggression, Maltreatment and Trauma 3,* 1, 269–99.

Calder, M. with Harold, G.T. and Howarth, E. (2004) *Children Living with Domestic Violence: Towards a Framework for Assessment and Intervention.* Lyme Regis: Russell House Publishing.

Cretney, M., Masson, J. and Bailey-Harris, R. (2003) *Principles of Family Law.* London: Sweet and Maxwell.

Dalton, C. (1999) 'When paradigms collide: Protecting battered parents and their children in the family court system.' *Family and Conciliation Courts Review 37,* 3, 273–96.

Department of Health (1999) *Working Together to Safeguard Children.* London: The Stationery Office.

Department of Health (2000) *Framework for the Assessment of Children in Need and their Families.* London: The Stationery Office.

Edleson, J. (1999) 'Children's witnessing of adult violence.' *Journal of Interpersonal Violence 14,* 8, 839–70.

Eriksson, M. and Hester, M. (2001) 'Violent men as good enough fathers? A look at England and Sweden.' *Violence Against Women 7,* 779–98.

Furniss, C. (1998) 'Family contact centres: The position in England, Wales and Scotland.' *Working Paper 6.* Leeds: University of Leeds.

Furniss, C. (2000) 'The process of referral to a family contact centre: policies and practices.' *Child and Family Law Quarterly 12,* 225–81.

Harrison, C., Mullender, A. and Thiara, R. (2002) *Challenging Violent Men.* Coventry: Coventry Domestic Violence Partnership.

Her Majesty's Government (2005) *Parental Separation: Children's Needs and Parents' Responsibilities. Next Steps.* London: The Stationery Office.

Hester, M. and Pearson, C. (1998) *From Periphery to Centre – Domestic Violence on Work with Abused Children.* Bristol: The Policy Press.

Hester, M. and Radford, L. (1996) *Domestic Violence and Child Contact Arrangements in England and Denmark*. Bristol: The Policy Press.

Hume, M. (2003) 'The relationship between child sexual abuse, domestic violence and separating families.' Paper presented at conference *Child Sexual Abuse: Justice Response or Alternative Resolution?* Australian Institute of Criminology, Adelaide, 1–2 May, 2004, accessed online June 2004, www.aic.gov.au/conferences/2003-abuse/hume.pdf

Humphreys, C. and Harrison, C. (2003) 'Focusing on safety: Domestic violence and the role of child contact centres.' *Child and Family Law Quarterly 15*, 3, 237–53.

Humphreys, C. and Holder, R. (2002) 'An integrated criminal justice response to domestic violence: It's challenging, but it's not rocket science.' *SAFE, The Domestic Violence Quarterly 3*, 16.

Humphreys, C. and Thiara, R. (2004) *Routes to Safety: Protection Issues Facing Abused Women and Children and the Role of Outreach Services*. Bristol: Women's Aid Publications.

Jaffe, P.G. and Geffner, R. (1998) 'Child custody disputes and domestic violence: Critical issues for mental health, social services and legal professionals.' In G.W. Holden, R. Geffner and E.N. Jouriles (eds) *Children Exposed to Marital Violence: Theory, Research and Applied Issues*. Washington DC: American Psychological Association.

Jaffe, P.G., Lemon, N.K.D. and Poisson, S.E. (2003) *Child Custody and Domestic Violence: A Call for Safety and Accountability*. Thousand Oaks, CA: Sage Publications.

James, M. (1994) 'Domestic violence as a form of child abuse: Identification and prevention.' *Issues in Child Abuse Prevention 2*, July. Accessed online (August 2004) at www.aifs.gov.au/nch/issues2.html.

Kaye, M., Stubbs, J. and Tolmie, J. (2003) *Negotiating Child Residence and Contact Arrangements Against a Background of Domestic Violence*. Nathan, Australia: Socio-legal Centre, Griffith University.

Kelly, L. (1994) 'The interconnectedness of domestic violence and child abuse: Challenges for research, policy and practice.' In A. Mullender and R. Morley (eds) *Children Living With Domestic Violence*. London: Whiting and Birch.

Kilsby, P. (2001) *Aspects of Crime: Children as Victims*. London: Home Office Crime and Criminal Justice Research Unit, Development and Statistics Directorate.

Lord Chancellor's Department (2001) *Guidelines for Good Practice on Parental Contact in Cases Where There is Domestic Violence*. London: Lord Chancellor's Department.

Maclean, M. and Eekelaar, J. (1997) *The Parental Obligation: A Study of Parenthood Across Households*. Oxford: Hart Publishing.

Mezey, G. and Bewley, S. (1997) 'Domestic violence and pregnancy.' *British Journal of Obstetrics and Gynaecology 104*, 528–31.

Mullender, A. and Morley, R. (eds) (1994) *Children Living with Domestic Violence*. London: Whiting and Birch.

Mullender, A., Hague, G., Imam, U., Kelly, L., Malos, E. and Regan, L. (2002) *Children's Perspectives on Domestic Violence*. London: Sage Publications.

NACCC (1994) *The Origins and History of the Network of Access and Child Contact Centres*. Nottingham: NACCC.

National Abuse Free Contact Campaign (NAFCC) (2004) *Response to a discussion paper, 'A New Approach to the Family Law System Implementation of Reforms'*, accessed online January 2005, at www.austdvclearinghouse.unsw.edu.au/r&r_docs/NAFCC_discussion_paper_response.pdf

Parkinson, P. and Humphreys, C. (1998) 'Children who witness domestic violence.' *Child and Family Law Quarterly 10*, 2, 147–56.

Radford, L., Sayer, S. and AMICA (1999) *Unreasonable Fears? Child Contact in the Context of Domestic Violence: A Survey of Mothers' Perceptions of Harm*. Bristol: Women's Aid Federation Publications.

Rai, D.K. and Thiara, R.K. (1997) *Re-defining Spaces: The Needs of Black Women and Children in Refuge Support Services and Black Workers in Women's Aid*. Bristol: Women's Aid Federation of England.

Saunders, H. (2001) *Making Contact Worse*. Bristol: Women's Aid Federation of England.

Saunders, H. (2004) *Twenty-Nine Child Homicides: Lessons Still to be Learnt on Domestic Violence and Child Protection*. Bristol: Women's Aid Federation of England.

Saunders, H. and Barron, J. (2003) *Failure to Protect?* Bristol: Women's Aid Federation of England.

Sloan, D. (2003) *Children in Need Census 2003, Social Factors Survey, Domestic Violence Analysis.* Available at www.cheshire.gov.uk

Smart, C. (2002) 'From children's shoes to children's voices.' *Family Court Review: An International Journal* 40, 3, 305–17.

Sturge, C. and Glaser, D. (2000) *Contact and Domestic Violence: The Experts' Court Report.* London: Family Law.

Wilson, M. and Daly, M. (2002) *Homicide.* New York: Aldine de Gruyter.

Wyndham, A. (1998) 'Children and domestic violence: The need for supervised contact services when contact with the violent father is ordered/desired.' *Australian Social Work 51*, 3, 41–8.

Chapter 10

Child Abuse and Domestic Violence in the Context of Parental Separation and Divorce

New Models of Intervention

Thea Brown

Introduction

An understanding of the relationship between child abuse, domestic violence and parental separation and divorce has been slow to develop, perhaps because of the confrontational issues involved. Parental separation and divorce are emotionally charged areas as are child abuse and domestic violence. Accepting that there is a relationship between all areas appears to have been difficult. The myth that child abuse and domestic violence in this context are merely allegations manufactured by one parent seeking a tactical advantage over the other in their intimate partnership dispute has obscured the reality of the relationship between child abuse, domestic violence and parental separation. It has delayed the achievement of much needed and more detailed knowledge.

However, recent improvements in understanding this relationship have led to the emergence of a number of new models of inter-organisational intervention for services working with children and their families on problems of child abuse and domestic violence in the context of parental separation and divorce. This chapter develops the theme of Christine Harrison's chapter (Chapter 9) in presenting perspectives on the role of child abuse and domestic violence (two types of family violence) in parental separation and divorce and some new programmes of intervention. In addition, principles to underpin the development of new models of intervention for child abuse and domestic violence in the context of parental separation and divorce in diverse social systems and communities are proposed.

Obstacles to understanding the relationship between child abuse, domestic violence and parental separation and divorce

One of the obstacles to understanding the relationship between child abuse and domestic violence and parental separation and divorce has been the way researchers and commentators have divided the reality of the family problems into distinct and unrelated areas of enquiry, with parental separation and divorce being seen as one area, child abuse as another and domestic violence as another again. As an understanding of the inter-relationship between these issues has taken shape, discussions about it have become part of the highly charged atmosphere that surrounds any public consideration of parental separation and divorce. In this area, debate and discussion take on the same emotional and blaming character as the disputes between the separating partners: for example, the gender polarisation of the individual marital dispute is repeated in the gender polarisation of the public debate.

Recognition of the increases in the annual breakdown rates of legal marriages followed by similar recognition of increases in annual breakdown rates of de facto marital partnerships is relatively recent. Attention was drawn to the societal challenge this posed by the pioneering divorce research team of Wallerstein and Kelly (1980) who undertook the first detailed study of the circumstances and aftermath of divorce by studying 60 divorcing families in the US. They pointed out that marital partnership breakdown rates had reached 30 per cent annually in the US by the 1980s, a figure that has been repeated and exceeded in many other countries subsequently.

Their explanations of the causes of the increase in marital breakdowns did not include the role of family violence, nor the role of child abuse or of domestic violence or both, despite the fact that they observed family violence and noted its existence. Although they described partners locked into marriages where they were 'demeaned, neglected and abused' (Wallerstein and Kelly 1980, p.11), they did not see either domestic violence or child abuse as causes of the marital collapse but rather as accompaniments to a partnership's disintegration. Their interpretation of family violence as incidental to the partnership breakdown, while not a major theme of the research, delayed the understanding of the role of child abuse and domestic violence in parental separation for many years.

Set alongside the increases in divorce rates internationally came an equally rapid increase in child abuse notification rates. As was the case with the divorce rates, the increase in child abuse notifications became apparent in the 1960s and

1970s and gathered further pace in the 1980s when it became of great concern to the child protection services internationally (Berliner and Conte 2002; Corby 2000; Howitt 1993).

Why child abuse notifications rose so rapidly during these decades remains unclear; however, in retrospect, it seems possible that the increases in child abuse notifications were related to the rise in the marital separation and divorce rate. At the time it was suggested that the rise was due to increased community awareness of child abuse as a result of the inter-disciplinary research, teaching, service provision and lobbying of researchers and practitioners such as Dr Henry Kempe, of the Kempe Center, Denver, US. While some have proposed that Kempe was merely the most visible element in a groundswell of professional concern for abused children (Corby 2000), explanations still centre around increased awareness driven by professional activity.

However, it is likely that the complementary rises in the incidence of the breakdown of marital partnerships and of child abuse notifications were linked at least in part to the changing position of women in society (Gordon 1992). As women received more education, had access to better contraception and had fewer children, infiltrated further into the workforce and gained better salaries and work conditions, obtaining or maintaining a marriage was no longer as necessary for child and maternal welfare. Divorce became easier to gain; economic support after divorce improved through state intervention and through work opportunities; problems could be admitted and marital breakdown allowed legally, socially and psychologically. Evidence for the increasingly acceptable costs of separation for women is provided by the finding that parental separation is usually instigated by women (Jordan 1996).

The growth in the rates of parental separation and divorce and in the notifications of child abuse led to an increase in the numbers of parental disputes over residence and/or contact involving allegations of child abuse by the 1980s (Thoennes and Pearson 1988). Explanations for the increase were framed within the discourse of the bitterness of the partnership disputes. First attempts at explanations suggested the allegations were false and that they had been initiated to gain an edge, possibly sharpened by revenge, in marital wars over property division and parenting arrangements for the children. A spate of research studies with small samples attempted to determine how much of this increase in residence and contact disputes with child abuse allegations was due to real child abuse and how much was due to false allegations. The debate over the truth and falsity of what were seen as only claims of child abuse had begun (Schudson 1992; Toth 1992).

A strand of this view, now discredited by research, remains entrenched today. Gardner proposed the Parental Alienation Syndrome as an explanation for the allegations of child sexual abuse made in this context, he maintained, by malicious parents (usually mothers) seeking to detach the child from the other parent (Gardner 1986). His is not the only construction of an image of the 'bad mother'. It has been a popular image in the child protection literature and practice, including work on parental separation and divorce, and it has been examined in detail by a number of researchers (Hay 2003; Hooper and Humphreys 1998; Humphreys 1997). Hooper and Humphreys (1998) suggest that mothers have been blamed for their children's sexual abuse, despite rarely inflicting it, because they were seen as responsible for their children's care, regardless of individual circumstances. Others support this view and extend it to all forms of child abuse, pointing out that mothers are the focus of professional intervention even when others are found to be the perpetrators (Corby 2000; O'Hagan and Dillenburger 1995; see also Chapter 8 in this book).

More recent research shows that child abuse and domestic violence separately and together lead to parental separation in a large and increasing number of marital partnerships. They are a cause of partnership breakdown and divorce, ranging in incidence in various studies from 60 to 80 per cent of partnership breakdown (FLPAG 2001). Moreover, child abuse and domestic violence do not stop following separation but continue afterwards (Hester and Radford 1996). There is also evidence to suggest separation leaves children vulnerable to instances of abuse, particularly sexual abuse, from new perpetrators. The precise mechanisms whereby this occurs have not been identified, but it appears that the marital or partnership status of the parents after separation does not affect the post-separation incidence of abuse (Wilson 2002).

It is not surprising that separating parents resort to socio-legal services for assistance. Yet the services surrounding family and private law and equivalent jurisdictions have managed separating and divorcing families where there is child abuse or domestic violence or both very poorly; the disputes have lingered in family and divorce courts, giving the appearance of even larger numbers due to the court's inability to resolve such disputes. Family and divorce courts have become arenas for the resolution of family violence without any accompanying awareness of their new role.

Allegations, abuse and abusers

As socio-legal services begin to develop more appropriate strategies for dealing with child abuse and domestic violence in the context of parental separation and divorce, it is essential for them to base their intervention on a firm base of knowledge derived from large-scale and rigorous research.

It is important to acknowledge that the majority of allegations made in this context are not fictitious. Taking all the different types of child abuse allegations together, the most recent findings (taken from the evaluation study of the new intervention programme known as Magellan, described more fully later in this chapter) show that just over one half of the allegations are reported to the court as substantiated by child protection services, meaning that professionals found evidence of the alleged abuse. Almost all of the substantiated abuse was found to be associated with domestic violence (Brown *et al.* 2001). In the other group, amounting to just under half of the cases, the child protection service reported that they found no evidence of abuse, but their substantiating levels were found to be affected by the willingness and the capacity of child protection services to investigate. When the service put a lower priority on these types of notifications, when it did not equip workers with the policies, procedures and knowledge to deal with them, substantiations were lower. In one study reviewing allegations where the child protection service had little willingness or capacity to investigate and where the inter-organisational case management processes between the court and the investigators was poor, some 22 per cent of allegations were substantiated. Subsequently, when the same service entered the new intervention programme, when willingness and capacity were improved, 52 per cent were substantiated on investigation (Brown *et al.* 1998, 2001).

Some allegations are false and evidence can be found showing that there is no abuse as opposed to findings that there is no evidence of abuse. However, rates of false allegations are low and vary between 9 and 12 per cent (Brown *et al.* 1998; Hume 1997; Thoennes and Pearson 1988). When the families where these occurred were investigated (Brown 2003), the allegations were found to be made by fathers slightly more often than by mothers (5:4). Most of these allegations were associated with long-term mental health problems and abusive backgrounds in the person making the allegations, although one-third of such allegations had no apparent explanation.

The abuse and its background differ from the abuse that is more commonly notified to child protection services. The differences require professional staff to be specially equipped to deal with a clientele who have particular problems concerning the abuse. If the professionals are not so equipped they will encounter difficulties and offer less effective and even damaging intervention.

The families are almost always two-parent families where both parents see themselves as actively involved in the children's care. While fathers have been reported to be largely missing in child protection practice, either actually absent or discounted by the services (Fleming 2002; Scourfield 2001), in this context both parents are combatants in an end-of-partnership dispute that includes the future care of their children. The families come from all socio-economic strata. Their three distinctive characteristics are: a high incidence of criminal convictions, to a greater extent for the men; a high incidence of unemployment that is in part related to their criminality; and a high incidence of family violence generally. This violence includes domestic violence, child abuse, child to parent violence,

violence in the extended family and a high incidence of violence towards the community. Professionals will find co-operative engagement difficult.

The nature of the child abuse is also different. The most common form, both reported and substantiated, is multiple type abuse, a category of abuse only recently used, and it occurs more frequently in this context than in others (Brown *et al.* 1998, 2001; Cawson 2002). Sexual abuse is more commonly reported, either alone or as one aspect of multiple type abuse (Brown *et al.* 1998, 2001). Physical abuse is reported and substantiated to the same extent as in other contexts but neglect is largely missing as a category and is unusual in this context. Also the abuse occurs in specific settings with abuse occurring on contact visits where the child is more vulnerable or at the changeover point prior to contact. Abduction can occur, and although it is regarded as a criminal offence rather than abuse, it can be the setting for abuse. Finally, child homicide can occur; it is rare but it does happen.

The perpetrators, and those who accuse them, are usually family members and here the basis for the gender war observed in parental separation and divorce becomes evident. The most common substantiated perpetrators are fathers (61%), with mothers being far less common (8%). The high prevalence of substantiated sexual abuse accounts in part for the gender bias towards males. Of concern is the high incidence of other family members identified as perpetrators (31%), including step-parents, grandparents and step-grandparents, uncles and siblings. Mothers are the most frequent source of the allegations; fathers are less likely to make allegations of any kind of abuse and other family members are infrequent accusers. However, professionals make some 12 per cent of the allegations (Brown *et al.* 1998, 2001).

Responding to abuse allegations

The socio-legal services in many countries have struggled to address these problems satisfactorily. Family and divorce courts and equivalent jurisdictions were not established with this problem in mind and they have found it difficult to respond appropriately. The most difficult aspect has been achieving inter-agency co-operation and co-ordination as so many different services have to be brought together to manage the problem. Such services, including private legal practices, public legal aid services, child protection services, police and the courts themselves, are separately established and operate under different legislative auspices, having different goals, programmes, procedures and professional groups each using their own professional and organisational languages.

The problems of inter-agency co-ordination in child protection have been known for many years (Hallett 1995; Lyon and de Cruz 1993) and in the context of parental separation and divorce the effects include lengthy delays in dispute resolution, case drift and poor outcomes regarding the protection of the children (Brown *et al.* 1998; Hester and Radford 1996; Hume 1997; Thoennes and Pearson 1988). The service system focuses on the parents' issues, rather than those of the child. Even when the problems for the child are acknowledged, the intervention offered is often not appropriate to and not helpful for the children (Hay and Brown 2004). The courts have been ignorant about domestic violence and its relationship to child abuse; they have tended to separate out domestic violence from child abuse and to simplify the management of the dispute by disregarding one or the other (Brown and Alexander 2006).

New interventions

In recent years, some courts have introduced new programmes to better manage these problems, an aspect of the trend in courts towards specialised judicial administration (King 1997). The first of these, the Magellan programme, introduced in Australia in 2003, was based on programme principles derived from research undertaken in 1995–7 (Brown *et al.* 1998), but it did not use a broader child protection theoretical model as it could have done.

The Magellan programme

The Magellan programme was initiated on an experimental basis by the Family Court of Australia in two Melbourne court registries in 1998 and then introduced nationally state by state from 2003. The principles underpinning the programme were as follows:

- an inter-organisational approach
- a focus on the children
- prioritising early intervention
- a judge-led and tightly managed time-limited approach
- court-ordered expert assessments including both a child protection investigation and a court family report
- court-ordered publicly funded legal representation for every child
- a court multi-disciplinary team.

The programme was designed by a committee representing the consortium of services that co-operated to provide the new programme, that is the Family Court of Australia, the Commonwealth Attorney-General's Department (the funder of the Commonwealth court system and of the state legal aid commissions), the state child protection service, the state police, the state legal aid commission, the Law Council of Australia and the team led by the author that carried out the formal evaluation of Magellan. The programme was designed to utilise a court staff team of two judges, a senior counsellor, assisted by six others to undertake family reports, and a court registrar. Cases were offered a place in the programme after the registrar and the senior counsellor (who normally reviewed all applications in relation to children's matters) determined if allegations of physical or sexual abuse were involved in the dispute. Protocols for co-operation between all participating services were developed in detail in advance. The committee met monthly to support and monitor the programme.

The programme for the disputes comprised four court events. All court events or hearings were held on the same day each week. The *first court event* was a preliminary mention presided over by the judge with the senior counsellor and registrar present. The judge explained the new programme and made a number of procedural orders as well as interim orders if required. At this hearing, the judge ordered the appointment of a legal representative for the child funded by legal aid and the child protection investigation, a report of which was to be returned to the court within five weeks. The report and the file were to be made available to the legal practitioners one week before the next hearing and the report was to be made available to the parents at the same time. The *second court event* was held seven weeks later if the case had not been resolved. At this time, the judge received the child protection report and ordered a report from the court counsellors assessing the family's functioning to be completed and returned to the court in seven weeks. Legal practitioners and parents were to be given the report one week before the next hearing which was planned for ten weeks ahead. The *third court event* was a pre-hearing conference led by the registrar and with the senior counsellor. The family, their legal advisors and other services, such as the child protection service, met at the informal conference to discuss views, reports, common ground, options, and ongoing concerns. The *fourth court event* was the trial or final hearing which took place ten weeks from the pre-hearing conference and which was conducted in the same way as all trials in the Family Court.

Within 18 months, all except one of the 100 cases were completed. The one outstanding case was delayed by an appeal to the Minister of Immigration over the resident status of the mother and children. The time delay in this case was so great that it was dropped from the study but then re-instated after a determination by the Minister placed it within the Australian jurisdiction.

The programme goals were achieved. Co-operation between the court and the child protection service improved substantially with all families being investigated, compared to only half previously, with the time taken for reports to be completed falling by one quarter to an average of 32 days, well within the programme's time frame, and with some 52 per cent of children where abuse had been alleged having had the abuse substantiated as opposed to 23 per cent previously. The police were involved in 51 per cent of the families and took legal action, primarily charging an offender, in 26 per cent of these cases, about twice as frequently as has been reported in other studies (Goddard 1988). Some 33 per cent of cases were resolved prior to family reports being ordered and some 5 per cent of cases had current reports on file. The completion of a family report produced a resolution based on the report for one-quarter of the cases where a report was carried out. These were primarily contact-only disputes as had been noted in the earlier study (Brown *et al.* 1998).

Reviewing outcomes from the 1998 study of the management of residence and contact disputes where child abuse allegations were involved (Brown *et al.* 1998) and comparing them with the outcomes in the 2001 Magellan study (Brown *et al.* 2001), the average number of court events fell from an average of five during the 1992–5 period covered in the first study to 2.95 in the 1998–2000 period covered in the later study. The time the process took fell from 17.5 months in the first study to 8.79 months in the second study. Similarly, the number of cases proceeding to a trial fell from 30 per cent in the first study to 13 per cent in the second study. The importance of these gains is evidenced by the link detected in the first study between the degree of children's distress, as assessed by the descriptions of the children's state of mind in reports from experts, including those from the child protection service, and the time spent in the legal process and the number of hearings taken during the process.

Final orders involving either supervised contact (26%) or no contact (15%) rose by one-quarter, as judged by the findings of another unrelated concurrent study (Rhoades, Graycar and Harrison 2000). Only 8 per cent of these orders were not by consent. The numbers of children showing high levels of distress fell dramatically from 28 in the first study to 4 per cent in the second but it must be acknowledged that the programme may not have been the only factor that was influential in producing this effect (Brown *et al.* 1998, 2001). The breakdown rate of final orders fell from 37 to 5 per cent, as measured no less than 12 months after final orders were achieved in each case.

With these results, the Commonwealth Attorney-General's Department authorised all state legal aid services to support the programme, thereby establishing a new policy allowing legal aid to fund legal representatives for all the children in these cases and to do so regardless of parental means. Also it allowed legal aid caps to the total grant to be exceeded for each and for any party.

The Columbus programme

One omission in the Magellan programme was the avoidance of the issue of domestic violence as a form of child abuse. In that programme, if an allegation of child abuse referred to domestic violence as well or to domestic violence that obviously involved the child, then the case was included. However, in disputes where only domestic violence was referred to, and where there was no mention of any impact of this on the child, the case was not included. Yet, domestic violence is regarded as abusive in its impact on children even if they are not directly involved and it is regarded as an indicator of likely child abuse in any context as well as in this particular context (Brown *et al.* 1998).

Thus, in 2001, the Family Court of Western Australia, the one state in Australia not covered by the Commonwealth family law legislation, introduced the Columbus programme. This was similar to Magellan but included domestic violence as a form of child abuse which represented another step forward in dealing more effectively with child abuse and domestic violence (Murphy and Pike 2003). Columbus was not able to attract as wide support from the relevant services as the Magellan programme; it gained the support of the state legal aid commission to fund legal representatives for the children but not the support of the child protection service or the police. Perhaps because of this, it did not incorporate expert child protection assessments.

It was staffed by a multi-disciplinary team of a judicial officer, with a magistrate rather than a judge, and a court counsellor, both of whom chaired a series of case conferences with a view to achieving a negotiated settlement. Although the project has not been completed, the early results show similar but less dramatic improvements when compared with the Magellan programme at the time of writing (Murphy and Pike 2003).

Principles underpinning future programmes

One jurisdiction in Canada has introduced an inter-agency programme based on Magellan but to date no others have commenced a specialised programme of such scope. However, other countries are moving towards new models of intervention in somewhat different ways. For example, New Zealand has introduced family law legislation that prohibits a parent with a conviction for domestic violence from seeking either a residence or contact order until they have given evidence of a minimum period free of domestic violence. In another development, the Australian Family Law Council (2004) has proposed that the Magellan programme be supported by the development of the court's own child protection service.

There is clear concern about the issue and some pioneering projects addressing it but, as yet, there has been no articulation of policy principles to underpin a child protection model of intervention for children involved in residence and contact disputes where child abuse and/or domestic violence have been alleged.

However, an examination of the projects undertaken to date and the relevant literature suggest some key principles which should inform any model. These are as follows:

1. *Children's safety and protection from harm should be the major consideration and should be maintained by the court as long as is required.* The safety of the children and their protection from harm should be given priority above other considerations and should be given precedence over maintaining a bond between the child and the parent. There is no evidence to show that maintaining a bond with an abusive parent contributes to a child's well-being but there is evidence to show that it does harm (Rogers and Pryor 1998). In the context of parental separation and divorce, children are especially vulnerable as they are ordered by courts regardless of their own desires to be with one or other parent when there is no protection afforded them by that court during this time. Children's protection should also be maintained as long as they require it by having court orders monitored by the court rather than by the parents.

2. *Domestic violence should be regarded as a form of child abuse.* Domestic violence has been shown to be damaging to children even when it is not directed at them. The effects it has on children demonstrate that it is not good parenting and therefore it cannot be argued as being separate from or irrelevant to parenting. Furthermore, the correlation between domestic violence and all forms of child abuse is high and, in the context of parental separation and divorce, especially high with one form of violence obscuring the other (Brown *et al.* 1998). Accepting domestic violence is the same as tolerating child abuse.

3. *Children and their well-being should be the focus.* The children and their well-being should be the focus of any decision-making rather than the well-being of the parents. Parents' needs for contact or residency should not be confused with children's needs.

4. *Children's views should be sought and placed before the court.* Children's views as to their situation should be sought when they are willing for this to occur and they should be placed before the court. Their views may be different from those of their parents and from those of other family members. Their views should not be sought if they are not to be made known to the court and if they will not be taken into consideration. Children should be able to speak to the judge if they wish and judges should be trained to undertake such discussions. It should be possible to treat children's views with confidentiality if to do otherwise would place them or their siblings in danger of further abuse.

5. *Children should be offered support during the proceedings.* It is clear that being part of a residence and contact dispute that may or may not include court proceedings is very distressing for the children and support from counselling agencies should be available to children to minimise their distress (Hay 2003). Counselling does not necessarily shape the children's views of their parents or the dispute and should not be

terminated on such grounds unless there is clear evidence that this is so. In such cases, alternative counselling should be immediately arranged.

6.   *Children should be treated with respect at all times.* Children are vulnerable at any time and especially so after parental separation. Resolution of a residence and contact dispute where children are interviewed by many professionals and experts should not further damage the children and they should be treated with respect at all times. They should not be compelled by the court to undertake activities that they regard as dangerous for themselves. All court and associated professionals should observe a child-respectful and child-safe code of behaviour.

7.   *All children should have a publicly funded legal representative, regardless of their parents' means.* All children should have a legal representative to act on their behalf and the legal practitioner should not be paid by the parents, either directly or indirectly. The child's legal representatives should be paid from public funds, for example from legal aid.

8.   *An inter-agency approach should be used.* As issues of child abuse require an inter-agency response (Brown *et al.* 2001; Hallett 1995; Lyon and de Cruz 1993), courts should mobilise an inter-organisational network including child protection services, police, legal aid, relationship counselling services for children and adults and contact centres. Such services require clear procedures and protocols to be developed between all services for their co-operative endeavours.

9.   *Programmes should be court led and judge managed with tight pre-set time lines.* Special programmes should be established by courts to deal with residence and contact disputes where child abuse allegations are involved and they should comprise a series of pre-set steps devised by the court and then tightly managed by the judge within pre-set time lines. The courts should take the initiative and lead in dispute resolution by mechanisms they have designed, based on courts' knowledge of the most effective means for resolution.

10.   *Early intervention should occur.* Special programmes should incorporate early intervention as this appears to contribute to resolution, as evidenced by both the Magellan and Columbus outcomes. Resources invested in intervention at the outset of a programme save resources in the longer term.

11.   *Child abuse and domestic violence allegations to be investigated immediately by expert forensic investigation staff.* One early intervention required is the immediate investigation of allegations of family violence. No decision-making can take place without a full investigation first, for the results of the investigation provide the basis for subsequent decision-making. Such investigations should be carried out by staff trained in forensic child protection and domestic violence investigation.

12. *A senior multi-disciplinary court team with expertise and training about child abuse and domestic violence should be used.* A multi-disciplinary court team should be used as the resolution and decision-making process requires the contribution of a number of areas of expertise. Furthermore, child abuse and domestic violence are complex areas where specialist knowledge is required. The secretive nature of the abusive behaviour places it beyond ordinary and easily accessible knowledge. Perpetrators of abuse entice ignorant professionals into a variety of responses that can develop into an unwitting collusion. Expert knowledge is required; senior staff should be used and they should receive special training.

Conclusion

Increased understanding of the role of child abuse and domestic violence in parental separation and divorce has informed several pioneering socio-legal programmes centred on courts and aimed at addressing the problem with effective services. To date, evaluations of these programmes have been encouraging and the models they provide have the capacity to stimulate developments elsewhere. As a wider range of initiatives emerge at the national and international levels, it should become possible to compare their effectiveness in terms of both processes and the outcomes achieved for children.

References

Berliner, L. and Conte, J. (2002) *Present State of Assessment and Treatment in the Field, a Paper presented by Invitation to the 14th International Congress on Child Abuse and Neglect.* Denver, CO: ISPCAN and the Kempe Children's Foundation.

Brown, T. (2003) 'Fathers and child abuse allegations in the context of parental separation and divorce.' *Family Courts Review 41,* 3, 367–80.

Brown, T. and Alexander, R. (2006) *Child Abuse and Parental Separation.* In press. Sydney: Allen and Unwin.

Brown, T., Frederico, M., Hewitt, L. and Sheehan, R. (1998) *Violence in Families: The Management of Child Abuse Allegations in Custody and Access Disputes Before the Family Court of Australia.* Family Violence and Family Court Research Program. Melbourne: Monash University.

Brown, T., Sheehan, R., Frederico, M. and Hewitt, L. (2001) *Resolving Family Violence to Children: The Evaluation of Project Magellan, a Pilot Project for Managing Family Court Residence and Contact Disputes When Allegations of Child Abuse Have Been Made.* Family Violence and Family Court Research Program. Melbourne: Monash University.

Cawson, P. (2002) *Child Maltreatment in the Family: The Experience of a National Sample of Young People.* London: National Society for the Prevention of Cruelty to Children.

Corby, B. (2000) *Child Abuse: Towards a Knowledge Base* (2nd edn). Buckingham: Open University Press.

Family Law Council (2004) *Family Law and Child Protection: Final Report.* Barton, ACT: Children's Services Committee, Family Law Council.

Family Law Pathways Advisory Group (FLPAG) (2001) *Out of the Maze: Pathways to the Future for Families Experiencing Separation. Report of the Family Law Pathways Advisory Group.* Canberra: Commonwealth of Australia.

Fleming, J. (2002) 'Just the two of us: The involvement of fathers in building stronger families.' *Developing Practice 4*, 60–9.

Gardner, R.A. (1986) *Child Custody Litigation: A Guide for Parents and Mental Health Professionals.* Cresshill, NJ: Creative Therapeutics.

Goddard, C. (1988) *Victoria's Protective Services: Dual Tracks and Double Standards.* Melbourne: Victorian Society for the Prevention of Child Abuse and Neglect.

Gordon, M. (1992) 'Recent supreme court rulings on child testimony in sexual abuse cases.' *Journal of Child Sexual Abuse 1*, 59–71.

Hallett, C. (1995) *Interagency Coordination in Child Protection: Studies in Child Protection.* London: HMSO.

Hay, A. (2003) 'The experiences of children in residence and contact disputes where child abuse allegations are involved.' A paper presented to *Child Sexual Abuse Allegations: The Justice Response.* Adelaide: Conference, Institute of Criminology.

Hay, A. and Brown, T. (2004) 'Children's views.' A paper presented to *Working Together for a Child Safe World.* Brisbane: 15th International Congress on Child Abuse and Neglect.

Hester, M. and Radford, L. (1996) *Domestic Violence and Child Contact Arrangements in England and Denmark.* Bristol: The Policy Press.

Hooper, C.A. and Humphreys, C. (1998) 'Women whose children have been sexually abused.' *British Journal of Social Work 28*, 581–99.

Howitt, D. (1993) *Child Abuse Errors.* New Jersey: Rutgers University Press.

Hume, M. (1997) *Child Sexual Abuse Allegations and the Family Court.* Unpublished Master's thesis, Humanities and Social Sciences. Adelaide: University of South Australia.

Humphreys, C. (1997) 'Child sexual abuse in the context of divorce: Issues for mothers.' *British Journal of Social Work 27*, 282–312.

Jordan, P. (1996) 'Ten years on: the effects of separation and divorce on men.' A paper presented to the *Fifth Australian Family Studies Research Conference*, Brisbane, Australia.

King, D. (1997) 'Judicial intervention.' *Family Advocate 19*, 4.

Lyon, C. and de Cruz, P. (1993) *Child Abuse, Family Law* (2nd edn). Bristol: Jordan Publishing Limited.

Murphy, P. and Pike, L. (2003) 'The Columbus Pilot in the Family Court of Western Australia: Some early findings from the evaluation.' A paper presented at the *Eighth Australian Institute of Family Studies Conference*, Melbourne.

O'Hagan, K. and Dillenburger, K. (1995) *The Abuse of Women Within Childcare Work.* Buckingham: Open University Press.

Rhoades, H., Graycar, R. and Harrison, M. (2000) *The Family Law Reform Act 1995. The First Three Years.* Sydney: University of Sydney and the Family Court of Australia.

Rogers, B. and Pryor, J. (1998) *Divorce and Separation: The Outcomes for Children.* York: Joseph Rowntree Foundation.

Schudson, C. (1992) 'Antagonistic parents in family courts: False allegations or false assumptions of child abuse.' *Journal of Child Sexual Abuse 1*, 111–13.

Scourfield, J.B. (2001) 'Constructing men in child protection work.' *Men and Masculinities 4*, 1, 70–89.

Thoennes, N. and Pearson, N. (1988) 'Summary of findings from sexual abuse allegations project.' In B. Nicholson and J. Bulkley (eds) *Sexual Abuse Allegations in Custody and Visitation Cases.* Washington, DC: National Legal Resources Center for Child Advocacy and Protection, pp.1–28.

Toth, P. (1992) 'All child abuse allegations demand attention.' *Journal of Child Sexual Abuse 1*, 117–18.

Wallerstein, J. and Kelly, J. (1980) *Surviving the Breakup: How Children and Parents Cope with Divorce.* New York: Basic Books.

Wilson, R.F. (2002) 'Fractured families, fragile children – the sexual vulnerability of girls in the aftermath of divorce.' *Child and Family Law Quarterly 14*, 1, 1–23.

Part Four

Working with Perpetrators

Chapter 11

Domestic Abuse Risk Assessment and Safety Planning in Child Protection – Assessing Perpetrators

Lorraine Radford, Neil Blacklock and Kate Iwi

Introduction

There is no doubt that domestic violence raises many issues of concern for child protection. Working with families living with domestic violence is challenging. Victims of domestic violence often feel trapped in a relationship with the perpetrator by a combination of force, fear, obligation and lack of options and they may leave and return on more than one occasion (Glass 1995). Professionals sometimes find this difficult to understand, can lose patience with mothers and lament their failure to protect children from living with abuse. Abusers can be volatile and frightening people who may threaten or intimidate social workers (Humphreys 2000). Child protection cases involving domestic violence often present with multiple issues and include cases where the adult victim as well as the perpetrator may have abused or neglected the child. Parents fearing the consequences of exposure to ongoing violence may evade contact with statutory agencies (Mullender 1996).

A shortcoming of the common assessment framework currently used in the UK is the very limited reference made to domestic violence. Even if identified, the violence may be subsumed under another issue or problem affecting the family (Hester and Pearson 1998). These problems are compounded by the historically established tendency in social work to deal predominantly with women so that, where there is abuse or neglect of a child, the woman is the focus of attention and little effort is made to challenge the male domestic violence perpetrator (Humphreys 2000; Milner 1993; O'Hagan and Dillenburger 1995; Stanley

1997). Practice in child protection has undoubtedly changed in the past few years so that the importance of supporting women and challenging men in the context of domestic violence is becoming more readily accepted. There is some disagreement over the extent of this change. Indeed it has been argued that social workers have taken the recommendation to challenge men too far by adopting a confrontational style to work with perpetrators at the same time as neglecting the support and protection of the woman (Milner 2004). We are not aware of any research on current social work practice that confirms this conclusion and it lies at odds with our own observations of the variations in practice. The purpose of working with perpetrators is not to 'demonise men' but to challenge the violence and get better protection for the victim (usually the woman) and the children. Properly assessing the violence in the specific context of the relationship is an important part of this process. In this chapter we discuss recent developments in domestic violence risk assessment and highlight as an example the practice developed within a voluntary sector project, the Domestic Violence Intervention Project (DVIP). The example illustrates how a gendered analysis of violence has informed practice but this does not predetermine a rigid, dogmatic approach to assessment. Risk assessment needs to draw upon a theoretically informed evidence base but it also needs to focus on the individuals involved rather than on assumed patterns of behaviour.

Risk or safety?

A risk assessment is a probability calculation that a harmful behaviour or event will occur. This involves an assessment of the frequency of the behaviour/event, its likely impact and who it will affect (Kemshall 1996). Our discussions and correspondence with practitioners in the UK involved in domestic violence risk assessment and management suggest that this work has developed from (at least) two sources – the spread of actuarialism in criminal justice and child protection systems and the development of risk assessment and safety planning in advocacy and refuge services (Legal Services Commission 2003). Both trends have been heavily influenced by developments in working with violence in the US (Garland 2002; Mullender 1996). Both trends also reflect broader developments in child protection work and a shift in focus from assessing the needs of looked-after children towards assessing all children's needs (see *Every Child Matters*, DfES 2003). These developments have had a profound impact on what social workers and other agencies do when working together to safeguard children.

Child protection and work with offenders has often included some assessment of risk, based upon clinical or professional judgement. Public service re-structuring, targeting and rationing over the past 20 years has brought about a greater emphasis on risk assessment, especially actuarialism, in the police, probation and the prison system (Kemshall 2002; Young 1999). Actuarial risk assessment derives from the insurance industry and it has spread rapidly to statutory agencies concerned to protect themselves from client-initiated court cases for compensation. Actuarial risk assessment draws upon research-based probability calculations to identify the likely level of risk, focusing especially on the most dangerous offender. Its purpose is to manage this risk by containing it and minimising the likelihood of further harm. Identifying different levels of risk allows practitioners to identify domestic violence and to match the level of risk or need (commonly high, medium or low risk) to the appropriately targeted level of resources. Targeting resources in this way however raises the possibility that efforts will become focused on the highest risk, most dangerous, but relatively rare cases, while the more usual 'everyday violence' (Stanko 1990) carries on undeterred. Risk assessment can be used as a rationing device.

In contrast to actuarial risk assessment are the developments based upon safety planning that have grown within advocacy services and refuges. Here the purpose of a risk (safety) assessment is to provide knowledge that will assist in safety planning with the victim and children. Understanding the victim's fears and experiences of living with the violence is a crucial step in getting her better protection. Focusing on safety means going beyond an assessment of the risk of further physical attack and repeat victimisation. Safety includes psychological safety and freedom from fear, creating peace at home. Safety can also be seen to include creating the space to recover from trauma and depression so that continuing confrontation with the triggers for traumatic re-living of the past do not undermine the recovery of both adult and child survivors of domestic violence. We borrow from the thinking behind the Assessment Framework (Department of Health 2000) in believing that an assessment drawing up this broad definition of safety and well-being is more appropriate for informing decisions about domestic violence and child welfare.

We need though to carefully consider who assesses risk, at what stage and then what action is taken as a result. Risk assessment requires time and resources for adequate staff training. Assessments have to be workable and not overly bureaucratic. There are also issues of competence and consistency to consider as a result of the outsourcing of risk assessment on to psychiatric, psychological and voluntary sector services. Informed decisions by commissioning services about the value of these partnerships depend upon a degree of shared knowledge about the risk assessment evidence base but we have observed a limited awareness of perpetrator assessment issues.

The evidence base for domestic violence risk assessment is growing but still rather limited. The research literature has drawn conclusions based on the following methods:

- Fatality reviews (Websdale 1999) and research conducted in prisons (Soothill *et al.* 2002). These are the atypical and least common cases of domestic violence which result in fatalities or in prosecution.

- Victimisation and crime surveys (e.g. Walby and Myhill 2002) or reviews of police or agency data (Campbell *et al.* 1998). The usefulness of these sources depends on what is reported and recorded. Children and young people as victims (or perpetrators) of crime are nearly always absent from crime surveys.

- Surveys of perpetrator characteristics (Gilchrist *et al.* 2003).

Factors commonly linked with a risk of further domestic violence in the research literature include:

- previous physical or sexual assaults (Walby and Myhill 2002)

- an escalation in the frequency and severity of violence (Websdale 1999)

- recent separation (Walby and Myhill 2002)

- either partner's threats and attempts to kill or to commit suicide (Websdale 1999)

- violence in pregnancy (Campbell *et al.* 1998)

- the perpetrator's possessiveness, jealousy, stalking and psychological abuse of the victim

- previous criminality or breach of court orders

- the degree of isolation and vulnerability of the victim – women aged 16 to 24 years report more domestic violence (Walby and Myhill 2002)

- child abuse and previous contact with a child protection agency.

This list is by no means exhaustive but many of these risk indicators can be found in the various domestic violence risk assessment tools and checklists that now exist (see for example the SARA, Spousal Assault Risk Assessment, Kropp *et al.* 1999; or Campbell's Danger Assessment Checklist, Campbell *et al.* 1998). Not all the assessments that are used have a firm evidential foundation. Risk assessment can never be wholly accurate nor infallible and cannot be used to predict whether or not an event will happen. Research on homicides and child deaths has shown that assessments cannot be used to predict even the worst outcomes (Sinclair and Bullock 2002). Searching for 'lethality indicators' can throw up a large number of 'false positives' because indicators of lethality are found in many relationships that do not result in homicide (Kemshall 2002).

At the other end of the risk scale, defining a perpetrator of abuse as 'low risk' is not an excuse for complacency. A central pattern in domestic violence is the escalation of abuse. What may be considered 'low risk' initially may change very rapidly – for example, on separation. This is a significant problem if risk assessment is used as a tool to ration resources. The process of risk assessment needs to be dynamic and open to review as circumstances can change. The possibility of change can be included up to a point in an assessment. Risk assessments often combine static and dynamic risk factors. Static risk factors focus on the history and past behaviour of the perpetrator and the nature of the past abuse. Dynamic factors consider the changeable characteristics of the perpetrator (such as attitudes) and of the context (such as separation) that can either raise or decrease the risk of further harm. These risk factors need to be understood as being associated with an increased likelihood of further violence rather than as being definitely linked or casual factors. Families and their circumstances are complex and tick-box risk assessments which aggregate numbers to determine how resources and staff are allocated to a case can be too mechanistic to respond appropriately to needs, safety and risk. Some individuals or groups may be more at risk than others as either victims or perpetrators but stereotyping groups or individuals is unhelpful and discriminatory. One woman from a minority group may be at greater risk due to her abuser's strong attachment to traditional gender roles, while another may be isolated due to language issues or immigration status. At face value, the service contact statistics might suggest that women from minorities are more vulnerable to abuse but the women's safety needs are very different in these two cases. Any risk assessment needs to focus on the individuals involved rather than purely on the patterns of abusive relationships. Assessments should not become substitutes for hearing what an individual has to say about her experiences and fears. Assessments also need to be fair and reasonable and able to withstand possible challenges in court.

The purpose of a domestic violence risk assessment in child protection is most commonly to gauge and to deal with the risks that the domestic violence poses for the well-being of the child. To date, however, domestic violence risk assessment has focused mostly on the risks to the adult victim. Our consultation with a range of agencies involved in domestic violence risk assessment in the UK (Legal Services Commission 2003) showed a need for assessments that were relevant to the issues that present in work with children and would take into account research findings on how children may be affected by living with the abuse (e.g. Hester, Harwin and Pearson 1998; McGee 2000). In particular, risk assessment needs to take the following into account:

- The possibility that if a parent is abused then the perpetrator may also be physically or sexually abusing the child.
- Children witness or overhear the violence and this can cause fear and other harm.

- Children who witness domestic violence are seldom passive bystanders. The perpetrator may try to draw them into the abuse, particularly into the drip-drip tactics of constant criticism and undermining. Alternatively, the children may intervene to protect the other parent or find other ways to try to manage the violence.

- Domestic violence can have a devastating impact upon the health and well-being of the victim. This can affect the victim's capacity to parent. The perpetrator's tactics of abuse may also include undermining her parenting and her relationship with the children.

- A number of factors (from the child's individual characteristics to her/his attachment to parents or to others outside of the family) can influence the impact that the domestic violence has on the child's welfare.

- The capacity for change to stop the violence and to support a healthy relationship able to address the emotional and developmental needs of the child.

There are a number of issues that make this work difficult to engage with. The particular challenges in domestic violence risk assessment and child protection include:

- how to assess the nature and impact of the domestic violence and its inter-relationship with other issues in the family affecting parenting, applying the broad definition of safety to include the child's emotional and psychological safety

- how to make sound judgements about the level of risk, the difficulty of identifying the high-risk cases where parents are 'unco-operative', there are multiple problems and where the children are very young

- how to approach cases where it appears both parents take part in the abuse

- how to assess the impact of the violence on the child's attachment to an abusive parent taking into account the possibility of a traumatic rather than an affective bond (Calder, Harold and Howarth 2004)

- dealing with tensions between the victim's and the children's needs and wishes.

Developing partnerships to move practice forward – DVIP's experience

The number of men referred to DVIP's domestic violence prevention programme by social workers through the period 1992–2000 was consistently at a worrying low rate (6.25% of total referrals or 12 out of 192 in 2001–2). This number remained low despite DVIP offering a service that was, at the time, free to social work departments. Domestic violence features in the lives of 37 per cent of children who are receiving social work interventions and 60 per cent of children on the 'at risk' register (Children in Need Census 2001). Given this, it was hard to see why social workers were en masse *not* referring, year after year.

During these years of low social service referrals, members of DVIP wondered what sort of service was needed for social services clients who had domestic violence issues that contributed substantially to the child protection risks. There was, of course, a cultural divide between domestic violence agencies and social work departments – part historical, but partly to do with the different 'primary client', resulting in different models of understanding and practice. Moving across this divide has required modifying the approach taken by DVIP to:

- understand the impact of domestic violence on children's lives and the necessity for a change in practice

- understand how their task and the institution in which they work shapes how social workers see these issues

- understand what was it about how DVIP worked that was problematic for social workers and how that is shaped by our task and the institution in which we work

- find individual social workers who could champion institutional change within their agency.

Social work is institutionally constructed to protect children and is predicated on historical perspectives of parental responsibility, especially in terms of mother-hood (Mullender 1996; Radford and Hester 2002). Domestic violence agencies on the other hand are predominantly focused on the welfare and safety of the victim, usually the mother in the first instance. This has led to institutional polar-isation where social work is child welfare focused and domestic violence agencies are victim focused. As a result, many domestic violence agencies see social workers as victim blaming (mother as failing to protect) and social workers see domestic violence specialists as blind to maternal responsibility.

In an attempt to move beyond this polarisation and increase perpetrator accountability in social work, DVIP developed joint working arrangements with two London boroughs (Westminster and Hammersmith and Fulham). In Hammersmith and Fulham, the driving concern was about responses to the number of notifications from police officers that children are present during domestic violence incidents (form 78s). In Westminster, their driving concern was that current interventions sometimes drove women further away from sources of support, together with a hope that non-statutory agencies could more easily engage with families who were often suspicious (an understatement) of social workers. Both local authorities shared DVIP's aim to make the perpetrator accountable in social work practice, bringing the abuser into treatment where appropriate. Each local authority worked with DVIP in very different ways with significantly different outcomes (see Blacklock 2004).

Joint working arrangements – elements common to both

DVIP offered four levels of response to local authority social service departments (SSDs): these were constructed to correspond to four risk thresholds which are described below.

Thresholds 1 and 2

- *Threshold 1* is where an incident has been reported to the department but the children were not present during the incident or were not aware of the incident. Also, there would be no history of involvement with social services and no previous referrals to the department.

- *Threshold 2* responds to reports where the children were present during (had witnessed or heard) the incident, and/or if there were previous F78s or SSD involvement. In these cases it is likely that the family would be contacted by a social worker by letter/phone call and a 'seven-day' (section 17) assessment would take place, resulting in a service plan, which would then be communicated to the couple.

In response to both these thresholds, DVIP would attempt to contact the man to offer an initial appointment. This involves a DVIP worker attempting to contact the alleged abuser by telephone and by letter. He would be asked to come in for a meeting with DVIP about the incident.

The purpose of this meeting is to:

- ascertain something of his version of the history of domestic violence, his attitude towards it, and his perception of the impact on the child(ren)

- make note of any indicators of particular concern in terms of risk

- explore the possibility of addressing his behaviour through appropriate means such as a perpetrator programme, substance misuse programme, parenting course and/or mental health intervention

- develop his motivation towards seeking further help.

DVIP would feed back to social services as to whether or not we were successful in contacting him and any particular concerns. In Threshold 2 assessments, DVIP would work within the time frame of the assessment and alongside the allocated social worker to ensure consistency of approach between the two organisations. As a result the man could go on to take up a place on DVIP's Violence Prevention Programme and further brief reports would be provided to social services on progress.

Thresholds 3 and 4 – standard risk assessment for child protection cases and full risk assessment in public law court proceedings

- *Threshold 3* is where the children are already on the child protection register or where registration is under consideration. At this level, a standard risk assessment (shorter version of the full risk assessment used for public law court cases) would be undertaken by DVIP. Social workers would consider referring to DVIP where the ending of the domestic violence would result in an increase in safety and possible deregistration of the children.

- *Threshold 4* covers referrals for full risk assessment in care proceedings where domestic violence is a contributing factor. This assessment provides the court with a greater understanding of the risk resulting from the domestic violence.

The assessment considers the perspectives of both parents and of the children through liaison with social workers and guardians. It includes between four and six hours of interview time with the alleged perpetrator and between two and six hours with the other parent. All DVIP risk assessment reports outline the history of domestic violence, risk levels and risk areas, they recommend treatment options, and include an assessment of whether interventions such as a perpetrator programme are likely to significantly reduce the risk. The DVIP's women's support service was offered to all women whose partners attended appointments at DVIP.

As soon as DVIP began to undertake risk assessments in public law cases, the court started to request dual assessments where they wanted the risk posed by both parents to be assessed. This brought a set of new challenges in terms of what was being assessed, for example our understanding of women's use of violence and what sort of approach should be used to address this. However, as a starting point, we needed to understand what was really happening in these relationships, who was doing what to whom, why, and what was the impact of this behaviour (Erwin 2004). The danger of failing to consider these issues is that we can end up mirroring what happened in the US where the introduction of mandatory arrest policies for domestic violence had the unintended consequence of radically increasing the number of dual arrests (Hirschel and Buzawa 2002; Miller 2001). Dual arrests would occur when police officers were faced with a situation where both parties had used physical violence. Victims of domestic violence who had defended themselves were being arrested and convicted of assaults and sentenced to treatment programmes.

In the UK, the framework for assessment used by social workers examines the parental relationship purely in relation to the child. It is not constituted to understand the dynamics and meaning of domestic violence, nor is social work institutionally configured to hold abusers accountable. This, we believe, leads to the number of requests for dual assessments and the tendency, when both parents have used violence, to see that violence as mutual. When used inappropriately, the paradigm of mutual violence is clearly detrimental to victims of domestic violence. The initial task in a dual assessment is to decide if there is a predominant (primary) physical aggressor (PPA). Faced with reports that both parties have used violence towards each other, DVIP needs to evaluate each party's experience and story separately. If it cannot be ascertained that one person has used violence purely in self-defence, then a number of other issues are explored.

First, what is the history of abuse? If someone has been subject to a period of violence and abuse and hits back, this does not have the same meaning nor does it require the same response. Second, the relative severity of the injuries needs to be considered. The injuries of a man with scratches to his face and a woman with a black eye and bruising round her neck need to be viewed differently. Third, the impact of the behaviour needs to be understood. This should include the accumulative impact of living in an abusive relationship and being subject to emotional and possibly sexual abuse. Fourth, the power relationship between the parties needs to be explored since this affects a range of other issues including the couple's expectations of each other, the authority, fearfulness and vulnerability within the relationship. The abuse of structural and historical power inequalities (for example, around gender, race, age or class issues) are often a significant part of the picture in the dynamics of domestic violence.

Understanding who is most fearful and who is most at risk from further injury provides meaning to the respective behaviours of each partner. The use of predominant physical aggressor terminology puts the violence into a context. It is a process that is gender-neutral, while taking into account the operation of gender among a range of potential power relationships within the specific relationship, paving the way for an assessment of the needs of and risks posed by each parent.

The risk assessment process at DVIP

At DVIP, safety planning and interventions to bring about change for both parents and children are key aspects of the risk assessment and risk management/harm reduction approach. Assessment and safety planning (for Thresholds

3 and 4 outlined above) is a three-stage process of initial assessment, time-limited intervention and reassessment of change (see Figure 11.1).

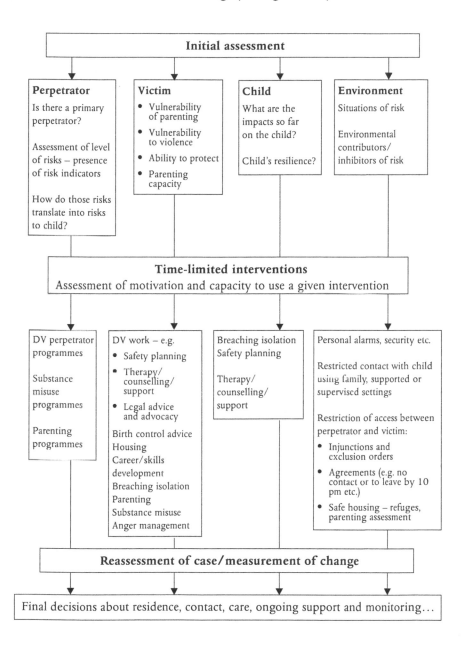

Figure 11.1 Assessment of current risk and harm

Risk assessment and safety planning in child protection cases

Separate interviews are arranged with the parents alongside the assessment of the children, which may be done either by DVIP's specialist children's worker or by the social worker working alongside DVIP. The first step is to gain as clear a picture as possible of the nature of the violence and its consequences. This takes into account the inevitable difficulties due to parents not being truthful or simply having different views about the violence and its consequences. It is often the case that both victims and perpetrators minimise the abuse. The credibility of different versions of the history of abuse and its impacts need to be estimated and weighed up. This is a delicate process involving assessment of evidence alongside clinical judgement which needs to be firmly rooted in observation. If there is a clear PPA then they can be seen as the key source of the risk being assessed. However, if both parents are substantially abusing each other, then the following steps need to be carried out with both parents.

The assessment of the current level of risk (from negligible to high) involves looking at the information gained about the violence in relation to static and dynamic risk indicators. The indicators considered include those common to other domestic violence risk assessments but with the additional focus on the impact of the abuse on the child and on parenting. The assessment considers developmental risk indicators (whether or not the parent also lived with violence as a child etc.), base rate behavioural risk indicators (such as the frequency of the violence, violence in pregnancy, extreme jealousy, breaches of court orders, etc.) and dynamic psycho-social variables (see Box 11.1). The assessment aims to build an understanding not only of the violence but also of the parents' attitudes towards the violence and the existence of any denial, minimisation, blame, remorse, empathy for the victim and child and any motivation for change.

Assessing the harm includes looking at the other parent's vulnerability to violence, their ability to protect the child and their parenting capacity as well as considering the vulnerability and harm to the children themselves. Living with domestic violence can have dire consequences for the health of a victim and this can impact on her capacity to shield the child from harm and her capacity to parent. The assessment considers how the parent coped with the abuse and the efforts taken to protect herself or the children.

The ability to protect the child from harm will be influenced by factors such as the degree of isolation of the victim, her awareness of the child abuse, her access to a support system, the quality of the relationship with the child and whether or not the perpetrator has made attempts to undermine her parenting. Finding out about parenting and empathy for the children from both parents includes asking the parents about their own experiences as children whether or not they see these as being relevant to their feelings about their own parenting

Box 11.1 Risk indicators

Examples of developmental risk factors

- Witnessing violence as a child.
- Parental intimidation, domination, mental abuse and shaming.
- Violence to peers encouraged.
- Experience of physical or sexual abuse as a child.
- Childhood conduct problems.

Examples of behavioural risk indicators (38 indicators are assessed)

- Violence in pregnancy.
- Any violence that caused injury needing treatment or hospitalisation.
- Use of weapons.
- Violence to people outside the immediate family.
- Stalking behaviour.
- Self-harm or attempted suicide.
- Escalating offence pattern.
- Violence or sexual abuse to children.
- Violence or sadistic treatment of animals.
- Threats to kill.
- Violation of court orders.

Examples of psycho-social variables

- Attitudes to acceptability of violence.
- Attitude to risk.
- Empathy for victim and children.
- Depression.
- Minimisation of the violence.
- Acceptance of responsibility.
- Remorse.
- Proprietariness.
- Co-operation with the assessment.

(see Box 11.2). It also allows for an understanding of the parent's sense of the children's needs and an exploration of any concerns or worries the parent may have about the children.

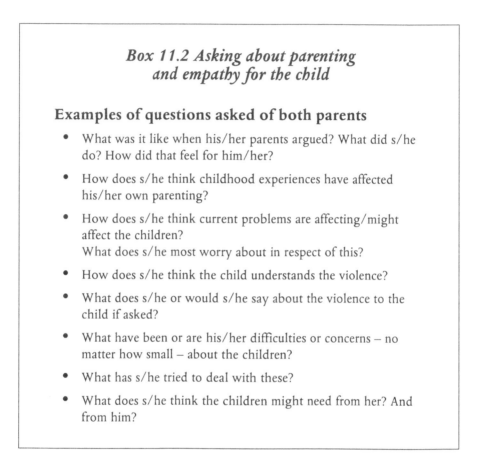

Box 11.2 Asking about parenting and empathy for the child

Examples of questions asked of both parents

- What was it like when his/her parents argued? What did s/he do? How did that feel for him/her?

- How does s/he think childhood experiences have affected his/her own parenting?

- How does s/he think current problems are affecting/might affect the children?
  What does s/he most worry about in respect of this?

- How does s/he think the child understands the violence?

- What does s/he or would s/he say about the violence to the child if asked?

- What have been or are his/her difficulties or concerns – no matter how small – about the children?

- What has s/he tried to deal with these?

- What does s/he think the children might need from her? And from him?

How does this risk relate to the risk to child? The assessment draws on the specialist children's worker or social worker's knowledge about what is known about the abuse to the child. In addition the assessment includes asking questions about how the children were involved, the degree to which they witnessed and overheard the violence, how the violence affected them, environmental contributors or inhibitors of risk and protective factors that helped the children to cope with the abuse (see Box 11.3). Working closely with the social worker or children's worker, a detailed analysis of the domestic violence in the context of the child's relationship with the violent parent helps with exploring to what extent the bond between parent and child is based upon love (affective) or upon fear (traumatic).

Box 11.3 Examples of contributors and inhibitors of risk for the child

- The child's age.

- Exposure to/awareness of the violence.

- Is there already significant harm?

- Nature of the attachment with non-abusing parent.

- Nature of the attachment to abusive parent and possibility of a traumatic bond – is he also abusive to the child? Does the child fear him? Does the child appear to identify with the abuser in order to remain safe?

- Does the child show behaviours which may result from the trauma of the domestic violence (e.g. bedwetting, night terrors, behavioural 'acting out')?

- How able is the child to resolve conflict?

- Has the child been able to take any control, e.g. call police, choose to stay with others etc.?

- Does the child have a good network of peer group relationships?

- Educational achievement of the child.

- Does the child have other non-abusive adult supports?

- Are there other factors compounding the child's vulnerability, e.g. disability?

The next stage involves assessing the scope for change with the victim (see Box 11.4), the perpetrator (Box 11.5) and the child and how to improve safety with time-limited interventions.

A range of options for improving safety are considered and interventions commonly include a mixture of individual safety planning, therapeutic or counselling support, legal advice and advocacy or practical help with finding paid work, housing or accommodation. Options for improving safety have to have relevance to the areas of risk and vulnerability identified.

Assessing the scope for change with the perpetrator involves considering his motivation and his capacity to move on from the abusive relationship (see Box

Box 11.4 Assessing victims' perspectives on change

Examples of areas covered

- Has she ever thought of leaving? What are her worst fears about leaving the relationship?

- What would have to change to make her feel safe in an argument – including safe enough to really speak her mind?

- Has he said he'll change before? Did he?

- Is he more violent now than when they were first together? If it carries on escalating that way, where would they be in two years' time?

- Does she think he will be violent again?

- What does she most fear happening in the relationship?

Questions like these:

- help you to see whether she appreciates the current risk to herself and her children

- give some indication of how she talks herself into and out of denial around this

- give a sense of what her strongest motivations to leave have been so far

- give information about her support system

- ask her to be realistic about the chances he'll change and to focus on safety rather than other issues as the main deciding factor in whether to leave or stay.

11.5). This explores with the perpetrator the nature of his abuse, how it may have changed in the course of the relationship and how it affects him, his partner and children. It is important to explore and record carefully how he describes the violent events to assess any denial or minimisation of the abuse and the level of empathy for the impact of the violence on the partner and the children.

When assessing the value and risk of trying time-limited interventions to keep the family together, the capacity for change (the perpetrator stopping his violence and the woman protecting the child) needs to be considered with reference to the resilience of the child.

Box 11.5 Assessing the perpetrator's motivation to change

- Spend time going through the inventory of abuse and discuss the forms his abuse takes.

- Ask him if he has ever said he will change or will not do it again. What happened?

- Ask how his violence affects him. List all of the costs and benefits…

- Ask how he thinks the partner would say she is affected by the abuse.

- Ask how his own family/community/peer group support him in stopping the abuse or in continuing it.

- Who does he talk to who he knows will wind him up? Who can talk him down?

These questions will help you assess:

- his levels of denial and minimisation and his understanding of his violence

- his appreciation of the risk he poses

- his levels of empathy for his partner

- whether he has sought help in the past, and whether the reasons that this did not work still apply

- some sense of his motivation and ability to try a time-limited intervention.

The final step in the assessment process involves measuring change after a period of intervention. This involves looking at indicators of change for the victim, the perpetrator and the child. The emphasis here is on assessing if there have been any tangible improvements in safety. For the victim, this includes issues such as having an improved support network, a demonstrable ability to implement safety plans to protect herself and her children from abuse. For the perpetrator, it includes indicators such as the violence stopping, a reduction of other forms of abuse, evidence of role shifts within the relationship towards greater equality, attendance and progress on a perpetrator programme. For the child, assessment will look for measurable improvements in symptoms of trauma, improved development in all areas, better understanding of the violence, improved family and peer relationships etc. In the end, of course, the risks to the children of keeping them in the family need to be weighed against the detriment of moving them to alternative carers.

The assessment process allows for the complexities of individual family circumstances to be taken into account while addressing and dealing with the domestic violence. Although there has not yet been an opportunity for independent academic researchers to evaluate this approach to risk assessment and risk management, we believe this enables a rigorous approach that is sufficiently flexible to increase safety and challenge perpetrators without resort to stereotypical pre-judgement. This approach has however developed in the context of mostly good and well-developed partnerships with other agencies in the locality. An assessment may crucially depend upon another practitioner's willingness to share information and to participate in an intervention. The most important aspect of an assessment is what happens next – what resources exist to help the family to increase their safety and to challenge the violence? There is clearly considerable scope to develop better and more widely available resources to support parents and children and for more perpetrator services working not just with offenders but also with the more commonly encountered domestic violence cases coming to the attention of child protection agencies and the family courts.

References

Blacklock, N. (2004) *Lost Opportunities: Domestic Violence, Social Work and Reporting: Domestic Violence Intervention Project*, www.dvip.org

Calder, M., Harold, G. and Howarth, E. (2004) *Children Living with Domestic Violence: Towards A Framework for Assessment and Intervention.* Lyme Regis, Dorset: Russell House Publishing.

Campbell, J., Soeken, K., McFarlane, J. and Parker, B. (1998) 'Risk factors for femicide among pregnant and non-pregnant battered women.' In J. Campbell (ed) *Empowering Survivors of Abuse: Health Care for Battered Women and Their Children.* Thousand Oaks, CA: Sage Publications.

Children in Need Census (2001). Available at www.dfes.gov.uk

Department for Education and Skills (DfES) (2003) *Every Child Matters.* London: The Stationery Office.

Department of Health (2000) *Framework of Assessment for Children in Need and Their Families.* London: The Stationery Office.

Erwin, T. (2004) *When is Arrest Not an Option? The Dilemmas of Predominant Physical Aggressor Language and the Regulation of Intimate Partner Violence.* Battered Women's Justice Project. Available at www.bwjp.org

Garland, D. (2002) *The Culture of Control.* Oxford: Oxford University Press.

Gilchrist, E., Johnson, R., Takriti, R., Weston, S., Beech, A. and Kebbell, M. (2003) *Domestic Violence Offenders: Characteristics and Offending Needs.* Home Office Research Study. London: Home Office.

Glass, D.D. (1995) *'All My Fault': Why Women Don't Leave Abusive Men.* London: Virago.

Hester, M. and Pearson, C. (1998) *From Periphery to Centre: Domestic Violence in Work with Abused Children.* Bristol: The Policy Press.

Hester, M., Harwin, N. and Pearson, C. (1998) *Making an Impact: A Reader on Children and Domestic Violence.* London: DOH/Barnardo's/NSPCC/School of Policy Studies.

Hirschel, D. and Buzawa, E. (2002) 'Understanding the context of dual arrest: Directions for future research.' *Violence Against Women 8*, 12, 1449–73.

Humphreys, C. (2000) *Social Work, Domestic Violence and Child Protection: Challenging Practice.* Bristol: The Policy Press.

Kemshall, H. (1996) *Reviewing Risk: A Review of the Research on the Assessment and Management of Risk and Dangerousness: Implications for Policy and Practice in the Probation Service.* Home Office Research and Statistics Directorate. London: Home Office.

Kemshall, H. (2002) *Understanding Risk in Criminal Justice.* Maidenhead, Buckingham: Open University Press.

Kropp, P., Hart, S., Webster, C. and Eaves, D. (1999) *The Spousal Assault Risk Assessment (SARA) Guide User's Manual.* Toronto, Canada: Multi-Health Systems Inc and BC Institute Against Family Violence.

Legal Services Commission (2003) *Expert Consultation on Domestic Violence Risk Assessment.* London: Millbank Tower, October.

McGee, C. (2000) *Childhood Experiences of Domestic Violence.* London: Jessica Kingsley Publishers.

Miller, S. (2001) 'The paradox of women arrested for domestic violence.' *Violence Against Women 7*, 12, 1339–76.

Milner, J. (1993) 'A disappearing act: Differing career paths of fathers and mothers in child protection investigations.' *Critical Social Policy 13*, 48–63.

Milner, J. (2004) 'From "disappearing" to "demonized": The effects on men and women of professional interventions based on challenging men who are violent.' *Critical Social Policy 24*, 1, 70–101.

Mullender, A. (1996) *Re-Thinking Domestic Violence: The Social Work and Probation Response.* London: Routledge.

O'Hagan, K. and Dillenburger, K. (1995) *The Abuse of Women in Child Care Work.* Buckingham: Open University Press.

Radford, L. and Hester, M. (2002) 'Overcoming mother blaming? Future directions for research on mothering and domestic violence.' In S. Graham-Bermann and J. Edleson (eds) *Domestic Violence in the Lives of Children: The Future of Research, Intervention and Social Policy.* Washington, DC: American Psychological Association.

Sinclair, R. and Bullock, R. (2002) *Learning from Past Experience: A Review of Serious Case Reviews.* London: Department of Health.

Soothill, K., Francis, B., Ackerley, E., Fligelstone, R. and Ranalli, G. (2002) *Murder and Serious Sexual Assault.* Police Research Series Paper 144. London: Home Office.

Stanko, E. (1990) *Everyday Violence.* London: Virago.

Stanley, N. (1997) 'Domestic violence and child abuse: Developing social work practice.' *Child and Family Social Work 2*, 3, 135–45.

Walby, S. and Myhill, A. (2002) 'Assessing and managing risk.' In J. Taylor-Browne (ed) *What Works in Reducing Domestic Violence?* London: Whiting and Birch.

Websdale, D. (1999) *Understanding Domestic Homicide.* London: Home Office.

Young, J. (1999) *The Exclusive Society.* London: Sage Publications.

Chapter 12

Are Men Who Use Violence Against Their Partners and Children Good Enough Fathers?

The Need for an Integrated Child Perspective in Treatment Work with Men

Marius Råkil

Introduction

This chapter will address an important question often neglected in the debate about how men's violence against their partners and children can be ended. Many men who use violence against their partner are also fathers. Is it possible to be a good father and a violent husband at the same time?

Violence against women and children represents a violation of both basic human rights and principles of gender equality. The women's movement and shelters for battered women have historically been the main agents for documenting the existence of violence against women and the magnitude of its impact as both a health and a social problem (Dobash and Dobash 1979; Mullender 1996). During the last few years, some of the Nordic countries have conducted national surveys that show violence against women and children to be of epidemic proportions (Heiskanen and Piispa 1998; Lundgren *et al.* 2001). Domestic violence is present to such a degree that it can be identified as a characteristic feature of our society with huge economic costs in terms of the medical and psychological problems it causes (Walby 2004). This has been well documented in the research literature ever since Lenore Walker introduced the term 'the battered woman syndrome' (Walker 1984).

Prior to the 1970s, victims of domestic violence were mainly dealt with by health services that had little or no knowledge of the specific features of men's violence against women. During the 1970s, the women's movement put men's violence against women on the agenda. The pro-feminist tradition emerged as a reaction to the psychiatric and psychoanalytic tradition of earlier decades. Pro-feminists argued that it is important to identify the male perpetrator as the problem, since men's violence is normalised and made invisible within a patriarchal context. The consequence of this viewpoint is also to see the behavioural and emotional reactions of woman survivors as normal reactions to an abnormal or unreasonable situation, not vice versa (Råkil 2002a). More recently, recognition has grown of ways of understanding domestic violence which acknowledge a range of patterns of violence (Johnson and Ferraro 2000). While violence towards women remains the dominant pattern (Walby and Allen 2004), women's violence towards men that is not only self-defence, the role of a man's female relatives in perpetrating violence against women, and same-sex violence have led to more differentiated understandings of significant but less common forms of domestic violence. This chapter will refer particularly to the dominant form of men's violence towards women, though within the service which is described this diversity is acknowledged through holding groups specifically for women who use violence against men or their children.

When men's violence against women was placed on the agenda, *the focus was initially on the woman* (Walker 1984). Although staff working in women's shelters also had contact with the women's children, the needs of these children were given relatively limited consideration. From the beginning of the 1980s, treatment programmes for men committing violence began to develop. This development illustrates a broadening of focus to include men. The first programmes were located in the US (Adams and Cayouette 2002). The American programmes have largely been psycho-educational in their structure, emphasising the need for men to 'unlearn' patriarchal attitudes, and replace these with learned relationship skills based on gender equality and respect for women's integrity and autonomy (Råkil 2002a). The research directed at programmes for perpetrators of domestic violence has remained focused on programme effectiveness, methodological problems and the relatively huge variations in drop-out rates (Daly, Power and Gondolf 2001; Green and Babcock 2001; Mullender and Burton 2001).

More recently, *children* exposed to violence in their homes have been included in the domestic violence agenda. With a few exceptions (Jaffe, Wolfe and Wilson 1990; Leira 2002, originally published in Norwegian in 1988), literature describing work with children exposed to domestic violence, or exploring how they are affected by it, is relatively recent (Eriksson 2001; Graham-Bermann and Edleson 2001; Hester, Pearson and Harwin 2000; Holden, Geffner and Jourlies 1998; Metell 2001; Romito, Saurel-Cubizolles and Crisma 2001). The body of documented knowledge in this area is still very limited (Peled 2000). This includes the issue of how knowledge about children's experience of violence by *their fathers or stepfathers* is included and integrated in the treatment of the men. At Alternative to Violence (ATV) in Norway, the integrating process has started and is ongoing. We know that children are both directly and indirectly severely affected by the violence perpetrated by their fathers or by those holding a father role in relation to the child.

The differential impact of violence

When we talk about children living with domestic violence, it is important to talk about *boys* and *girls*. This gender differentiation is significant because boys and girls exposed to similar forms of domestic violence may cope with violence in different ways, often developing in different directions. However, this picture is ambiguous. Much of the research shows very diverse responses to violence from boys and girls with no clear-cut pattern emerging (Mathias, Mertin and Murray 1995; O'Keefe 1996). Some studies show girls with more behavioural and emotional problems than boys (Davis and Carlson 1987), while others show the opposite. Rosenberg (1984) found that when there was a low level of parental violence, boys used more aggressive coping strategies and girls were more passive. However, when the violence was chronic and severe the opposite was the case. Other research suggests a more clearly differentiated pattern (Hotaling and Sugarman 1986; Jaffe *et al.* 1990; Saunders 1995). These studies often argue that, as a result of the cultural codes which shape gender roles, boys tend to cope with life events in a more externalising way or by directing their attention towards others; while girls, more often than boys, tend to cope with life events by internalising, or directing their attention towards themselves. One consequence of this gendered difference is that boys are likely to handle the experience of being exposed to violence by acting out and trying to take control over others. Girls, on the other hand, tend to handle similar experiences by drawing their attention and attributions towards themselves (asking 'what did I do wrong?'). An implication of this observation is that boys who are witnessing violence in their own homes represent a high-risk group for developing a problem with violence themselves, particularly if they have also been the subject of direct physical abuse (Hughes 1988; Spaccarelli, Sandler and Roosa 1994), though care needs to be taken to acknowledge that this is a pattern rather than a predictive behaviour. Many young men who have lived with violence are committed to being, and in fact are, non-violent in their adult relations (see Mullender and Morley 1994).

While the research about gendered responses by boys and girls to living with violence and abuse is ambiguous, Kelly (1994) makes the point that this does not make gender irrelevant. Children are growing up witnessing (usually) male dominance and female subordination and their gender identities will in some way be affected by this. She argues that, 'We need a framework which takes gender as a critical factor, but which allows for differences within, as well as between, the responses of girls and boys' (p.49).

Experiences of the young people referred to Alternative to Violence (ATV) tend to confirm the picture of boys with greater problems with aggressive behaviour. At ATV's treatment programme for adolescents (aged 10 to 18), approximately 90 per cent of the clients are boys. Seventy to eighty per cent of the total client group report having significant experiences of witnessing violence in their family of origin (Bengtson *et al.* 2002). One implication of this is that we need to interpret boys' and male adolescents' acting out behaviour as 'symptoms' of a 'masculine' coping strategy which attempts to manage the experience of witnessing violence. This process is often handled differently by girls. It can sometimes be more of a challenge to identify girls' reactions to witnessing violence (or boys who also have experiences of depression and loss), as such responses are not usually as visible as those of young people who are expressing their reactions more aggressively. Both patterns of behaviour need to be responded to in order to provide help for girls and boys who have witnessed violence by their fathers or stepfathers.

Alternative to Violence (ATV) in Norway

Alternative to Violence (ATV) is a professional treatment and research centre which was established in 1987. The ATV practitioners are mainly psychologists working with violence within the family on a full-time basis. The ATV treatment models have a pro-feminist value base, and the therapeutic work includes both individual and group treatment. At present ATV runs a range of different programmes:

- a treatment programme for *men* who are violent towards their partners including specific sessions for *men who are fathers*
- a partner service offering service and support for the *partners* of men attending ATV's programme for men, and for the women in contact with the Women's Shelter in Oslo
- a treatment service for *women* who use violence against their partner and/or children
- a treatment service for the *children* of the men or women attending the above mentioned programmes and services

- a treatment programme for *adolescents* who have developed problems with violence.

The 'backbone' of ATV's work is the treatment programme for men, although the well-being and security of the women and children are the primary concern of the centre. However, it is acknowledged that the responsibility for the violence lies with the perpetrator who is almost always the male parent within the family. The violence will therefore not end until men end their violent behaviour.

There are a number of reasons why ATV has taken on these various projects. There are a limited number of positive interventions to support women and children affected by men's violence within the family. Knowledge about domestic violence is only partially integrated into the public health-care system in Norway. Another important rationale for the different projects within ATV can be found in the way the organisation conceptualises family violence. At present ATV considers that, in order to challenge men's violent behaviour effectively, *those working with the men need first-hand knowledge on how men's violence affects their partners and children.*

Men's pathway into the ATV treatment programme

The referral process for the men's treatment programme adopts a low threshold, requiring only a phone call to register with the programme. ATV is contacted by 150–200 new men each year. Approximately 60 per cent make the contact themselves, often after being 'referred' by their partner or as a result of reading about ATV in the newspaper. Approximately 40 per cent are referred through an official body (e.g. the police, social workers, doctors, children's services, shelters for battered women, the psychiatric system, priests, emergency units, prisons, and so on).

The ATV programme is designed to offer men either individual or group treatment after an initial individual assessment phase of three sessions. The assessment consists of a semi-structured interview with a primary focus on the man's violent behaviour. In addition, the Symptom Check List-90 (SCL-90; Derogatis 1975) is usually administered. Neither the individual work nor the groupwork is set within a fixed time frame. Clients who start in group treatment have to commit to the group, but different members join and end their stay in the group at different points in time. Both the men attending individual treatment and those attending a group go through a four-phased treatment programme (described below) at varying rates. Some men take longer than others to acknowledge violence as a substantial problem and to assume responsibility for their violence. Others require more time to work through the aspects of their personal history that are connected to their violent behaviour, such as having witnessed violence by their own fathers as children. Using the data of all men recruited to the ATV programme over the last ten years, the average duration of individual treatment is ten months (one session per week), and 1.5 years for men in group treatment (involving a two-hour weekly meeting).

In order to assist the men to end their violence, practitioners must be trained to recognise the wide variety of ways in which men commit violent acts, including physical, psychological, sexualised, and property violence. Special attention is given to the various forms of psychological violence, which include explicit and implicit threats of violence, mental degradation and intimidation, controlling and isolating behaviour, and pathological jealousy. It is in the psychological violence that we find the foundation of men's violence against women: the power and control strategies that keep her in the subordinate position in order to support a man's perception of manhood, womanhood, and intimacy. In this context, psychological violence can be seen as the basis for all other forms of violence.

The ATV model for work with men

The ATV model of treatment revolves around four phases that men need to pass through (Råkil 2002b). The overall goal of this work is to assist men to assume responsibility for their violent behaviour. The *first phase* involves focusing on the *violence*. From the first meeting, the violent behaviour is explicitly addressed. The main aim of this first phase of treatment is to acknowledge the violence as an actual reality. The violence has to be *reconstructed in a very detailed way*, in terms of what happened, where did it happen, how it happened, and to whom. The reconstruction work must be based on awareness of the language that is used in this setting. It is of paramount importance that the violence is talked about as violence, and not reformulated into concepts like 'we had a fight/we were quarrelling', which defocuses the gendered and power-abusing features of violence. This 'mapping' process also includes detailed questions about the children: their presence, if they were not present where they were, and their reactions to the violence. The reconstruction work described is motivated by the understanding that men's violence against women and children is harmful and dangerous. The mapping is also based on knowledge about *the magnitude and the degree of dangerousness*, in order to be able to assess proper safety precautions (Davies, Lyon and Monti-Catania 1998). This implies that we need to develop safety planning with the violent men, which is separate but parallel and co-ordinated with the work with their partners.

This work on the reality of the violence forms the necessary basis for the ensuing work on changing the men's violent behaviour. It is very difficult to change behaviour if it is not considered problematic. The violence becomes apparent and real to the client by talking about it in a direct and serious way.

Through detailed and investigative questions about the violence itself, it becomes difficult for the client to mentally protect himself from the reality of his violence. This approach requires that the person undertaking this work conducts it with respect and professionalism. The tasks of this first phase also involves working against the invisibility, which is one of the basic characteristics of men's violence towards women and children.

The *second phase* is about focusing on *responsibility*. Through the process of detailed reconstruction of the violent behaviour, it becomes apparent that the violent acts are rational and controlled, indicating that the violence is actually a chosen act among many other alternative actions. In turn, this implies that a man has the option of choosing other, non-violent acts instead. Part of the work on responsibility includes focusing on denial, minimisation, externalising and frag- mentation, which are common features of men's talk about their violent behav- iour (Adams 1988; Isdal 2000; Isdal and Råkil 2001). These cognitive mecha- nisms are not exclusively worked on in this phase of the work. Together with the focus on responsibility, they are dealt with and made a central issue throughout the entire working process. The outcome of the two first phases of the process should be an internalised awareness in the perpetrator summed up by the quote: 'the violence I have committed is actually my behaviour which I am responsible for. Thus, I am the only person who can change that behaviour' (ATV service user).

The work of the two first phases forms the necessary basis for going on into the *third phase* of the process which focuses on *psychological connections* between personal history and present use of violence. Topics such as a man's current life situation, his attitudes towards men and women, his social learning and personal perceptions of masculinity and intimacy and his significant historical experiences are explored in this phase. Many men who use violence in intimate relationships have witnessed and/or experienced domestic violence themselves as children. This work offers the possibility for the violent man to explore the child's position through his experience of witnessing his own father's violence. It helps him to actually *see* how the violence is affecting his children as well as his partner. To work through those aspects of each man's personal history which involve violence is seen as crucial to preventing recidivism in the long term (see Scott and Wolfe 2000). A focus on these experiences results in a process that is anti-fragmentative, connecting past and present experiences of fathering and the effects of violence.

The *fourth phase* entails a focus on the *harmful consequences of violence*. Through the processes described above, the client learns that his violent behaviour is not the result of a loss of control or a response to his partner's behaviour. He becomes able to acknowledge that the violence is about himself, his attitudes, and his own emotional and social self-perceptions, which in turn are often rooted in the lack of recognition of his own feelings of powerlessness, shame and inferiority. The difficulties in recognising the effects of violence and abuse are seen to be linked to both to his own personal social learning history and to the cultural context with its imperatives regulating the standards for masculinity and femininity.

Integrating men's violence with images of fatherhood

In recent years and as noted above, studies of children's experiences of living with domestic violence have gained greater attention. In the Nordic countries there has been relatively little systematic focus on children exposed to domestic violence. We maintain a split 'image' of men as *abusive fathers* on the one side, and men as *loving fathers* on the other (Eriksson 2001). It is difficult to acknowledge that many fathers are also men who impose their violence on women and children. This split image is illustrated by the lack of co-ordination between the criminal courts and civil courts in cases of child contact and domestic violence. While some violent men are convicted in the criminal courts, the civil court give the very same men parental responsibility, accompanied by demands from the court that the mother do her best to co-operate with him over parenting duties (see Chapters 8 and 9).

This 'split image' is also experienced on an individual level. The evidence from treatment is that many men struggle to integrate the reality of their violence with their role as practising fathers. When men seek treatment for their violent behaviour, they often present themselves as victims of their partner's unreasonable conduct. As mentioned earlier, men's approaches to describing and explaining their violent behaviour are characterised by externalisation ('her behaviour is the reason why I used violence'), denial and fragmentation (which involves removing the violence from its social and situational context, and presenting it as something without impact or consequences). The use of these 'strategies' constitutes a failure to acknowledge responsibility. One aspect of this refusal to take responsibility involves overlooking the children, and the effects of the violence on them. Men often describe the children as *not* being affected by the violence, and deny its impact on their life situation, self-perception or development. These ways of handling the violence (both the description and explanations) function to protect men from the psychological pain and disturbing reality that the violence represents. One important consequence of dealing with the violence in this way is that violent fathers don't talk about the violence with their children. The consequences for the child of being left alone with such traumatic experiences are well known. One possible outcome is that the child may attribute the causes of the violence to himself/herself. Other examples are loyalty conflict, confusion, ambivalent feelings towards both parents, feeling abandoned, betrayed, unhappy and fearful (Peled 2000).

Implications for intervention with violent fathers

ATV's work focusing on abusive men as fathers has a long history. However, after ATV started to work directly with children living with domestic violence, this work was intensified. We, like many professionals in this field of work, know that children are both directly and indirectly profoundly affected by violence perpetrated by their fathers or those holding a father role in relation to the child. This fact made it necessary to ask the question: are abusive fathers good enough fathers? This is a complex question which requires a nuanced rather than simplistic approach.

On a moral level, the majority of people would agree that violent fathers are not good enough fathers, particularly in the light of the research evidence of harm to children (Hester *et al.* 2000; Mullender *et al.* 2002). Does this mean that their 'right' to parent, and their contribution to positive parenting, is extinguished by their violence? The answer to this question may be more equivocal, though it is one with which all child protection professionals in this area need to engage. Clearly, for child protection professionals, where there is violence there needs to be an assessment of current safety, the impact of recent violence, and the dangers of future violence. In this arena, the risk assessment process outlined in the previous chapter (Chapter 11) is particularly helpful, outlining the complex range of issues which need to be taken into account in relation to men, women and children in making such assessments. The views of children themselves are also significant and these can range from being quite clear that they want nothing to do with violent fathers or father figures through to confused and ambivalent feelings towards their fathers. There are also some who are clear that they want an ongoing relationship with their fathers (Peled 2000). Clearly, whatever the child's wishes, the adults concerned (including professionals) need to ensure that children (and their mothers) are not placed at risk of further harm through contact, and should identify what arrangements and processes are required to create a situation of both physical and psychological safety. It is also evident that when children are given space to explore their experiences, either individually or in groups, their attitudes, feelings and wishes may shift and change (Peled and Edleson 1992).

The options inevitably vary and require individual evaluations of each situation. For many child protection professionals, it is still not axiomatic that cases of domestic violence are cases of 'not good enough' fathers. Traditionally, the practice has been to question the mother's caring abilities at the first assessment. When the focus in these cases is shifted to the father's violence as a primary problem, it becomes more obvious that the demands for behaviour change should be directed at the father or the person holding the father role. Hence, we would argue that a standard for all treatment programmes for perpetrators of domestic violence should include a focus on parenting and fatherhood for men with children.

Recently ATV started to set up a specific group for men who are fathers. The intention of this group is to develop our understanding of children's perspectives in our work with men and their violent behaviour. We also aim to focus more on fatherhood as a part of their problem with violence. We intend to eschew the previously described 'split image' of men as both abusive fathers and loving fathers and work with a more integrated model. Our experiences with violent men, abused women and their children have indicated that interventions with men need to focus on more than the men themselves and their violent behaviour. Interventions also need to address:

- men's perceptions of themselves as fathers
- how the violence is affecting the father–child relationship
- how the violence is affecting the mother–child relationship
- how the child is affected by the violence itself on both a short- and long-term basis
- the basic psychological needs of the child in a developmental perspective and how these needs are violated by the presence of violence.

The ongoing work with fathers recognises that this is a dynamic process in which some men will demonstrate a capacity to change, and others will not (Mullender and Burton 2001; Scott and Wolfe 2000). Reviewing men's ongoing capacity to parent will require that they can engage in detail in the exploration of the issues raised above and demonstrate an ability to take responsibility for their past role and the steps which would be required to create new and safer solutions for any future fathering role.

The experience of the work at ATV suggests that this programme provides a positive direction for work with perpetrators and arises directly from the experience of working with children. However, Peled (2000) has pointed out that the developments in this area of work with perpetrators are still marginal and require evaluation about their effectiveness. While we have considerable evidence of harm to children, we have little systematic evidence about the effectiveness of rehabilitation programmes for men as fathers. The work of the Domestic Violence Intervention Project discussed in the previous chapter has also explored the issue of risk assessment, alongside work with perpetrators, and this project has recently opened a supervised contact centre which will allow the exploration of whether supervised contact provides a safe context for contact with fathers who have used violence. This provides a further model for working with and assessing fathers in this area.

A consequence of an increased focus on the role of abusive men as fathers should be a closer collaboration between men's intervention programmes, child protection services and other key agencies such as health services and the courts in identifying the risks for children and the effects of violence on children in general. Our view is that to be an abusive father implies not being a *good enough* father. Children are affected in serious ways by their fathers' violence and men need to take full responsibility for their violent behaviour in order to be good enough fathers. Children *need* non-violent fathers. Children *deserve* a childhood without the presence of violence.

For more information about ATV, please see www.atv-stiftelsen.no or contact us at:

Alternativ til Vold (ATV)
Korsgata #28b
Oslo 0551, Norway
Email: post@atv-stiftelsen.no

References

Adams, D. (1988) 'Stages of anti-sexist awareness and change for men who batter.' In L. Dickstein and C. Nadelson (eds) *Family Violence: Emerging Issues of a National Crisis.* Washington DC: American Psychiatric Press, pp.63–97.

Adams, D. and Cayouette, S. (2002) 'Emerge: A group education model for abusers.' In E. Aldarondo and F. Mederos (eds) *Batterer Intervention Programs: A Handbook for Clinicians, Practitioners and Advocates.* New York: Civic Research Inc.

Bengtson, M., Bugge Pedersen, B., Steinsvåg, P. and Terland, H. (2002) 'Noen erfaringer med å etablere en terapeutisk relasjon til ungdom med volds-og aggresjonsproblemer [Establishing a therapeutic relation to adolescents with violence and aggression problems].' *Journal of the Norwegian Psychological Association 39,* 13–20.

Daly, J.E., Power, T.G. and Gondolf, E. (2001) 'Predictors of batterer program attendance.' *Journal of Interpersonal Violence 16,* 10, 971–91.

Davies, J., Lyon, E. and Monti-Catania, D. (1998) *Safety Planning With Battered Women: Complex Lives/Difficult Choices.* Thousand Oaks, CA: Sage Publications.

Davis, L. and Carlson, B. (1987) 'Observation of spouse abuse: What happens to the children?' *Journal of Interpersonal Violence 2,* 3, 278–91.

Derogatis, L.R. (1975) *Symptom Checklist-90-Revised (SCL-90-R).* Minneapolis, MN: NCS Assessments.

Dobash, R.E. and Dobash, R. (1979) *Violence Against Wives. A Case Against the Patriarchy.* New York: Macmillan Publishing.

Eriksson, M. (2001) 'Om vårdnad, boende och umgänge.' In B. Metell (ed), *Barn som ser pappa slå* (ss.104–37) [About child custody, cohabitation and fathers' access to their children (pp.104–37)]. Stockholm: Gothia Publishing Company (in Swedish).

Graham-Bermann, S.A. and Edleson, J.L. (2001) *Domestic Violence in the Lives of Children. The Future of Research, Intervention, and Social Policy.* Washington DC: American Psychological Association.

Green, C. and Babcock, J. (2001) *Does Batterer's Treatment Work? A Meta-Analytic Review of Domestic Violence Treatment.* Paper presented at the 7th International Family Violence Research Conference, July, Portsmouth, NH.

Heiskanen, M. and Piispa, M. (1998) *Faith, Hope, Battering. A Survey of Men's Violence Against Women in Finland.* Helsinki: Statistics Finland.

Hester, M., Pearson, C. and Harwin, N. (2000) *Making an Impact: A Reader.* London: Jessica Kingsley Publishers.

Holden, G.W., Geffner, R. and Jourlies, E.N. (1998) *Children Exposed to Marital Violence.* Washington DC: American Psychological Association.

Hotaling, G.T. and Sugarman, D.B. (1986) 'An analysis of risk markers in husband to wife violence: The current state of knowledge.' *Violence and Victims 1,* 2, 101–24.

Hughes, H. (1988) 'Psychological and behavioral correlates of family violence in child witnesses and victims.' *American Journal of Orthopsychiatry 58,* 1, 77–90.

Isdal, P. (2000) *Meningen med volden [The Meaning of Violence].* Oslo, Norway: Kommuneforlaget Publishing Co.

Isdal, P. and Råkil, M. (2001) 'Umulige menn eller menn med muligheter [Impossible men or men with possibilities? Treatment of men who use violence against women].' In B. Metell (ed) *Barn som ser pappa slå [Children witnessing their fathers' violence* (pp.68–103)]. Stockholm, Sweden: Gothia Publishing Co.

Jaffe, P., Wolfe, D. and Wilson, S. (1990) *Children of Battered Women.* Newbury Park, CA: Sage Publications.

Johnson, M. and Ferraro, K. (2000) 'Research on domestic violence in the 1990s: Making distinctions.' *Journal of Marriage and the Family 62,* 4, 948–63.

Kelly, L. (1994) 'The interconnectedness of domestic violence and child abuse: Challenges for research, policy and practice.' In A. Mullender and R. Morley (eds) *Children Living with Domestic Violence.* London: Whiting and Birch.

Leira, H.K. (2002) 'Course in child and youth rights – a model of group intervention with children and young people who have experienced violence in the family.' In M. Eriksson, A. Nenola, and M.M. Nilsen (eds): *Kön och våld i Norden. Rapport från en konferens i Køge, Danmark, 23–24 november 2001.* København: Nordic Council of Ministers.

Lundgren, E., Heimer, G., Westerstrand, J. and Kallioski, A.-M. (2001) *Slagen Dam. Mäns våld mot kvinnor i jämställda Sverige – en omfangsundersøkning.* Brottsoffer-myndigheten och Uppsala Universitet [Battered woman. Men's violence against women in the Swedish society of gender equality: A national survey. University of Uppsala, Sweden].

Mathias, J., Mertin, P. and Murray, B. (1995) 'The psychological functioning of children from backgrounds of domestic violence.' *Australian Psychologist 30,* 1, 8–15.

Metell, B. (ed) (2001) *Barn som ser pappa slå [Children witnessing their fathers' violence* (pp.68–103)]. Stockholm, Sweden: Gothia Publishing Co.

Mullender, A. (1996) *Re-thinking Domestic Violence: The Social Work and Probation Response.* London: Routledge.

Mullender, A. and Burton, S. (2001) 'Dealing with perpetrators.' In J. Taylor-Browne (ed) *What Works in Reducing Domestic Violence?* London: Whiting and Birch.

Mullender, A. and Morley, S. (eds) (1994) *Children Living With Domestic Violence.* London: Whiting and Birch.

Mullender, A., Kelly, L., Hague, G., Malos, E. and Iman, U. (2002) *Children's Perspectives on Domestic Violence.* London: Routledge.

O'Keefe, M. (1996) 'The differential effects of family violence on adolescent adjustment.' *Child and Adolescent Social Work Journal 13,* 1, 51–68.

Peled, E. (2000) 'Parenting by men who abuse women: Issues and dilemmas.' *British Journal of Social Work 30,* 1, 25–36.

Peled, E. and Edleson, J. (1992) 'Multiple perspectives on groupwork with children of battered women.' *Violence and Victims 7,* 4, 327–46.

Råkil, M. (2002a) 'En introduksjon til feltet menns vold mot kvinner.' In M. Råkil (ed) *Menns vold mot kvinner. Behandlingserfaringer og kunnskapsstatus.* 17–30. Oslo: Universitetsforlaget. ['An introduction to the field of men's violence against women.' *Men's Violence Against Women. Clinical Experiences and Current State of Knowledge.* 17–30. Oslo: Scandinavian University Press.]

Råkil, M. (2002b) 'A Norwegian integrative model for the treatment of men who batter.' *Family Violence and Sexual Assault Bulletin 18*, 6–14.

Romito, P., Saurel-Cubizolles, M.-J. and Crisma, M. (2001) 'The relationship between parents' violence against daughters and violence by other perpetrators: An Italian study.' *Journal of Violence Against Women 7*, 12, 1429–63.

Rosenberg, M. (1984) Inter-generational family violence: a critique and implications for witnessing children.' Paper presented at the 92nd Annual Convention of the American Psychological Association, Toronto.

Saunders, D. (1995) 'Prediction of wife assault.' In I.J. Campbell (ed) *Assessing Dangerousness: Violence By Sexual Offenders, Batterers, and Child Abusers.* Thousand Oaks, CA: Sage Publications, pp.68–95.

Scott, K. and Wolfe, D. (2000) 'Change among batterers: Examining men's success stories.' *Journal of Interpersonal Violence 15*, 8, 827–42.

Spaccarelli, S., Sandler, I. and Roosa, M. (1994) 'History of spouse violence against mother: Correlated risks and unique effects in child mental health.' *Journal of Family Violence 9*, 1, 79–96.

Walby, S. (2004) 'The real cost of domestic violence.' *SAFE Domestic Abuse Quarterly 11*, 15–18.

Walby, S. and Allen, J. (2004) *Domestic Violence, Sexual Assault and Stalking: Findings from the British Crime Survey.* Home Office Research Study 276. London: Home Office Research, Development and Statistics Directorate.

Walker, L.E. (1984) *The Battered Woman Syndrome.* New York, NY: Springer Publishing Co.

Chapter 13

Men's Use of Violence and Intimidation Against Family Members and Child Protection Workers

Brian Littlechild and Caroline Bourke

Introduction

Fear of violence and aggression can affect many of those involved in situations where child protection procedures are being deployed. This fear can be found in abused children themselves (Briere 1992; McGee 2000); in non-abusing family members, usually women, who may also be subject to similar types of violence and/or intimidation (McGee 2000; Smith 1989); and also among child protection workers (Littlechild 2000; Stanley and Goddard 1997, 2002). Interpersonal violence is not only a common feature of service users' personal lives (Social Services Inspectorate 1995), but also characterises the professional lives of social workers, as evidenced by the work of Pahl (1999) and NISW (National Institute for Social Work 1999), among others. This chapter will set out the nature and effects of these fears where domestic violence, child abuse and violence against child protection workers may be involved, the similarities between certain types of male violence towards those in their informal and formal networks, and the implications of avoiding the resulting issues in assessments and interventions.

The chapter focuses on the risks to child-care workers from the power/control dynamics exhibited by male abusers. Although women are also capable of abusive and violent behaviour towards workers, particularly when children are being taken into care, the aim here is to explore the links between men's violence to women and children and their abusive behaviour towards professionals. The chapter will also examine the types of risk assessment and risk management processes and policies which might best be introduced to protect workers and non-abusing family members and therefore, potentially, the children within a household. The evidence used here derives mainly from UK reports and research but its relevance stretches beyond the UK.

While such violence may not be a major feature of all child protection work, it is a significant feature in a number of the most serious cases. There is extensive evidence from inquiries into child deaths that such violence, and the fear engendered by it, is frequently present within the sets of relationships surrounding these situations (Bridge Child Care Development Service 1997; Dingwall, Eekelaar and Murray 1983; Guardian 2000; Mullender and Morley 1994; Newham Area Child Protection Committee 2002; O'Hagan and Dillenburger 1995).

The adverse effects of threats and violence against children, women, and child protection professionals are now well documented (Littlechild 2000; Mullender and Debbonaire 2000; Mullender and Morley 1994; O'Hagan and Dillenburger 1995; Pahl 1999; Smith and Nursten 1998). For mothers, these can include an inability to protect herself or her children (Edwards 1996), as evidenced in the situation of Beverley Lorrington within the relationship in which Jasmine Beckford eventually died (London Borough of Brent 1985). The power/control dynamics which produce fear of a violent man can be the same for abused children, other abused family members (particularly women), and the child protection workers involved (Littlechild 2002b; O'Hagan and Dillenburger 1995). While similarities in the means by which such fear is induced in mothers and children has been recognised within inquiries into child deaths (Department of Health 1991; O'Hagan and Dillenburger 1995), these types of behaviour have not been recognised as also being employed against child protection workers as a means of gaining power and control over them. Such strategies can be employed to prevent workers from intruding and investigating to too great an extent into abuses taking place in the family; with most of the victims of intimidatory strategies – as opposed to direct physical violence and threats made in front of colleagues – being female workers (Littlechild 2000, 2002b). The correlation between violence to children and violence to staff is indicated by Humphreys' (2000) finding that, in the 32 cases of child protection investigations she studied, 11 contained reports of violence and abuse to staff.

Similarities in the types of violence experienced by abused children and the experiences of social workers abused by parents are apparent in a review of associated research (see Mudaly and Goddard 2001; Stanley and Goddard 1997, 2002). It has been suggested that there may be links between the different forms of violence against children, mothers and workers in certain individual cases, and that the use of such control strategies needs to be identified and confronted (Humphreys 1999, 2000; O'Hagan 1997; Stanley and Goddard 1997).

The term 'violence' is used in relation to violence against staff throughout this chapter to denote situations of perceived threat and aggression as well as physical violence. This definition is employed in the government's National Task Force on Violence Against Social Care Staff (Department of Health 2000), which used the European Commission's definition DG-V (3): 'Incidents where persons are abused, threatened or assaulted in circumstances relating to their work, involving an explicit or implicit challenge to their safety, well-being or health' (Department of Health 2000, p.2).

The effects of violence and threats on workers

The Department of Health (1991) review of findings from inquiries into child deaths found that, in a number of the cases, threats of violence from violent males against staff had significant effects on the workers and the child protection process (see also Bridge Consultancy 1991; Guardian 2000; London Borough of Greenwich 1987; London Borough of Lambeth 1987; Newham Area Child Protection Committee 2002). Concerns about how such violence – and in particular male violence – can negatively affect child protection assessments and decision-making processes have been raised by a number of authors (Farmer and Owen 1995, 1998; O'Hagan and Dillenburger 1995; Reder, Duncan and Gray 1993; Stanley and Goddard 2002). Dingwall *et al.* noted as long ago as 1983 how:

> a violent man may sufficiently intimidate (the predominately female) front line staff in health visiting and social work to prevent them from discovering maltreatment (e.g. of father of Stephen Menheniott 1979, who instilled fear in the whole of his small island community). (p.101)

More recently, the child protection inquiry report into the death of Ainlee Walker found that workers from the different agencies were deterred from visiting the family due to threats of violence to staff, and that such threats contributed to the deliberate and effective concealment of Ainlee's abuse from the workers and agencies (Newham Area Child Protection Committee 2002). The Bridge Child Care Development Service report (1997) into the circumstances surrounding the death of Rikki Neave suggested that there are often links between violence towards staff and others in a family's network. Awareness of these can alert professionals to relevant areas in risk assessment and risk management in child protection work.

O'Hagan and Dillenburger (1995) concluded that child-care professionals may avoid men because of anticipated violence, and that workers' avoidance of aggressive and violent men is a feature in a number of child abuse death cases: 'Violent men consistently dominate the 35 inquiry reports produced since 1974, and have, with few exceptions, been responsible for the deaths of the children in those reports' (p.145) and that: 'It is obvious...how the avoidance of men can and often does constitute an abuse of women, but avoidance also seriously exacerbates the paramount task of protecting the child' (p.146).

Under-reporting violence

As with child abuse and domestic violence against women, the true extent of violence against health and social care staff is unknown, as a high proportion of such incidents do not get reported. All forms of violence against social work staff are under-reported, but particularly intimidation and threats (Brockmann 2002; Brockmann and McLean 2000; Norris 1990), and racial harassment and abuse (Norris 1990; Smith 1988). Norris quotes a study from a metropolitan borough that found that 115 staff had experienced 'racial assault', but that issues of ethnicity and race were poorly served and not mentioned at all in many responses from local authorities in his research. Smith (1988) found significant under-reporting of violent incidents against black staff, and attributed it to distrust of how managers would deal with any such report. Brockmann (2002) suggests that decisions by staff from ethnic minorities not to report may be due to strategies of resistance, such as denial.

Under-reporting by staff is caused by several factors: lack of certainty about what constitutes violence, abuse and unacceptable behaviour; whether staff believe they will be taken seriously by managers or not; whether they will be given supportive and effective responses, or blamed for in some way 'asking for' the violence, and/or seen as 'weak' workers; and whether staff believe it is 'part of the job' to have to experience and endure such behaviour (Littlechild 2002b; Norris 1990; Rowett 1986). However, support for workers experiencing such violence is often poor or non-existent; in this respect, their experiences resemble those of women who suffer domestic violence (Dobash and Dobash 1992; McGee 2000; Mullender and Morley 1994). Goddard (1996) found that scant, if any, attention was paid to the impact of service users' behaviour on staff in social work agencies.

The nature, extent and effects of violence against staff

Findings from the British Crime Survey (Budd 1999) confirm that social work is a high-risk occupation. Social workers and probation officers were particularly at risk while working – 9.4 per cent had been assaulted, and 9.5 per cent had been threatened, among the highest incidences across all the groups, apart from physical assaults against the police (24.6%). This study also found that social workers appeared to be at higher risk of repeat victimisation than many other occupational groups. The National Institute for Social Work (NISW) review of the research (1999) confirmed that social care staff experience violence and abuse more often than staff in many other occupations. In common with Budd's findings, Littlechild's research (2000, 2002a) suggests that physical violence from adult clients in child protection work is comparatively rare, but other forms of 'indirect violence', as one respondent referred to it, occurred frequently.

Threats of further actions from clients had the greatest effects, especially when this appeared to the worker to be focused individually against her/himself and sometimes on their family, rather than on their role as an agency representative. In the US, Horejsi and Garthwait (1994) found that nearly all of the workers in their survey had experienced work-related violence in the previous 12 months, and consequently two-thirds considered seeking other employment. The effects were largely psychological, with fear having the most serious effects on themselves and their behaviour. Such findings are consistent with those of Smith and Nursten (1998) and with Littlechild's studies (2000, 2002a).

Findings from this latter piece of research indicate that male clients may use threats to try to deter the child protection professionals involved, and that these threats can have a major impact on individual workers. Staff also reported their experiences of attempting to communicate with children through a screen of aggression and violence which some abusers of children used to keep the protection workers at bay. This resonates with Farmer and Owen's (1995, 1998) findings that, in three out of five situations where children had suffered neglect, or physical or emotional abuse, the mothers were also subjected to violence by their male partners (see also Chapter 8 by Elaine Farmer). They concluded that when women who live with violent men are clearly unable to protect themselves, the chances of them being in a position to protect their children may be remote. Workers and agencies appear to have little appreciation of the nature or effects of such behaviour either on the workers themselves, or on the protection of the children involved (Littlechild 2000, 2002a, 2002b).

Men are the most frequent perpetrators of threatening behaviour, such as sustained and personalised verbal abuse and threats, following workers in the street or in cars, and threats of violence to professionals' families. These forms of violence can produce some of the most severe effects on worker victims (Brockmann and McLean 2000; National Institute for Social Work 1999). Littlechild (2000, 2002a) found that these types of situations were usually not one-off incidents, but part of a set of dynamics and threats that built up over time, and which can best be described as 'developing violent scenarios'. Some of the patterns of power and control utilised by some abusers for inducing fear in victims are similar to patterns identified in men's stalking of women (Budd and

Mattinson 2000; McGee 2000). Furthermore, the intrusion of child protection workers into his domain of power and control can be seen by the dominant male in the family as a risk to the family structure and his part within it (Wilmot 1998).

Social workers and the child protection agencies they work for often focus their intervention on the non-abusing parent (Farmer and Owen 1998). This practice has generated concerns that blame falls on the non-abusing parent which in turn can increase their anxiety and fear (Stanley 1997). The dominant pattern appears to be to avoid or minimise the effects of the man's abuse of the mother (Humphreys 2000). The effects of men's avoidance of responsibility, and their frequent aggression, are often not confronted by practitioners (see also Hearn 1998; Humphreys 1999, 2000; Littlechild 2000, 2002b).

Responses to violence

Social workers and their employing agencies often fail to recognise the types of threat present within males' power/control patterns that can disempower and intimidate both them and other family members. The role of child protection social workers places them at greater risk due to the role conflict and ambiguity present in their role, in which social workers are required to investigate possible abuse, and put themselves in a powerful and potentially controlling role, while simultaneously offering a supportive role working in 'partnership' with parents (see Department of Health 1995). Consideration of such matters led Hethering-ton *et al.* (1997) and Corby (2000) to question the viability of social workers being able to carry out these functions simultaneously. Parents often experience social workers' child protection role as controlling, powerful and judgemental, while perceiving that they themselves have very little power or control (see for example National Institute for Social Work 1999). Such perceptions of the child protection social work role are closely linked to parents' displays of aggression and violence. Stanley and Goddard (1997) suggest that the complex set of dynamics within abusive families can draw the worker into the role of victim, which means they are unable to challenge the abuse, or utilise procedures properly, and that, at times, workers appear to indulge in self-deception and denial of violence.

Male abusers often use control strategies based upon threats of violence and other dire consequences if family members reveal the secret of the abuse to any 'outsiders'. When their power is threatened by the scrutiny of outside statutory agencies, abusers can attempt to maintain control by preventing children and other family members reporting the abuse, and/or frightening workers in order to keep them at bay. Men's strategies of power/control over members of their family can include threats of further violence, persuading the abused person that they will not be believed if they approach others, and that they will be seen as responsible for family break ups (see Mullender and Debbonaire 2000). Victims are often caught up within control strategies that over time have inculcated a feeling that the violence is their fault, rather than the abuser's responsibility (Mullender and Morley 1994; Smith 1989; Walker 1977). Similarly, work with families may be ineffective because assumptions are made about shared blame for the violence which can place the women at greater danger; women may also be prevented from communicating openly and honestly as they may have been threatened with reprisals from their abuser. While the precise means may differ, the use of power/control mechanisms to intimidate others in the family's informal and formal networks is a key mechanism used by violent and controlling males. Where abusers use threats of violence within their sphere of influence it is sometimes possible to identify a 'control/threat continuum' within the abuser's networks as a risk factor for the child where the power/control continuum targets two or all three from among the child, the informal and formal networks.

In Littlechild's (2000) research, workers reported that, in the main, too little was done to deal with service users' violence against themselves and non-abusing family members. A number of workers believed there needed to be more systematic and structured responses to clients who were aggressive and violent. Some staff who had experienced violence considered that the response of their agency had been inadequate, and that the issues arising from these types of behaviour were not confronted in child protection conferences or plans.

Developing guidance and policies

Child protection procedures and guidance usually fail to include considerations of how to incorporate knowledge of the impact of male violence into the assessment of risk or child protection plans; for example, the UK government's core assessment record proformas associated with the *Framework for the Assessment of Children in Need and Their Families* (Department of Health *et al.* 2000) and the associated *Family Pack of Questionnaires and Scales* (Cox and Bentovim 2000) omit to address this issue. Incorporating assessment of parental violence and how it may affect interventions was recommended by James in 1994. These recommendations were never acted upon; in fact, it has been ignored to considerable extent in the framework. The Department of Health guidance, *Protecting Children* (1988), considered that professional dangerousness occurs when 'a social worker is allowed to avoid contact with the child or family due to unacknowledged fears for personal safety' (p.12).

However, this isolated reference to the damaging effects of violence does not appear in the current guidance. A Department of Health (1991) review of findings from child abuse death inquiries found that, in a number of the cases, threats of violence against staff had significant effects on the workers and the child protection process. For example, the Kimberly Carlile inquiry team recommended that: 'Every effort must be made to make sure that the social worker's assessment, on which might hinge the safety of a child, is not disarmed by the possibility of violence, or the fear of its possibility' (p.71). If this issue is not addressed more systematically in assessment and child protection plans, dangers for women, children and workers will persist.

Supervision and support from managers is a key factor in reducing stress for workers (Gibbs 2001; Jones, Fletcher and Ibbetson 1991), and in dealing with issues of aggression and violence within families, and against workers (Stanley and Goddard 2002). Experiences of supportive reactions of managers and employing agencies persuade staff to report intimidation and violence. Such positive experiences will also change workers' views that some forms of violence are not sufficiently serious to report, or that clients have justifications for being violent. Supportive responses from senior staff will provide clear messages that acceptance of violence is not 'part of the job', and should dispel concerns that managers will not fully support the worker or take actions to deal with the behaviour from clients (Norris 1990).

These shifts might be achieved by the following approaches:

- Acknowledge that some abusive males use threats and/or physical violence as a way of keeping other family members from revealing the abuse to 'outsiders', or professionals, and that this needs to be included in risk assessments and treatment plans.

- Incorporate screening protocols within national and local assessment frameworks which acknowledge some males' power/control strategies, and their effects on children, non-abusing family members, and child protection workers.

- Provide greater impetus to formulate child protection plans which assess and address directly abusers' power/control strategies.

- Provide appropriate support for women, children and workers who are subject to such behaviour which, where possible, allows them to move at their own pace to deal with the issues, within a clearly stated set of procedures that acknowledges their fears.

- Develop strategies to aid victims of violence to disclose continuing violence without fear of exacerbating the risks. If they do not, and the need for protection and empowerment of these groups is neglected, this may affect the protection of the child involved.

- Support workers to ensure that they do not deny or fail to acknowledge such dynamics through ignorance, fear, lack of support and supervision, or inadequate checklists that do not address these issues.

- Continue the work of the UK government's National Task Force on Violence Against Social Care Staff (Department of Health 2000), with the remit of monitoring agencies' progress on increasing reporting of violence against staff, and promoting developments to increase their safety, well-being and confidence.

- Provide clear definitions and systems of reporting the identified types of violence and aggression; such as 'any incident in which an individual worker, as s/he experiences it, suffers verbal abuse, physical abuse, homophobic abuse, disablist abuse, sexual or racially motivated harassment, verbal abuse or threats in circumstances relating to their work'.

- Managers need to encourage reporting of such behaviours verbally and in writing, and respond to such reports sympathetically and supportively. The real nature and effects of such aggression are often not fully appreciated in agencies because incidents are not recorded and collated in ways which allow an understanding of the full picture, or enable risk management procedures to be put into place (Macdonald and Sirotich 2001; Norris 1990; Rowett 1986; UNISON/British Association of Social Workers 1997).

- Reports should include the victim's suggestions for improvements in policies and procedures – currently this is often not the case in agencies' reporting procedures.

- Put clear procedures in place establishing who will deal with the perpetrator, how, and with what (if any) involvement from the victim. There is little evidence that agencies work to set limits and boundaries with service users where they have used violence or intimidatory and threatening behaviour. This issue is also rarely addressed in the literature on violence against staff.

- Make clear who in the agency has:
  - the responsibility to support workers in order for them to carry out their child protection functions effectively when faced with aggression and violence from clients
  - the responsibility to assess over time and incorporate learning from workers' reports of violence, and feed back to all staff what actions have been taken to reduce the identified risks.

The employing agency should ensure their staff are aware of the legal provisions that affect their protection. The Health and Safety at Work Act 1974 requires employers to make their workers as safe as reasonably possible; at the same time, however, the Act requires workers to not put themselves in situations of risk, which raises some interesting points about whether workers can to refuse to carry out work where there is real risk of violence without clear and appropriate support from their agency. The General Social Care Council (2002) *Codes of Conduct and Practice for Social Care Workers and Employers of Social Care Workers*, which social workers registered with this body from 2004 will be required to comply with, states that social workers must follow practice and procedures designed to keep them and other people safe from violent and abusive behaviour. The codes also require workers to inform their employer or the appropriate authority about any physical, mental, or emotional difficulties that might affect their ability to do their job competently and safely, and not to put themselves or other people at unnecessary risk. The Protection from Harassment Act 1997 (available at www.opsi.gov.uk) was introduced to counter the phenomenon of stalking of women, but is available for use by all, including workers. The Act contains civil and criminal remedies which can be invoked when someone experiences conduct that can amount to them being 'harassed' by, or fearing violence from, another person on at least two occasions. Harassment can include behaviour that produces stress and fear in the victim. Individuals can seek an injunction to stop the harassment, and if it is severe, the police can bring forward a criminal prosecution.

Conclusion

In the light of the evidence of the extent and effects of violence from some men against family members and social workers, agencies need to acknowledge and consider the effects on child-care assessments and interventions. Such considerations need to start from a recognition of not only the fearful effects that such men can produce in their partners, but also the similarities between certain types of male violence towards members of their informal and formal networks.

This chapter has developed arguments for addressing the risk of violence to staff posed by a small but significantly threatening number of service users. There appears to be reluctance to openly acknowledge the use and effects of violence by men in their interactions with child-care professionals, and, as evidenced in a number of child abuse death reports, fears of making things worse by raising the matter with the family and violent abuser. It has been suggested that there may be links between these different forms of violence in individual situations, and that particular elements of the situation where men may be using such control strategies need confronting. Men's attempts to frighten and disempower workers or non-abusing family members then become important matters to be dealt with in assessment, through staff support, support for non-abusing family members, and in interventions. Agencies and individual workers need to ensure that they are trained and knowledgeable about the impact of male violence in families where abuse is occurring, so that their approaches and methods do not allow such effects to continue and intensify. They also need an understanding of the types of power/control strategies which can affect the protection of abused family members.

The child's needs for safeguarding and protection from abuse need to be at the centre of any such set of strategies; but for this to happen, the shifts in policy and practice described above need to be taken on board by agencies. If we can incorporate our knowledge of the problems caused by such men's violence into child-care policy and practice, rather than seeing domestic violence as a separate issue from the protection of children, we will be able to protect abused children, abused family members, and social work staff more effectively.

References

Bridge Child Care Development Service (1997) *Report on Behalf of Cambridgeshire County Council Social Services Department.* Cambridge: Cambridgeshire County Council.

Bridge Consultancy (1991) *Sukina: An Evaluation of the Circumstances Surrounding Her Death.* London: Bridge Child Care Consultancy.

Briere, J.N. (1992) *Child Abuse Trauma: Theory and Treatment of the Lasting Effects.* London: Sage Publications.

Brockmann, M. (2002) 'New perspectives on violence in social care.' *Journal of Social Work 2*, 1, 29–44.

Brockmann, M. and McLean, J. (2000) *Review Paper for the National Task Force on Violence Against Social Care Staff.* London: National Institute for Social Work Research Unit.

Budd, T. (1999) *Violence at Work: Findings from the British Crime Survey.* London: Home Office/Health and Safety Executive.

Budd, T. and Mattinson, J. (2000) *The Extent and Nature of Stalking: Findings from the 1998 British Crime Survey.* London: Home Office Research, Development and Statistics Directorate.

Corby, B. (2000) *Child Abuse: Towards a Knowledge Base.* Buckingham. Open University Press.

Cox, A. and Bentovim, A. (2000) *The Family Pack of Questionnaires and Scales.* London: Department of Health.

Department of Health (1988) *Protecting Children: A Guide for Social Workers Undertaking a Comprehensive Assessment.* London: HMSO.

Department of Health (1991) *Child Abuse Deaths: A Study of Inquiry Reports 1980–1989.* London: HMSO.

Department of Health (1995) *The Challenge of Partnership in Child Protection.* London: Stationery Office.

Department of Health (2000) *A Safer Place: Report of the Task Force and National Action Plan on Violence Against Social Care Staff.* London: Department of Health.

Department of Health, Department for Education and Employment, Home Office (2000) *Framework for the Assessment of Children in Need and Their Families.* London: Stationery Office.

Dingwall, R., Eekelaar, J. and Murray, T. (1983) *The Protection of Children: State Intervention and Family Life.* Oxford: Basil Blackwell.

Dobash, R.E. and Dobash, R.P. (1992) *Women, Violence and Social Change.* London: Routledge.

Edwards, S.S.M. (1996) *Sex and Gender in the Legal Process.* London: Blackwell Press.

Farmer, E. and Owen, M. (1995) *Child Protection Practice: Private Risks and Public Remedies.* London: HMSO.

Farmer, E. and Owen, M. (1998) 'Gender and the child protection process.' *British Journal of Social Work 28*, 545–64.

General Social Care Council (2002) *Codes of Conduct and Practice for Social Care Workers and Employers of Social Care Workers.* London: General Social Care Council.

Gibbs, J.A. (2001) 'Maintaining front-line workers in child protection: A case for refocusing supervision.' *Child Abuse Review 10*, 5, 323–35.

Goddard, C. (1996) *Child Abuse and Child Protection: A Guide for Health, Education and Welfare.* South Melbourne: Church Livingstone.

Guardian (2000) 'Couple jailed for neglect of five children.' *The Guardian,* 21 March.

Hearn, J. (1998) *The Violences of Men.* London: Sage Publications.

Hetherington, R., Cooper, A., Smith, P. and Wilford, G. (1997) *Protecting Children: Messages from Europe.* Lyme Regis: Russell House Publishing.

Horejsi, C. and Garthwait, C. (1994) 'A survey of threats and violence directed against social protection workers in a rural state.' *Child Welfare 73,* 2, 173–9.

Humphreys, C. (1999) 'Avoidance and confrontation: social work practice in relation to domestic violence and child abuse.' *Child and Family Social Work 4,* 77–87.

Humphreys, C. (2000) *Social Work, Domestic Violence and Child Protection: Challenging Practice.* Bristol: The Policy Press.

James, G. (1994) *Study of Working Together 'Part 8 Reports'.* London: Department of Health.

Jones, F., Fletcher, B. (C.), and Ibbetson, K. (1991) 'Stressors and strains amongst social workers.' *British Journal of Social Work 21,* 5, 443–70.

Littlechild, B. (2000) *I Know Where You Live: How child protection social workers are affected by threats and aggression. A study into the stresses faced by child protection workers in Hertfordshire: with notes on research into Finnish social workers' experiences.* Hatfield: University of Hertfordshire.

Littlechild, B. (2002a) *The Management of Conflict and Service User Violence Against Staff in Child Protection Work.* Hatfield: Centre for Community Research, University of Hertfordshire.

Littlechild, B. (2002b) 'The effects of client violence on child protection networks.' *Trauma, Violence and Abuse 3,* 2, 144–58.

London Borough of Brent (1985) *A Child in Trust – The Report of the Panel of Inquiry into the Circumstances Surrounding the Death of Jasmine Beckford.* London: London Borough of Brent.

London Borough of Greenwich (1987) *Protection of Children in a Responsible Society: The Report of the Commission of Enquiry into the Circumstances Surrounding the Death of Kimberley Carlile.* London: London Borough of Greenwich/Greenwich Health Authority.

London Borough of Lambeth (1987) *Whose Child? The Report of the Public Inquiry into the Death of Tyra Henry.* London: London Borough of Lambeth.

Macdonald, G. and Sirotich, F. (2001) 'Reporting client violence.' *Social Work 46,* 2, 107–14.

McGee, C. (2000) *Childhood Experiences of Domestic Violence.* London: Jessica Kingsley Publishers.

Mudaly, N. and Goddard, C. (2001) 'The child abuse victim as a hostage: Scorpion's story.' *Child Abuse Review 10,* 6, 428–39.

Mullender, A. and Debbonaire, T. (2000) *Child Protection and Domestic Violence.* Birmingham: Venture Press.

Mullender, A. and Morley, R. (1994) 'Context and content of a new agenda.' In A. Mullender and R. Morley (eds) *Children Living with Domestic Violence.* London: Whiting and Birch.

National Institute for Social Work (1999) *Violence Against Social Workers. Briefing Paper 26.* London: NISW.

Newham Area Child Protection Committee (2002) *Ainlee: Chapter 8 Review.* London: Newham Area Child Protection Committee.

Norris, D. (1990) *Violence Against Social Workers.* London: Jessica Kingsley Publishers.

O'Hagan, K. (1997) 'The problem of engaging men in child protection work.' *British Journal of Social Work 27,* 25–42.

O'Hagan, K. and Dillenburger, K. (1995) *The Abuse of Women Within Child Care Work.* Buckingham: Open University Press.

Pahl, J. (1999) 'Coping with physical violence and verbal abuse.' In S. Balloch, J. McLean and M. Fisher (eds) *Social Services: Working Under Pressure.* Bristol: The Policy Press.

Protection from Harassment Act (1997) Available at www.opsi.gov.uk

Reder, P., Duncan, S. and Gray, M. (1993) *Beyond Blame: Child Abuse Tragedies Revisited.* London: Routledge.

Rowett, C. (1986) *Violence in Social Work*. University of Cambridge Institute of Criminology Occasional Paper No. 14. Cambridge: University of Cambridge.

Smith, F. (1988) *An Analysis of Violence Towards Staff in a Social Service Department*. London: Croydon Social Services.

Smith, L. (1989) *Domestic Violence: An Overview of the Literature*. London: HMSO.

Smith, M. and Nursten, J. (1998) 'Social workers' experiences of distress – moving towards change?' *British Journal of Social Work 28*, 351–68.

Social Services Inspectorate (1995) *Domestic Violence and Social Care*. London: Department of Health.

Stanley, N. (1997) 'Domestic violence and child abuse: developing social work practice.' *Child and Family Social Work 2*, 3, 135–145.

Stanley, J. and Goddard, C. (1997) 'Failures in child protection: A case study.' *Child Abuse Review 6*, 1, 46–54.

Stanley, J. and Goddard, C. (2002) *In the Firing Line: Violence and Power in Child Protection Work*. Chichester: Wiley.

UNISON/British Association of Social Workers (1997) *Dealing with Violence and Stress in Social Services*. Birmingham: UNISON/BASW.

Walker, L.E. (1977) 'Battered women and learned helplessness.' *Victimology 2*, 525–6.

Wilmot, C. (1997) 'Public Pressure; Private Stress.' In R. Davies (ed) *Stress in Social Work*. London: Jessica Kingsley Publishers.

List of Contributors

Dr Jo Bell is a researcher at the University of Central Lancashire and Lecturer in Child and Adolescent Development in the Faculty of Health and Social Care at the University of Hull. She has extensive experience of research on sensitive issues with young people and families.

Neil Blacklock is Development Manager of the Domestic Violence Intervention Project, West London, which he founded.

Caroline Bourke is a senior lecturer, teaching Child Welfare/Protection and Family Violence, and the Programme Leader for BSc (Hons) Social Work at the University of Hertfordshire. Her background has been in children and families social work, predominantly in child protection. She has a long-standing interest in child protection and violence within families and researches family violence, particularly in Slovenia.

Dr Jan Breckenridge is a Senior Lecturer in the School of Social Work at the University of New South Wales, Australia, and is the Director of the Centre for Gender-Related Violence Studies there. Jan has worked, taught and researched in the areas of domestic and sexual violence, gender issues and child abuse for 25 years. She is co-editor of a number of books on sexual and domestic violence.

Dr Thea Brown is Professor of Social Work and Director of the Family Violence and Family Court Research Program at Monash University, Melbourne, Australia. Her research and policy development in child abuse and domestic violence in the context of parental separation and divorce has been published internationally.

Jane Ellis is currently a final year doctoral student in the Centre for the Study of Safety and Wellbeing at the University of Warwick. Her PhD incorporates research into violence against women and 'primary prevention' programmes along with an evaluation of a domestic violence programme for schools. She has a background of working with children and young people in both formal and non-formal educational settings and is a governor at a community primary school.

Dr Elaine Farmer is Professor of Child and Family Studies and Head of the Research Centre for Family Policy and Child Welfare in the School for Policy Studies at the University of Bristol. She has a background in social work and has researched and published widely on fostering, residential and kinship care, reunification and child protection.

Dr Christine Harrison is Senior Lecturer in the School of Health and Social Studies at the University of Warwick; Deputy Director of the Centre for the Study of Safety and Wellbeing and Director of a Masters Social Work Course. Sha has co-ordinated and taught child-care social work at qualifying and post-qualifying levels for the last 15 years, and regularly teaches on programmes for other professionals. As well as having substantial practice experience in child care, she supervises workers at a hostel for women offenders and is a member of the management group of Coventry Rape and Sexual Abuse centre. Research related to physical, emotional and sexual violence towards women and children, and the issues this raises for promoting their safety, is a theme running throughout various aspects of her work over recent years.

Dr Marianne Hester is Professor of Gender, Violence and International Policy at the University of Bristol. She has carried out research into many aspects of gender and violence, including work on domestic violence, children, and street prostitution, often comparing the UK, Denmark and China. She is Visiting Professor at the China University of Political Science and Law, Beijing, and Patron of South Tyneside Women's Aid.

Claire Houghton is a leading advocate for the rights of children and young people experiencing domestic abuse in Scotland. She worked for more than a decade as the National Children's Rights Worker with Scottish Women's Aid. She is currently working as a consultant with the Scottish Executive as Children's Services Policy Manager in the Violence Against Women Unit.

Dr Cathy Humphreys is Reader in the School of Health and Social Studies at the University of Warwick and Director of the Centre for the Study of Safety and Well-Being. A social worker by training, she has worked in both England and Australia. In 2006 she will be appointed to the Alfred Felton Chair in Child and Family Welfare at University of Melbourne.

Kate Iwi is Manager of Children's Services at the Domestic Violence Intervention Project (DVIP) in London. Her background is in psychology, forensic psychotherapy and child protection and she has previously worked with perpetrators of domestic violence for nine years. She has co-written DVIP's manual for domestic violence intervention which is used widely across the UK and Europe.

Dr Brian Littlechild is Associate Head of School of Social, Community and Health Care Studies/Centre for Community Research at the University of Hertfordshire. He originally specialised as a social worker and manager in children and families work. He has carried out research on inter-agency domestic violence work, and the effects and management of violence from service users on child protection work and workers.

Dr Audrey Mullender is Principal of Ruskin College Oxford and holds a Professorship in Social Work at the University of Warwick. During her distinguished research career she has published on the topics of domestic violence, post-adoption issues for birth relatives and groupwork theory, and has authored 16 books.

Dr Lorraine Radford is Head of Research at the NSPCC, based in London, England. Her particular areas of research interest include the impact of domestic violence upon children and parenting, safe child contact arrangements, risk assessment and, more recently, violence and health. She is Senior Research Fellow at Roehampton University, London, where she previously taught courses on crime, violence and children's rights.

Marius Råkil is Director of the Men's Treatment Programme at Alternative to Violence (ATV), Oslo, Norway, the oldest domestic violence treatment programme in Europe. He is a trained psychologist and has been working in the treatment of violent men for the last 15 years. In addition to lecturing and teaching, he has written articles and edited a book in Norway on domestic violence. He can be contacted at marius.raakil@mobilpost.com

Claire Ralfs is the Director of Community Education and Training at Relationships Australia, South Australia. Claire's work as a front-line worker, manager and trainer has focused on groups for whom violence, discrimination and abuse are key factors in their marginalisation and involvement in community services. She is presently enrolled in a doctoral programme at the University of South Australia, investigating the impact of skills-oriented professional education on the quality of service delivery.

Nicky Stanley is Professor of Social Work at the University of Central Lancashire. She is a trained social worker who researches in the areas of women's and young people's mental health, child protection and domestic violence. She is co-editor of *Child Abuse Review*.

Subject Index

Author Index